The Albert Plan
To Save America

DAN ALBERT

To the millions who have fought to gain and retain the freedoms that we have enjoyed in this great nation we call The United States of America: may we succeed in preserving the liberty that you have given life, limb and fortune to secure.

CONTENTS

Introduction

After the terrorist attacks of 9/11, we heard much about the potential for terrorist sleeper cells already established throughout our land, and the danger of imminent follow-up attacks through the mobilization of such sleeper cells by radical Islamist jihadists. My thought at the time was that, in order to be prepared to counteract such terrorist sleeper cells, We the People should establish or join what I call "Freedom Cells."

I then realized that, in order to save our nation from the much broader problems that we face, We the People need a plan that the patriots that organize into Freedom Cells can use as a roadmap to clamor for the bold, comprehensive and transformational changes needed to correct the many problems created by the entrenched establishment political class and their globalist cronies.

A NATION IN DISTRESS

Liberals, globalists and radical environmentalists threaten to destroy our nation. Iran, North Korea and radical Islamic jihadists pose a clear and present danger. The entrenched establishment political class has exported American jobs and imported legal and illegal immigrants to displace millions more American workers. There are more than 100 million unemployed or underemployed Americans.

1

Escalating global debt threatens a global financial collapse that globalists will use as an opportunity to introduce a New World Order. Our nation is in distress. Has the United States reached a point of no return? Can America be saved?

After 9/11, I was very concerned that our nation may have reached the point of no return, or was very close to it. The failure of the administrations of Presidents George W. Bush and Barack Obama to secure our borders, and their decision to downplay the threat of radical Islamic terrorism by embracing Islam as a "peaceful religion" has certainly brought us closer to the point of no return, and exposed our nation to the danger of radical Islamic jihadists entering our country as Trojan horse "civilization jihadists."

A BOLD, COMPREHENSIVE, TRANSFORMATIONAL PLAN

Patriots everywhere are asking the same question: What can we do? We are aware of the need, and are prepared to commit to doing what we must do to take our country back. We the People must get behind a comprehensive plan to restore American sovereignty, American prosperity and American exceptionalism.

I believe that we can save America from the course that we are on, but it will take a movement to strip the federal government of the power that it has stolen from the states and the people. It will take a rising up of like-minded patriots behind a sensible plan in order to peacefully restore the balance of power intended by our founders so that we may avoid the uprising that will certainly come if the tyranny of the federal government is permitted to continue beyond the point of no return.

Many candidates for political office have put forth plans of one sort or another, but none of the plans that I have seen have been bold and comprehensive enough, and each has been tied to the political aspirations of the candidates that published each plan. Please forgive me if it sounds prideful that I include my name as part of this plan. Unlike political candidates that will present their

2

plans with their names on them, I am an ordinary citizen that is not seeking elective office that happens to have a plan to correct the course that we are on. This plan will not only save America, it will restore the greatness and uniqueness of America as the leader of the free world. My hope and intent is that this plan, or one of similar magnitude and direction, will gain traction as We the People take the necessary steps to take our country back.

Since this is a "beta edition" of a plan that will no doubt experience multiple revisions as the conversation continues, I need not seek to publish a perfect plan, as the urgent need at present is for a good plan that we can improve upon along the way. Please pardon my poor writing, and the numerous errors that I am sure will escape my attention. I am sure there will be numerous corrections in the next edition, but for now I trust that you will give consideration to the bold proposals that I make in this plan to restore our Republic and our lost liberties.

In this plan, I make numerous proposals for amendments to the Constitution that will correct some of the usurpations of power by our federal government that our founders forewarned that a strong federal government would foist upon its people. It will take constitutional amendments in order to permanently correct some of the overreach of our oppressive federal government, but We the People can aggregate our voices and actions in order to compel our states to take the corrective actions that they presently have the power to take in order to mitigate federal usurpations.

A CALL TO ACTION

We the People must clamor for immediate, specific action to restore the balance of powers intended by our founders and free our people to enjoy personal and economic liberty. Democrats don't have a monopoly on community organization. We must organize ourselves so that we may speak as one, and move as one in order to implement this plan to save America.

We have grown weary of the election cycle promises made that never gain traction and are soon forgotten by politicians that become assimilated into the political class. There are a few good ones that seem to be able to maintain principled positions, but few are able to resist the elixir of incredible power that has been aggregated by the Washington elite.

It has been said that power corrupts, and that absolute power corrupts absolutely. The entrenched establishment political class has such a thirst for acquiring and maintaining power that they will stop at nothing in furthering that end. The political elite are incapable of yielding any small measure of power back to the states or to the people, and so, like sheep being led to the slaughter, we march forward to the demise of our great nation.

The first step in taking our country back is for We the People to become organized to mobilize millions of patriots to become engaged and to stay engaged until after the job is done and beyond. It is not for the faint of heart. The second step is to overwhelm the Republican Party with patriots dedicated to what I call "Transformational Conservatism." The entrenched establishment political class is the minority, We the People that our seeking to restore our constitutional Republic are the silent majority.

Armed with truth, conservatives can beat Democrats at their own game of community organization. By getting organized, we can take over the Republican Party and use it as a vehicle to implement the bold, transformational changes that are needed to save our divided nation and restore economic liberty and prosperity. We must repudiate liberalism and the entrenched establishment political class. We must repudiate globalism and crony capitalism. We must also repudiate radical environmentalism.

We the People must dismantle big government and pursue the limited government that our founders envisioned. We must trust the free market to solve the problems that we face, and reduce our dependence upon government. We must reverse the degradation of our personal liberty, our freedom of speech, our freedom of religion and our right to keep and bear arms. When we restore our lost liberties, we will see an unleashing of the free market that will allow Americans to exercise our God-given natural rights enshrined in our founding documents.

If We the People don't take our country back, who will? If not now, when? Is there not a cause? When the people fear the government, there is tyranny, but when the government fears the people, there is liberty. May we restore our lost liberty to our great nation!

PART I

A Nation in Distress

ONE

To Destroy America

TRUTH AND FREEDOM ARE UNDER
RELENTLESS ATTACK BY LIBERALS,
ENVIRONMENTALISTS AND GLOBALISTS

If the foundations be destroyed, what can the righteous do?
 – Psalm 11:3

Building something requires much planning, design, coopera-
tion, hard work, time and resources. It is easier and quicker to
destroy something, or to tear something down, than to build it. We
have seen video of demolition experts bringing buildings down,
reducing what took years to build to a pile of rubble in less than a
minute. The most dramatic example of the destruction of buildings
that took years to plan, design and build is when terrorists brought
down the world trade center buildings in less than an hour.

Judeo-Christian values and the principles of freedom that are
the underpinning of the United States Constitution form the bedrock of Western Civilization, and are under relentless attack by liberals, environmentalists and globalists. There are forces at work,
some willful and some unwitting, that work together to threaten the
destruction of our nation, and all of Western civilization.

Our nation is in distress. In order to save America, We the
People must give careful scrutiny to the trends, policies and people
that contribute to the undermining and destruction of America, and
we must take immediate, decisive action to thwart those that would
destroy America. We must identify the major forces that undermine
the foundation of our country and identify specific actions that We
the People can take to preserve our Republic.

LIBERALISM IS DESTROYING AMERICA

Throughout most of history, if one was described as being liberal, one was being described as generous. Generous in giving materially to those that lack. One could also be described as liberal, if one was generous in the consideration of the dissenting points of view of others. Over the last hundred and fifty years, the progressive left has managed to hijack the term and to change the meaning so much that to be liberal today is to be almost the exact opposite of what it meant to be liberal for centuries.

The biblical instruction to "let your liberality be known to all men" or the promise that "the liberal soul shall be made fat" were references to a generosity that all people were at liberty to demonstrate in their lives. Liberals today are quite illiberal in the generosity that they show to others that do not share the progressive political ideals that have become synonymous with liberalism. Only those that are marching in lockstep with progressive ideology and action are accepted as liberal today.

The All-Out War Against Judeo-Christian Values

When Alexis de Tocqueville came to America to discover the secret of America's greatness, he concluded that America was great because America was good. Tocqueville observed the uniqueness of America's goodness when he visited America's churches. He further warned that America would cease to be great if America ceased to be good. One cannot help but wonder if our nation is now declining in greatness because our nation is hell-bent on destroying the foundation of goodness that made our nation great.

Our nation seems to have arrived at that point of choosing whether America will continue to be good. What we are seeing in our nation is the wholesale abandonment of the Judeo-Christian values upon which our great nation was founded. There is an open and growing hostility toward Christians and the God of the Bible that, if not reversed, will utterly destroy the foundation upon which our nation stands. If we continue to permit the liberal left to hijack the character of our nation, and allow them to shake their collective fist in defiance to God without standing up to them, we will have lost the soul of America.

Political Correctness: Liberalism Embracing a Lie

In accepting the false doctrine of political correctness, Americans have placed such a premium on the avoidance of offending others at all cost, that we have abandoned the rugged individualism that built our country. People are simply afraid to speak the truth for fear of offending some established or newly discovered victim group. Truth is lost in a constant cacophony of mumbo-jumbo and psychobabble. Instead of being at liberty to draw sharp distinctions between truth and error, we are stuck in a quagmire of trying to figure out how to water down the truth so that it doesn't offend the feeble-minded liberals trying to destroy our country.

It turns out that the "I'm okay, you're okay" philosophy of life is absolutely wrong. I'm not okay, and you're not okay if we deceive ourselves constantly. There is evil in the world. Not everyone can be a winner in Little League. Truth is truth, no matter how creative and convoluted people get in twisting the truth into lies that are dangerous and destructive.

One of the most glaring examples of damage to our country that has come from pursuing the path of political correctness at all cost is the way that our nation has mishandled screening for potential terror threats. After 9/11 happened, President George W. Bush responded with a "hug a Muslim" policy. Instead of looking to moderate Muslims to draw the distinction between themselves and radical Islam by denouncing acts of terror and those that commit them, and explaining how what they believe about Islam and the Koran is different from what the radical extremists believe, our leaders pursued the politically correct path of trying to convince us that Islam is a peaceful religion.

While encouraging moderate Muslims to enumerate and demonstrate the differences between the way they believe and the way terrorists believe, our nation should have recognized the threat of radical Islam and enacted responsible security measures based upon the reality that all of the perpetrators of the acts of terror committed on 9/11 were Muslims. Political correctness quickly shut down the possibility of profiling Muslims in screening for potential terror threats. Instead of doing the reasonable thing and scrutinizing all Muslims entering the country, we diluted the effort by screening everybody for fear of offending the very Muslims that should have been eager to demonstrate loyalty to our nation.

The problems presented by political correctness gone crazy in this country manifest themselves in countless ways. Common to all politically correct actions and statements is that political correctness almost always involves an embedded lie in each politically correct action or statement. To dismantle the politically correct argument, we must simply identify the manner in which the underlying liberal argument is embracing a lie, and expose the lie.

Welfare and the Redistribution of Wealth

Liberal policies that tax the producers in our economy at an exorbitant level and redistributes to those that are less productive have created an increasing dependency of millions of Americans upon federal and state welfare programs. The percentage of Americans that have an entitlement mentality, expecting increasing levels of subsidy by the federal and state government, has risen to such a level that it threatens to destroy our nation.

Liberals have intentionally created modern-day plantations of Americans that are enslaved by the programs that were created to supposedly assist them in becoming independent. Millions have become dependent upon handouts, and are no longer interested in a hand up from poverty. Liberal policies have made it too easy for some to remain in poverty instead of working.

The liberal strategy of creating massive groups of voters that essentially are tempted to vote themselves a paycheck instead of supporting policies that would give them greater opportunities for liberty is rapidly approaching a tipping point. There is a limit to how much tax-and-spend redistribution of wealth liberal policies that We the People will tolerate before we say enough is enough. The time has come that We the People must demand radical change.

Deficit Spending and Addiction to Debt

The dangerous habit that Congress has of spending far more than the U.S. Treasury receives in tax revenue, and the ease with which Congress raises the national debt limit is not a problem that is limited to liberals in Congress. Too many Republican members of Congress talk about balancing the budget and reducing spending during reelection, but then fail to take appropriate steps to reduce spending year after year.

There has to be a point when this madness will reach the point of no return, when our country will be not only bankrupt, but incapable of correcting the problem. If we have not already passed the point of no return, we are dangerously close. We the People have grown weary of members of the entrenched establishment political class of both parties spending our nation into oblivion.

Overregulation

Government at all levels seems to be on a suicidal mission to completely shut down productive output in this country. Ask any businessperson how much more difficult it is today to start or grow a business, or even to continue in business within the current regulatory environment. Businesses are being swamped with unnecessary and costly regulation that puts American businesses at a huge disadvantage in competing with international businesses. Liberal policies that are based upon the false premise that government knows best are choking off productivity and job creation.

Big business has no problem surviving in an overregulated environment, for onerous regulations are easier for big business to manage with than for small business. One could argue that there is an unholy alliance between big government and big business to drive small business out of our economy. You don't have to look very far to see that all of the small mom-and-pop businesses are being rolled up into national or international chains of businesses that have consolidated almost every business sector.

Entrepreneurship is being threatened with extinction, as more and more impediments to small business creation are erected. This does not bode well for the continuation of American capitalism, for the golden goose that has created the vast majority of jobs in this country has been sacrificed on the altar of liberal ideology.

Public Education

Liberalism has completely overtaken the public education system in this country, and has been producing an inferior product at ever-increasing cost. The dumbing down of American students with liberal indoctrination has created a generation of kids that lack the critical thinking skills for success in today's world. A high school diploma today is worth less than an eighth grade education was seventy-five years ago.

We are raising a generation of snowflake children that have no sense of the history of this nation that then attend liberal universities at great cost with high levels of student loan debt to earn what for most will turn out to be useless degrees. Instead of learning logic and reasoning, as well as job skills, kids learn to be politically correct and to become little social justice warriors.

RADICAL ENVIRONMENTALISM IS DESTROYING AMERICA

The American economic engine is seizing up because we have allowed the false theology of radical environmentalism to hamstring the productive elements of society. The false theology of radical environmentalism denies a Creator, worshiping the creation instead. The logical conclusion of the false doctrines of radical environmentalism will lead to advocacy for the depopulation of the earth and of the restoration of the environment to the pre-human state that the most radical of environmentalists believe harmoniously existed before humans appeared on the scene and ruined everything.

The truth is that God created an incredibly resilient earth, and placed an abundance of resources within our reach to empower us to fulfill his command to be fruitful and multiply and have dominion over the earth. Radical environmentalism teaches the false doctrine that the earth is fragile, and that humans are destroying the planet. The truth is that humans are not destroying the planet, and we probably could not do so even if we tried.

The myth of man-made climate change that is destructive to the planet is not remotely scientific. Climate change alarmists have changed from warning against global cooling, to warning against global warming, and when trends did not support either scenario, they decided to go with the mantra of climate change.

Where I was raised, people would say that if you don't like the weather, wait a little while and it will change. The weather is always changing. The climate is always changing. We don't have enough recorded history to scientifically demonstrate that what we have experienced over the past hundred years does not fall completely within the range of climate change over the past six millennia.

Scientists that lie are not scientists, they are liars. Much of what is called science today is not science, but rather unproven theories at best or malicious lies at worst. Dr. Michael Guillen has written a wonderful book, *Amazing Truths-How Science and the Bible Agree*, in which he brilliantly demonstrates that science and the Bible are the ultimate power couple. Science is no threat to the Bible. The Bible, on the other hand, has through the writings of the Apostle Paul warned against false science:

O Timothy, keep that which is committed to thy trust, avoiding profane and vain babblings, and oppositions of science falsely so called.

      – 1 Timothy 6:20

Some that have professed themselves to be scientists have made the assertion that increasing CO_2 levels will make the earth uninhabitable within a short period of time. I don't think that anyone has scientifically established what the optimum level of CO_2 is for the planet, but I have seen an assertion in writing somewhere that the optimum CO_2 level for plants is five times the current level of CO_2 in the atmosphere today.

Given the evidence that the earth was at one time much more lush and green than it is today, it isn't hard to believe that optimum levels of CO_2 for plant life is far greater than it is today. Doesn't it make sense that environmentalists, those that advocate for "green" proposals for the planet, would want to see the earth actually become more green and lush with a greater abundance of plant life?

Where is the scientific evidence that an increase in CO_2 levels will bring about the melting of the polar ice caps to such an extent that it will lead to significant increases in sea levels? If there happened to be scientific evidence that a certain level of CO_2 would bring about a certain degree of melting of polar ice caps that would then bring about a certain increase in sea level, then where is the proof that mankind would be worse off with higher sea levels and more plant life? Wouldn't this be a value judgment?

Climate alarmists seem to argue that human activity has increased the levels of CO_2 in the atmosphere to such an extent that we have to take dramatic action to reduce human activity in order to reverse the trend. During the Fort McMurray fires in western Canada, I became curious about how the volume of carbon emissions from those fires compared to the volume of carbon emissions resulting from human activity.

When I looked online for the answer to that question, I came across a report about peat-bog fires in Indonesia that collectively generated almost as much carbon emissions as the entire United States economy generated for the period of time considered. It is also important to note that volcanic activity can dwarf the level of CO_2 emissions by all human activity worldwide. Evidently bovine flatulence is also a huge generator of carbon emissions. If methane gas passed by cattle is a problem, imagine what hundreds of millions of bison and buffalo created for carbon emissions back when there was much less human activity.

When human activity was more limited hundreds of years ago, humans were also more limited in controlling great forest or prairie fires from consuming hundreds of thousands of square miles. When considering the impact of human activity on the climate, particularly industrial activity that is heavily dependent upon fossil fuels, we should also consider the ways that human activity likely brought about reductions in CO_2 emissions. Climate alarmists point to CO_2 emissions from the burning of fossil fuels by humans as the primary driver of what they assert is a crisis of climate change, but they never seem to include any offset to CO_2 emissions that comes from increased human population and activity. An honest scientific approach to the impact of human activity on CO_2 emissions would include all relevant data.

If we consider the numerous ways in which carbon emissions have risen and fallen naturally over the millennia, and the capacity that mankind has to mitigate any actual negative impact that human activity has on our environment, then we should not worry too much about the climate change alarmist fearmongering that extreme environmentalists and globalists are trying to cram down our throats. Those that think that we should build spaceships to go to Mars because our planet is dying should be free to spend their time and resources doing so, but We the People should simply try to be good stewards of the abundance that God has given us.

GLOBALISM IS DESTROYING AMERICA

We must distinguish between globalization and globalism, and the globalists that use the realities of globalization to pursue globalism. Dictionary.com offers a simple definition for globalism that I think works well for the purposes of this section. They define globalism as "the attitude or policy of placing the interests of the entire world above those of individual nations." I believe that this captures the essence of what globalism is, and the implications for the national sovereignty of individual nations. If globalists achieve the ultimate objective of globalism, which is global governance by the United Nations, or some other supra-national successor global entity, then they will have succeeded in destroying the constitutional republic known as the United States of America.

Although it is more difficult to come up with a very simple definition for globalization that most people would agree with, most definitions that come up in a Google search involve the free flow of goods and services, people and capital on a global scale with rapidly advancing technology, including communication and transportation. There is no element of globalization that is inherently wrong or destructive when considered individually. Most elements of globalization can be summed up simply as human progress in the harnessing of human potential to improve our world.

Elements of globalization are being employed by globalists to pursue the path that globalism leads to: global governance in the form of a New World Order that globalists dream of. The problem for the United States is that our leaders have yielded much of our national sovereignty and national competitive advantages by placing global interests ahead of our national interests and permitting American business to be hammered by international competition because liberal policymakers have effectively bound and gagged American enterprise.

TWO

Barack Obama's Strategy to Destroy America

We Have the Liberty to Infer Strategy From Obama's Statements and Actions

We are five days from fundamentally transforming America.

– Barack Obama

There is little question in the minds of many patriotic Americans that the actions and policies of Barack Obama have been destructive and disastrous for our nation. On October 30, 2008, just prior to his election as president, Barack Obama said "we are five days from fundamentally transforming America." Many of us that believed before he was elected that he would be very bad for our nation have been blown away by the extent of the devastation that Barack Obama has caused to our nation. I have personally been astounded by how many lawless, treasonous and unconstitutional actions Barack Obama has been able to get away with.

Many Americans believe, as I do, that Barack Obama has been implementing an intentional strategy to destroy America. Notwithstanding anything he might say to indicate otherwise, we can infer from many of his statements and actions that he is intentionally causing damage to our nation by any and all means available to him. I use the present tense when asserting that he is intentionally causing damage to our nation because, even since leaving office, he continues to demonstrate by his actions and statements that he is still pursuing his strategy. Many books will be written detailing the egregious actions of the most anti-American and lawless president we have seen to date, but we should consider a few highlights.

AIDING AND ABETTING RADICAL ISLAM

Barack Obama and then Secretary of State Hillary Clinton are largely responsible for the Arab spring, and the rise of ISIS. When the Iranian Green Movement sprang up in response to the alleged fraudulent Iranian elections in 2009, Barack Obama refused to give any support to that movement, but instead decided to cozy up to the Iranian leadership. Barack Obama decided to not allow a feeble freedom movement to move him off the course he was pursuing to secretly open negotiations with Iran that ultimately led to a very dangerous nuclear deal.

Barack Obama sadly missed the best opportunity since the overthrow of the Shah of Iran in 1979 to support the freedom movement in a country that had become the largest state sponsor of terrorism. In response to calls made by the leaders of the Iranian Green Movement for the United States to choose to take a stand for democracy or for the totalitarian Iranian regime, Barack Obama said "I've made it clear that the United States respects the sovereignty of the Islamic Republic of Iran, and is not interfering with Iran's affairs."

This failure by Barack Obama to support freedom stands in stark contrast to the way he handled the protests in more moderate Muslim nations such as Egypt and Libya. Obama was very quick to use the fact that hundreds of thousands of Egyptians gathered in Tahrir Square and in other locations in Cairo in January, 2011 as a basis to call for the resignation of President Hosni Mubarak. Where was the respect for the sovereignty of Egypt, and the exercise of restraint in interfering with Egypt's affairs?

Barack Obama and Hillary Clinton did not call for regime change when the opportunity presented itself to undermine the Iranian component of the "axis of evil" defined by President George W. Bush, yet later called for regime change in the more moderate states of Egypt and Libya, resulting in the rise to power of the radical Muslim Brotherhood in Egypt and the creation of a power vacuum in Libya that has permitted ISIS and other radical groups to establish radical Islamist strongholds in Libya from which they can conduct operations in the region.

By no means perfect, for no dictator is, Muammar Gaddafi had made great strides in transforming Libya from a nation blacklisted by the United Nations as a terrorist state to a status of having a restoration of full diplomatic relations with the United States. Libya had accepted responsibility for the 1988 bombing of Pan Am flight 103 over Lockerbie, Scotland, and had agreed to pay restitution to the families of the victims. Libya had abandoned the pursuit of weapons of mass destruction, and was instead making great strides in becoming a moderate Muslim nation that was accepted in the international community.

The Obama-Clinton foreign-policy initiatives that were being employed to support the Arab spring movement and the overthrow of the governments of moderate Muslim nations used the protests and civil war that sprang up in Libya in 2011 as justification for the United States and NATO to support the Libyan rebels in the over-throw of Gaddafi. The Obama-Clinton foreign-policy justification for the Libyan action, purported to be based upon supporting a movement for democracy, may have indeed been a fig leaf for covering up the true motivation behind the actions of the United States and NATO to bring about regime change.

In an email to Hillary Clinton dated April 2, 2011, Sydney Blumenthal lays out the motivation for French president Nicolas Sarkozy to "commit France to the attack on Libya." According to Blumenthal, Sarkozy's plans were driven by "a desire to gain a greater share of Libyan oil production, to increase French influence in North Africa, to improve his (Sarkozy's) internal political situation in France, to provide the French military with an opportunity to reassert its position in the world, and to address the concern of his (Sarkozy's) advisors over Gaddafi's long-term plans to supplant France as the dominant power in Francophone Africa." In the email produced to Judicial Watch in response to its FOIA request, Blumenthal pointed out to Hillary Clinton that Gaddafi was planning to use his substantial gold reserves to "establish a pan-African currency based on the Libyan golden Dinar" in order to "provide the Francophone African countries with an alternative to the French franc."

Barack Obama and Hillary Clinton opted to not overtly or covertly support the Iranian Green Revolution, but later overtly, and quite probably covertly supported regime change in Egypt and Libya. Although at the time, Barack Obama was touting the success of his foreign-policy regime change actions without the use of US boots on the ground, it is implausible to believe that, given the Obama-Clinton regime change strategy, the United States did not have CIA operatives on the ground in those countries stoking the fires of "democratic" protests.

The Obama-Clinton foreign-policy strategy failed to capitalize on the opportunity to undermine the totalitarian regime of the most ardent supporter of radical Islamic terrorism while undermining moderate Muslim nations and bringing about regime change that dramatically increased the risk of radical Islamic terrorists establishing strongholds in those countries. The Obama-Clinton foreign-policy gave rise to and supported the Arab spring, which is nothing more than a movement for radical Islamic jihad to gain ground in the Middle East at the expense of moderate Muslim nations. Barack Obama praised the Arab spring as a democracy movement, but nothing could be further from the truth.

The Obama-Clinton strategy to enhance and accelerate the blossoming of the Arab Spring kicked into high gear with the apparent decision to facilitate the supply of arms to the Syrian rebels that would later become ISIS. The administration was banned from supplying arms to the Syrian rebels, but there is very strong evidence that the CIA was aware of or monitoring the movement of arms from the port of Benghazi to ports in Syria. Indeed, it would not take much imagination to conclude that there was a direct link between gunrunning to Syria and the attack on our consulate in Benghazi and the resulting deaths of four Americans. Such a scheme could explain why the Obama-Clinton administration was lying about the cause of the Benghazi attack. Barack Obama and Hillary Clinton knowingly deceived the American people by falsely attributing the Benghazi attack to an internet video.

Lieutenant-General (retired) Michael Flynn, former Director of the Defense Intelligence Agency (DIA), in a much-publicized interview on Al Jazeera indicated that the rise of ISIS was a willful decision by the Obama administration. According to a memo declassified by the efforts of Judicial Watch, the Obama administration, other Western nations, gulf countries and Turkey supported the Salafist, Muslim Brotherhood and Al Qaeda in Iraq consortium against the Syrian regime. The memo also stated that "if the situation unravels there is the possibility of establishing a declared or undeclared Salafist principality in eastern Syria, and this is exactly what the supporting powers to the opposition want, in order to isolate the Syrian regime."

The notion that Barack Obama supported the establishment of ISIS and the caliphate is supported by the inaction of Barack Obama when ISIS began to gobble up territory in Iraq. Obama could have used the air power at his disposal to wipe out the fledgling ISIS troops when they made their initial incursion into Iraq, but he simply looked the other way and dismissed ISIS as a JV team.

The crowning moment of Barack Obama's strategy to aid and abet radical Islam was the negotiation and execution of the Iran nuclear deal and the simultaneous conveyance of pallets of cash and who knows what else Barack Obama promised the Iranians. Throughout the entire Iranian fiasco it was obvious that Barack Obama and his accomplice John Kerry were determined to sign a deal with Iran, regardless of the cost to the United States. There is no room for doubt in my mind, but I believe that history will judge

Barack Obama to have aided and abetted radical Islam when the sum total of all of his statements and actions are brought to light.

INCITING RACIAL DIVISION

As the first bi-racial president in American history, Barack Obama had the opportunity to continue to assuage racial wounds and tensions that had been dissipating for many decades, as the United States became a post-racial nation. If it were not for the race baiting of certain members of the black community, and vestiges of racism such as the NAACP, affirmative action and other race-based institutions, the United States in 2008 was about as free of racial problems as we will probably ever be.

Instead of contributing to the healing process, Barack Obama intentionally incited racial division every time he had an opportunity to encourage racial harmony. Early in his administration, when the black professor was arrested at his home for refusing to cooperate with the Cambridge, Massachusetts police that were simply doing their jobs, President Obama incited racial division by calling the Cambridge police officers stupid and asserting that the arrest of the black professor was motivated by racial discrimination.

Without knowing the facts, or perhaps knowing the facts and misapplying the facts, Barack Obama saw a situation that involved white police officers arresting a black man and asserted that racism was involved. To me, what Barack Obama did in that situation is a perfect example of how we should define racism. His reaction was a racist response to something that a colorblind person would never fall for. That episode proved to me that Barack Obama is a racist and a race baiter, and that holding a "beer summit" with the Cambridge policeman and the professor will not excuse.

Barack Obama was back to race baiting when George Zimmerman shot and killed Travon Martin in self-defense. By stating that if he had a son, he would probably look like Travon Martin, and getting the Justice Department involved in investigating the circumstances of the shooting without a reasonable basis, Obama was again stirring up racial division when he could have been calling for calm.

It seems to me that Barack Obama, Eric Holder and Loretta Lynch pursued a strategy of trying to stir up racial division with the way they handled these events, as well as those involving Michael Brown in Ferguson, Freddie Gray in Baltimore and Eric Garner in New York City in order to create discord and distrust among American citizens over fabricated issues of race. These efforts created a crisis in law enforcement, with the federal government overreaching with direct involvement in law enforcement in certain communities and creating distrust between law enforcement and the black community. Riots in Ferguson and Baltimore were the result, along with the beginning of the Black Lives Matter movement.

All of this inciting of racial division and the sowing of distrust of law enforcement by the black community led to multiple shootings of law enforcement personnel, and the handcuffing of law enforcement in cities like Baltimore. These manufactured crises were also used by the Obama administration to establish greater federal control over local law enforcement in certain cities through the execution of consent decrees foisted upon targeted cities.

In addition to all the above examples of inciting racial division, Barack Obama and his cohorts wearied us with constant accusations of racism for simply criticizing the policies of Barack Obama. We the People have learned that lesson, and we will not cower to those accusations anymore. The liberal agenda of following up that pattern of characterizing criticism of Barack Obama as racism with the next stage of characterizing criticism of Hillary Clinton as sexism or misogyny was thankfully denied liberals.

That dog won't hunt anymore. We the People will not accept the brushoff by liberals characterizing criticism of members of any of their constituent victim groups as racism, sexism, misogyny, xenophobia, Islamophobia or any other label that they want to place upon the conservative criticism of liberal policies. It's time to hold the left accountable for their bad policies and blatant lies.

UNRESTRAINED SPENDING AND BORROWING

President George W. Bush may have started the spending spree with the TARP bailouts at the end of his term, but Barack Obama wasted no time in accelerating spending and borrowing to staggering levels. Trillions of dollars were wasted, and it was all borrowed money. Much of that borrowed money served to create asset bubbles in housing and in the stock market, as well as corporate debt. The national debt virtually doubled under the presidency of Barack Obama. Those chickens will soon come home to roost, and I believe that the global financial collapse that may come as a result of cumulative policies of massive spending and borrowing will be the intended result of Barack Obama, his cronies and the globalist elites like George Soros that hold the puppet strings.

The entrenched establishment political class has a spending problem. They can't seem to help themselves from spending other people's money in order to acquire and retain power. There are those that pursue spending and borrowing in order to implement what amounts to a Cloward and Piven strategy on steroids to not only collapse the United States financial system, but to cause a global financial collapse that will usher in a New World Order. Barack Obama wasn't too concerned about balancing the budget or reducing the national debt because he was implementing a strategy to take down our country.

OBAMACARE

I will have much more to say about Obamacare in my chapter on Free Market Healthcare, especially the very obvious out-of-the-box solution that I propose to not only reverse the damage to our healthcare system caused by Obamacare, but to completely transform our healthcare system. The important truth about Obamacare for the purpose of this chapter is that the Affordable Care Act was not designed to provide better healthcare to all at lower cost, but rather it was designed to quickly move the best healthcare system in the world to a single-payer system.

Obama was lying through his teeth when he told Americans that the average family would see a reduction in health insurance cost of $2500 per year, that you could keep your doctor if you wanted to and that illegal aliens would not receive health insurance benefits under Obamacare. It turns out that Congressman Joe Wilson of South Carolina was absolutely correct when he said "you lie" during Obama's speech to a joint session of Congress.

It may have been impolite and disrespectful for Congressman Wilson to say that at that time, but he was right. Our representatives should have more boldly challenged Obama throughout his presidency, such as calling his bluff when he played the government shut-down card and blamed Republicans. We would not have suffered as much damage at the hands of Obama if Congress had stuck to their guns and allowed Obama to try to inflict as much pain from his government shut down as he could. Congress caved, and we have endured the ravages of Obamacare.

OPEN BORDER POLICY

One of the more obvious efforts by Barack Obama to undermine the national security and sovereignty of the United States was his blatant disregard for his duty to enforce immigration law and to enforce border security. Not only did the Obama administration tie the hands of border patrol agents, Obama in essence advertised that our borders were open to massive illegal immigration to our country. Just prior to the 2016 election, Obama, during an interview, implied that illegal aliens could vote without adverse consequences by saying that "if you vote, you're a citizen."

Obama did everything he could possibly do to make it easy for illegals to enter the country and to stay in the country. The open borders and catch and release policies of the Obama administration led to the senseless deaths of innocent American citizens at the hands of illegal alien criminals.

REFUGEE RESETTLEMENT PROGRAM

Barack Obama aggressively pursued ever-increasing numbers of refugees entering the United States from countries that were known to produce radical Islamic terrorist jihadists. We have good reason to believe that Obama intentionally gave rise to and aided the Arab spring in order to create a refugee crisis in Syria and Libya so that jihadists would have a free pass to enter our country with minimal vetting by the United Nations.

We have a growing problem of an increasing population of refugees that adhere to sharia law, which is incompatible with our Constitution. In some parts of the country there are significant populations of Muslim refugees that not only refuse to assimilate, but demand that we cater to their sharia-based Islamic culture. Additionally, there is a growing problem of disease such as tuberculosis among refugee populations. The majority of refugees from Islamic countries will become permanent wards of the state.

Immigration in this country used to be based upon permitting immigrants to come to America that are in good health and that have something to offer to make life in America better for all. Since the 1964 Immigration Act, we have seen a dramatic change in our immigration patterns that result in a serious burden to our economy and culture. This trend was dramatically accelerated and exacerbated during the Obama administration to the great detriment to our economy and culture.

MUSLIM BROTHERHOOD IN OUR MIDST

Before the George W. Bush administration, the Muslim Brotherhood was infiltrating our government. In his book, *Infiltration*, Paul Sperry quite thoroughly documents how the Bush administration embraced Muslim Brotherhood organizations and operatives, even placing many in sensitive national security positions, despite the terrorist attacks of 9/11.

The full extent of the manner in which Barack Obama expanded the influence of Muslim Brotherhood operatives in the various security agencies of the country will not be known for some time. The fact that Obama failed to designate Muslim Brotherhood as a terrorist organization, as other nations have, is of great concern. The problem with Muslim Brotherhood and all such organizations is that they claim to be moderate Muslims while practicing deceit that is sanctioned by the Koran. They pursue what they call civilization jihad in order to infiltrate our government and society for future action against our free society.

The fact that Obama toppled the moderate Mubarak regime in Egypt and replaced it with the Muslim Brotherhood government, and the temper tantrum that he threw when that Muslim Brotherhood government was toppled by more moderate leaders speaks volumes about Obama's loyalty to radical Islam above moderate Islam. We the People need a thorough, top-down, evaluation of all of our national security and military departments in order to purge the civilization jihadists from our midst.

TEARING DOWN OUR CULTURE

Barack Obama hates flyover country, and has a disdain for Americans that "bitterly cling to their guns and religion." Obama, like all leftists, simply does not understand that the majority of hardworking patriotic Americans love faith and freedom. We love our families, and we love our country.

Starting with his appointments to the Supreme Court and all of the lower federal courts, Obama aggressively pursued an agenda to fundamentally transform the culture of our nation. While campaigning for president, Barack Obama claimed to be against gay marriage, but it wasn't long after he became president that he changed his tune. Through judicial activism, Obama and his legions of culture warriors managed to upend the definition of marriage that has stood since creation as a foundational pillar of civilized society. Not satisfied with that victory, Obama had to poke us in the eye with a sharp stick by foisting upon us a transgender policy that we were completely unprepared for.

Without warning, we were all of a sudden distracted by Obama and his corporate cronies at Target and the NBA that were suddenly making unreasonable demands that we put our young girls at risk of having men that claim to be women entering bathrooms and locker rooms in schools, sporting events and Target stores. It was overwhelming, and completely unnecessary. Such cultural jihad was designed and intended by Obama to undermine what it means to be an American.

EVISCERATING OUR MILITARY

Notwithstanding anything that Barack Obama may have ever said to indicate otherwise, I firmly believe that he has not only a lack of respect for our military, but he has a disdain for our military. Early in his presidency, Barack Obama began dismantling our military. There was an exodus of people from the military after Obama was elected, and he accelerated the departure of many high-ranking officers. It is safe to say that the majority of our military men and women had the same disrespect for Barack Obama as he had for the military.

During his two terms in office, Obama managed to demoralize our servicemen and women by showing great weakness on the world stage, permitting gays to openly serve in the military and even opening the door for transgender individuals to serve. The Obama administration even authorized the performing of sex change operations on military personnel at taxpayer expense.

And let's not forget the humiliating capture and subsequent release of U.S. Navy personnel by the Iranians, all of which may have been choreographed by the Obama administration and the Iranians in order to enhance the Iranian image at a time when Obama was finalizing the nuclear deal with Iran. Obama's final act of disrespect toward our military was when he made the unprecedented decision just before leaving office to bring every single one of our carrier groups into port at the same time, making our aircraft carriers more vulnerable to attack than ever.

WAR ON THE MIDDLE CLASS

The Obama years have resulted in a shrinking of the middle class. Obama and his leftist globalist cronies love the elites and love the enslaved impoverished dependent constituents that they derive their power from. They absolutely hate middle class ordinary Americans with a passion. Barack Obama has waged jihad against middle class Americans. More than anything else, We the People must find a way to revitalize the middle class of this great country, and in so doing we must present a path to the slaves of the Democrat Party that are dependent upon government so that they too can become part of the middle class.

Most patriots were hoping and praying to see the last day of the destructive and tyrannical presidency of Barack Obama, and were greatly relieved to see that day come. Unfortunately, that day was not the last opportunity that Barack Obama will have to pursue his strategy to destroy America. As former President, Obama is already actively undermining our country. Time will tell, but I think we have seen just the beginning of a very activist former president that is determined to do anything and everything within his power to undermine and destroy our nation.

In addition to the plans that Barack Obama and Eric Holder are implementing to impact our elections going forward, and the criticism of President Trump that Barack Obama has already been putting forth, we face the prospect that a future Democrat president will nominate Obama to the Supreme Court. We should also recognize the possibility that Michelle Obama could one day run for president, effectively making Barack Obama co-president if she were to be elected president.

On a global scale, Obama would be the perfect anti-American candidate to be secretary general of the United Nations, a body that is so anti-American and such a threat to our national sovereignty that I will call for the United States to withdraw from the United Nations in a later chapter. We also shouldn't rule out the possibility that Obama someday reveals that he was a closet civilization jihadist that intentionally gave rise to the Arab spring, ISIS and the Islamic caliphate, which would make him a popular choice to become the leader of the caliphate.

I expect that there will be many books written that will elaborate on many of the reasons I have for believing that Barack Obama was implementing a strategy to destroy America. I have presented just a few of the reasons that I infer from the statements and actions of Barack Obama that he was indeed seeking to destroy America in any way that he possibly could. I also believe that, one way or another, Obama will find a way to continue his campaign to destroy America for many years to come. He is a leftist ideologue that will not be content to remain on permanent vacation with his celebrity and globalist elite friends.

THREE

Constitutional Crisis

We the people are the rightful masters of both Congress and the courts, not to overthrow the Constitution but to overthrow the men who pervert the Constitution.

– Abraham Lincoln

Our nation faces a Constitutional crisis of a magnitude that, until now, was unimaginable to most Americans, and certainly to our founding fathers. The balance of powers designed and established by our founders in the Constitution has been completely turned upside down through a series of usurpations of power. There must be a point of no return, and if we have not passed it, we are dangerously close to it.

We the People must take immediate, decisive action if we want to save our country from ceasing to exist as we know it. We must recognize where we have strayed from our founding principles and documents and identify the actions we must take to restore our constitutional republic.

THE FEDERAL GOVERNMENT HAS USURPED THE RIGHTS OF STATES

The federal government has trampled upon the power of the states and the people from whom it derives its power. The federal government has overwhelmed states with burdensome regulations and federal mandates. The federal government has restrained the states from protecting our borders and enforcing immigration law, and has continued to require states to accept refugees under the United

33

Nations Refugee Resettlement Program with no assurance of protection from terrorist infiltration. The ability of the states to assure the integrity of elections has been undermined, resulting in the dilution of the legal vote of legal citizens.

The federal government has very few enumerated powers that were delegated to it by the Constitution. The tenth amendment reserved all powers not delegated to the federal government to the states or to the people. The federal government has completely ignored the Constitution and has accrued to itself powers that the founders intended to deprive the federal government of in order to protect the states and their citizens from tyranny.

THE EXECUTIVE BRANCH HAS USURPED THE POWER OF CONGRESS

The Framers of the Constitution invested Congress with the greatest degree of power among the three branches of government. The legislative branch was given the power to make laws, including the power to raise revenue through taxes, and to spend those revenues. The power of the purse, along with other congressional powers, were designed and intended to keep a check on the power of the president and the executive branch.

The primary functions of the president are to enforce the laws established by Congress, and to function as the commander-in-chief of the Armed Forces of the United States. President Barack Obama doubled down on the prior usurpations of the executive branch by willfully and egregiously failing to enforce the laws of the United States, and by usurping the power of Congress by legislating through executive order.

Executive overreach by the president and the entire executive branch, especially the unelected runaway bureaucratic administrative state, has been permitted by an impotent legislative branch. One of the ways that Congress has failed to use its power to check the abuse of power by the executive branch is the failure of Congress to use the power of the purse to rein in executive overreach. Congress has permitted out-of-control spending, an escalation of the national debt and the printing of trillions of dollars by a Federal Reserve that Congress refuses to hold accountable.

JUDICIAL TYRANNY

Federal Courts have usurped the power of the president, Congress and of the states. The Supreme Court of the United States has unconstitutionally created law out of thin air. By the vote of five justices, the Supreme Court has overridden the laws of numerous states and God's law by concluding that the Constitution grants individuals of the same sex the right to be married in the eyes of the federal government.

Instead of discerning and applying the original intent of the text of the Constitution given to us by the founders, liberal justices have permitted ideology to subvert the Constitution, threatening the very foundation of our Republic.

The power to legislate from the bench was not granted to the judicial branch by the Framers of the Constitution, yet the Supreme Court assumed a legislative role in rewriting the affordable care act by reinterpreting the language and intent of the law in a manner that permitted it to pass constitutional muster. This was done even after Barack Obama unconstitutionally modified the law.

During the early days of the presidency of Donald Trump, a federal district judge struck down a valid executive order of President Trump related to immigration from seven nations that were known to pose a threat of radical Islamic terrorism. This was done despite very clear law that grants the president the power to make such a decision about immigration. The lower court decision was upheld by the Ninth Circuit Court of Appeals. Two federal judges then struck down a revised executive order by President Trump that was carefully worded in order to survive such a challenge. This overreach by the federal judiciary has become too common.

In his brilliant book, *Stolen Sovereignty*, Daniel Horowitz not only exposes the judicial coup of the left, but he provides the prescription for fixing the problem. The Constitution created the judicial branch of the federal government and defined the role of the Supreme Court, but it also gave Congress the power to establish all lower courts and to define the jurisdiction of those courts. Horowitz points out that Congress has the power to rein in the runaway judiciary by stripping the lower courts of jurisdiction over matters of election law, immigration, citizenship and other means of societal transformation that the left has been using to fundamentally transform our nation through the tyrannical judicial branch.

A HOUSE DIVIDED

And if a kingdom be divided against itself, that kingdom cannot stand. And if a house be divided against itself, that house cannot stand.

  –Mark 3:24-25

Our nation is divided by a fierce battle between conflicting worldviews that threatens to destroy America as we know it. On the one hand, liberals advocate for abortion, same-sex marriage, tax-and-spend big government, wealth redistribution, dependency upon government by our citizens, greater regulation and intrusion by government into the lives of citizens and businesses and a greatly diminished global role of the United States.

On the other hand, conservatives advocate for traditional Judeo-Christian values like the sanctity of life, traditional marriage, limited government, strict enforcement of the original intent of the Constitution and Bill of Rights and the free-market system that has been the basis for American prosperity and exceptionalism.

We are a divided nation, and we are becoming more sharply divided as time passes. Jesus plainly taught that a house divided against itself cannot stand, so we would be wise to find a way that

36

we may be less divided as a nation, or to find a way to peacefully divide our nation into two or more nations.

Many of the issues that divide our nation could be peacefully resolved by restoring the division of power between the state and federal governments given to us by the founders. If the federal government withdrew itself from education, welfare, housing, labor and other functions that properly belong to the states, each state could adopt liberal or conservative policies that citizens could support or reject by moving to a state that represents their values.

Instead of feeding an increasingly tyrannical federal government with more and more power by allowing the federal government to dictate virtually every aspect of our lives, if we restored power to the states and encouraged states to differentiate themselves based upon the people of each state choosing to govern themselves in a manner they deem most desirable, we would see a dramatic reduction in the division that we now have.

The constitutional crisis that we face is one of the fundamental causes, if not the primary cause of the divisions that cause the people of our nation to be so polarized. Had the federal government not accrued vast amounts of power that the founders intended to deprive the federal government of, there would not be so much at stake when we hold elections for president, vice president, senators and congressmen. If most of the power was vested in the states and We the People, our federal government would lack the power and the fortitude to oppress states and their citizens.

With the proper division of powers, the entrenched establishment political class and the bureaucratic state that they have created would simply not exist. Unelected judges and bureaucrats would not be able to wreak havoc with our economy and the pursuit of happiness by each citizen. There would be no judicial or bureaucratic tyranny, for the states would not put up with it.

If we had a weak executive branch and an even weaker judicial branch, as our founders intended, Congress would not endure the battering and abuse by the executive and judicial branches that they now endure. A massive transfer of power from the states to the federal government occurred when the Seventeenth Amendment, which provided for the direct election of senators, was ratified, for senators became unaccountable to the states and began to accrue power to the federal government at the expense of the states. The Senate became dysfunctional, Congress became dysfunctional and power transferred from the Congress to the executive and judicial branches.

The net effect of the distortion of our Constitution by the usurpations of power by the federal government is the dilution of states' rights, and the individual rights of United States citizens. The constitutional crisis that we now face has developed over the years by the actions of an entrenched establishment political class with an unquenchable lust for power. If We the People do not restore the balance of power intended by the founders by dramatically reducing the power of the federal government and returning it to the states, and also dramatically reducing the power of the executive branch and the power of the judicial branch and returning it to Congress, then we will have the divided nation that we deserve.

FOUR

The Promise and Perils of President Donald J. Trump

THOSE THAT SEE ONLY THE PROMISE OF
DONALD TRUMP ARE JUST AS BLIND AS
THOSE THAT SEE ONLY THE PERILS OF
DONALD TRUMP

Great peace have they which love thy law: and nothing shall offend them.

– Psalm 119:165

Sometimes our greatest strengths can be our greatest weaknesses. Donald Trump is no different than the rest of us in this regard. All we can do is to try to maximize our strengths and minimize our weaknesses. Donald Trump seems to have a strength in recruiting good people to work for him, but he doesn't seem to permit any room for constructive criticism or for the promotion of ideas that go against his stated position. Trump is very defensive.

Donald Trump seems to have a thin skin, but he is a fighter that is more than willing to get into the ring with anybody, or any number of adversaries. He has a habit of saying outlandish things, sometimes perhaps for dramatic effect, but whether he intends to be or not, he is very transparent. He also seems to be a patriotic American that truly loves his country.

We the People must give President Trump a fair shot to lead our nation through these perilous times. We must recognize that it is impossible for us to hold him to account for every misstep that he makes, every outlandish thing that he says or every decision that half of the nation disapproves of. Virtually everything that he does will offend or displease half of the nation. The same could be said of Barack Obama. We the People must give him some room to operate, but we must vigorously oppose him when he chooses to go down a path that is clearly not in the best interest of our nation.

FOR THOSE THAT SEE ONLY THE PROMISE

Those that see nothing but the promise of Donald Trump will find it very difficult to admit to and discuss any problems or concerns with the statements and actions of Donald Trump. We should take a dim view of such people and heavily discount everything they have to say about their assessment of Trump and his administration. Anyone that refuses to offer or condone any form of criticism of Trump loses all credibility, in my view, unless they are obviously constrained about what they are free to say or admit to because they work directly for Donald Trump.

We only enhance our opportunity to reach the hearts and minds of liberals if we can honestly assess any candidate or elected official against objective standards of truth instead of behaving like Democrats by defending every indefensible word or deed of any elected official, regardless of the office or the person. Liberals that actually love truth and are open to the truth will be easier to win over if they see us put truth above blind loyalty.

I would like to encourage fellow conservatives and patriots to not be found exercising blind loyalty to a fallible human being, but rather to be known for seeking out the truth and taking a stand for truth and righteousness, no matter the cost. Donald Trump is our duly elected president, and we should generally support him and pray for his safety, but we should also hold him to account for fulfilling his promises and doing the right thing. We can be generally supportive while also voicing our concerns, when necessary, about the statements, actions and policies of President Trump and his administration.

Obamacare Repeal and Replace

We should be very concerned about the way Donald Trump and his administration have responded to congressional efforts to pass legislation to repeal and replace Obamacare. Although it is true that, in almost every instance when Trump promised during his campaign to repeal Obamacare, he promised to do so in the context of repealing and replacing Obamacare, that is not what most Republican congressmen and senators promised their constituents in order to win election.

While campaigning, most Republican congressmen and senators, particularly those in the Freedom Caucus, promised their constituents to fully repeal Obamacare, without even referencing the notion that a repeal of Obamacare would be tied to a replacement for Obamacare. Even RINO Majority Leader Mitch McConnell promised to repeal Obamacare "root and branch." When Republicans won majorities in the House and Senate, they passed bills that would completely repeal Obamacare, which Barack Obama vetoed. Those attempts did not include any effort to replace Obamacare, as voters would have strenuously objected to such efforts.

Now that Republicans control both houses of Congress and the presidency, the fact that they can't get a standalone repeal bill passed proves that they were only passing repeal bills for show while Obama was president, knowing that Barack Obama would veto each bill. Donald Trump and the Republican-controlled Congress have bought the narrative of Barack Obama and the Democrats that, in order to repeal Obamacare, it must be replaced with something. If Republicans replace Obamacare with anything, it will only make the problems created by Obamacare worse, and then Republicans will own the results and be blamed for it.

When the Freedom Caucus was successful in shutting down the early attempts in the house to pass a repeal and replace bill, President Trump made a critical error in chastening the members of the Freedom Caucus for failing to support the Paul Ryan bill, when he should have been thanking the Freedom Caucus for saving him and the entire Republican Party from taking the blame for the disaster that would have resulted from the Ryan healthcare bill. Trump also made the critical error of calling for primary challenges to all of the Freedom Caucus members that voted against the Ryan bill, which was echoed by many of Trump's supporters.

I am grateful that the Freedom Caucus held firm, and that they managed to make progress with the help of Donald Trump to put forth a bill that was much better than the Paul Ryan bill, but I am concerned that the browbeating that the Freedom Caucus took from Trump caused them to give up ground that they should not have given up. This is one of the perils of Donald Trump, for he sometimes forgets who his friends are, like when he derided the Jewish reporter at a press conference for being against him when in fact the Jewish reporter was trying to support him.

I was delighted when Donald Trump came out and said that if the Senate couldn't come up with a bill to repeal and replace Obamacare, that they should simply put forth a bill to repeal Obamacare, and then work on what to replace it with later. This is a much better approach than what Mitch McConnell suggested doing, of working with Democrats to come up with a bill to repeal and replace Obamacare if Republicans couldn't agree on a bill. Engaging in such an effort with Democrats would only result in a bill to try to repair Obamacare, which might slow the process down a little, but will not stop the inevitable collapse of the health insurance and healthcare markets caused by Obamacare and any replacement or repair efforts.

Headlines on the morning of July 18, 2017 revealed that with Senators Mike Lee and Jerry Moran joining Senators Rand Paul and Susan Collins in opposition to Mitch McConnell's bill to repeal and replace Obamacare, the bill was effectively dead on arrival, and would not garner the votes to even debate the bill. Donald Trump tweeted his response by saying "we were let down by all of the

Democrats and a few Republicans. Most Republicans were loyal, terrific & worked really hard. We will return!"

Trump seems to imply by his tweet that Republicans that were opposed to the disaster of a pork-barrel insurance company bailout bill that was crafted by Mitch McConnell and lobbyists in backroom negotiations were somehow obstructionists that were disloyal to Trump and his agenda to make America great again. Trump just doesn't get the fact that the Freedom Caucus in the house and conservative senators have been fighting to keep him from making a colossal mistake.

Trump's blindness to this and the blindness of some of his supporters that criticize the Freedom Caucus represent one of the greatest perils of the Trump presidency. Instead of using the bully pulpit to criticize the House Freedom Caucus and conservative senators trying to fulfill the campaign promises that they made to fully repeal Obamacare, Trump should use the bully pulpit to call for the removal of Mitch McConnell and Paul Ryan from leadership and to praise the efforts of the House Freedom Caucus and like-minded senators.

If Congress fails to immediately repeal Obamacare, any effort to repair or replace Obamacare will continue the slow march to a government controlled, single-payer healthcare system, which is what Democrats were seeking when they passed Obamacare in the first place. The fear of the unknown has the Trump administration and Congress frozen like deer in headlights, not knowing which way to go. Democrats are gleeful that Republicans are unwittingly trying to commit political suicide by tinkering with the time-bomb that Democrats set back in 2010.

Congress should simply repeal Obamacare, transfer Medicaid and Medicare to the states, get the federal government completely out of healthcare and let the free market sort things out, as it would generate a better solution than anything Congress will do to try to repair or replace Obamacare.

Draining the Swamp

Early in the presidential campaign, Donald Trump and Ted Cruz shared the anti-establishment lane among the candidates that were seeking the Republican nomination for president. To the great consternation of the entrenched establishment political class, the two most prominent anti-establishment candidates consistently combined for over 60% of the Republican primary vote. As the nominee, Donald Trump promised numerous times to "drain the swamp," if elected.

The great danger for anyone going to Washington to serve in elected office is that, despite the best of intentions to change Washington, Washington usually changes the individual. Both Trump and Cruz showed great promise to be able to resist the temptation to join the swamp instead of draining the swamp. Although Trump alienated Cruz by falsely accusing his father, they seem to have made amends since then.

In order to successfully drain the swamp, President Trump needs the Freedom Caucus in the House, and what amounts to the Freedom Caucus in the Senate in senators Ted Cruz, Mike Lee and Rand Paul. Instead of criticizing the Freedom Caucus and their like-minded colleagues in the Senate, Trump should use the bully pulpit to criticize and cajole RINOs Paul Ryan and Mitch McConnell.

Instead of calling for primary challenges to members of the House Freedom Caucus and their like-minded conservative colleagues in the Senate, Trump should call for primary challengers to McConnell and Ryan and all of their RINO compatriots. How Trump handles his relationships with the Freedom Caucus house members and the handful of senators that tea party activists sent to Washington will tell us all we need to know about whether Trump will drain the swamp or not.

Trump calling for primary challenges to Freedom Caucus members and endorsing Luther Strange, Mitch McConnell's candidate in the Republican primary for Jeff Sessions' former Alabama

Senate seat, may be strong indicators that Trump is not committed to draining the swamp after all, but We the People must continue to be cautiously optimistic that Donald Trump will prove to be a true anti-establishment president until he establishes a clear trend that proves he is not.

Spending and Debt

While campaigning for president, Trump promised to shake things up in Washington, but he did not run as a true conservative. Conservatives have no right to expect him to be a fiscal, social and defense conservative, but we can certainly clamor for him to be as conservative as we can get him to be. We should be concerned about the lack of emphasis by Donald Trump on the spending problem that the federal government has, and the serious threat that our national debt poses to our nation.

Trump certainly shows some concern for spending, such as when he made a few phone calls to negotiate a lower price on Air Force One and on the F-35, but on the other hand, he seems to think that the federal government should lead the way in spending $1 trillion on infrastructure. We'll see how this plays out, as Trump speaks about a private-public partnership to get the job done. He has the potential to advocate for reducing spending and getting our debt problem under control, but We the People must hold his feet to the fire on getting our fiscal house in order.

The Trump Train

Donald Trump has already been elected president, so we don't have to support him on everything he comes up with. As we seek to restore American prosperity and American sovereignty, indeed to make America great again, we need not blindly endorse everything that Donald Trump or his administration proposes or supports. I like the way that Vice-President Mike Pence supports Donald Trump without saying or acting like he wants everyone to join what people have called the "Trump Train." Mike Pence maintains his credibility without undermining Trump.

Mike Pence was put in a difficult position to have to come out and be a cheerleader for the disastrous bills to repeal and replace Obamacare that Paul Ryan and Mitch McConnell tried to foist upon America. It seems to me that it went against everything that Mike Pence previously stood for. I give him a pass because he was trying to be a loyal foot soldier, although he is the only one within the administration that can publicly oppose the president and not be fired. Those that blindly pushed the flawed Paul Ryan and Mitch McConnell Obamacare repeal and replace bills and criticized the Freedom Caucus for not supporting such disastrous legislation have no excuse, and no credibility.

We need to maintain a healthy balance of being supportive of President Trump and his administration when they are going in the right direction, and opposing those things they pursue that are not in the best interest of our nation. Our nation needs a more educated citizenry that do much more than vote. It seems to me that, if you are not 100% in agreement with everything that Trump says, does or wants to do, you are not on the "Trump train."

The Trump Agenda

We must also be careful about signing onto what people call the "Trump Agenda." Donald Trump can make speeches about making America great again or draining the swamp, but when it comes to specifics, the devil is in the details. Trump supporters, and even Donald Trump himself would have a hard time consistently articulating specific action steps that together form the essence of what would be called the Trump agenda, and even if they could, the agenda and the prioritization of it must necessarily change.

Trump has made some excellent speeches that were written beforehand and that he read by teleprompter. We must recognize that for what it is, and not as a clear and certain articulation of his agenda at any point in time, for anything that Trump says is subject to revision. The statements and actions of Donald Trump prove that he is very flexible and willing to change, which sometimes is a good thing, but at other times is simply Donald Trump being double minded or going back on his word. Even if we like what Trump is saying, we should not expect to pin him down on the details, unless We the People can successfully hold his feet to the fire.

We can't go wrong by saying that the Trump agenda is to make America great again, to put America first and to drain the swamp. If we define the Trump agenda in those generalities, we can expect that most Americans would agree with that agenda. The problem is that when you put meat on the bones and get more definition of what the specifics of any agenda or plan are, Americans will start lining up along partisan lines.

I have great hope that many of the specific actions that Trump will take, or that Congress will have the gumption to take, will actually start to demonstrate to many Democrats that the failed liberal policies of the past have done nothing to help them, and that the country under the leadership of Donald Trump is actually moving in a direction that is better for them. Winning the hearts and minds of a good number of deceived Democrats is what We the People will need to do to break the stranglehold that liberals have on many Democrat victim groups.

Trump: Nationalist or Globalist?

Donald Trump communicated volumes when he stated that he is a nationalist and a globalist. I took his statement at face value, but there are some Trump supporters that sincerely believe that when Donald Trump makes a statement like that, that he somehow is toying with people's minds or trolling certain people. I certainly hope that Donald Trump knows that a nationalist puts the interests of the nation above the interests of all other nations, and that a globalist puts the interests of the nation behind the global interests of all nations collectively. By definition, a nationalist cannot be a globalist, and a globalist cannot be a nationalist. Trump should know this.

I took what Donald Trump said as indicative of his desire to be all things to all people, to please everyone. I took it as indicative of Donald Trump's belief that he can do a deal with anyone because he is Donald Trump. This is dangerous thinking.

We should be concerned about some of the deals that Donald Trump the dealmaker would get our nation into. Instead of moving the United States Embassy in Israel from Tel Aviv to Jerusalem as Trump promised in his campaign, it seems that he believes that by dispatching Jared Kushner to the Middle East, that a deal between Israel and the Palestinians for a two-state solution can be brokered during his administration. Instead, Trump should have recognized the reality that a two state solution is impossible, and he should have announced the relocation of the embassy as promised.

We should be very concerned about the role that Trump has allowed his daughter Ivanka and son-in-law Jared Kushner to have in his administration, as well as the addition of many globalists to his team. The departures of Steve Bannon and Sebastian Gorka may also signal a move away from the anti-establishment, anti-globalist agenda that won Trump the presidency. We the People must clamor for Donald Trump to repudiate globalism and to drain the swamp of the entrenched establishment political class. We must hope and pray that he does not turn out to be a globalist after all.

Donald Trump's Worst Enemy

We can sometimes become our own worst enemy, and it sure seems that Donald Trump has demonstrated the validity of that truism. None of the "Never Trumpers" or Trump haters or those that spew vitriol and hatred against Trump can come anywhere close to causing the damage to President Trump than the damage that Donald Trump causes to himself. This is true because of the sheer impact that the statements and actions of Donald Trump have upon his ability to govern. Taken as a whole, the entrenched establishment political class, and what is known as the deep state probably represents the greatest threat to President Trump, but no single individual can cause more damage to his presidency than Donald Trump himself.

FOR THOSE THAT SEE ONLY THE PERILS

Those that see nothing but the perils of Donald Trump will likewise find it very difficult to admit to and discuss any good that Donald Trump has accomplished or proposes for our nation. When trying to win the hearts and minds of Democrats, we will do well to freely admit that Trump has his flaws, but ask that they also admit to the positive attributes of Donald Trump.

Donald Trump is Patriotic

One thing that is abundantly clear to me is that Donald Trump is a patriot that loves his country. Some of the patriotic statements and actions of Donald Trump took place decades ago, when he was a Democrat. The same can be said about the generosity of Donald Trump and the compassion that he has been known to show others in need. Donald Trump may be a ruthless negotiator at times, but he has also demonstrated many times that he has a heart of gold.

Trump is Shaking Things Up

Our nation is in distress for so many reasons, and we need things to dramatically change if we are going to save our Republic. Extreme ideological liberals probably think that our nation is going in exactly the right direction, but even most average hard-working Democrats are acutely aware that our nation is in serious trouble. The majority of Democrats should have no trouble seeing the necessity of draining the swamp and repudiating the entrenched establishment political class. They may not understand the causes of our problems and know what the solutions are, but I think that many of them are glad to see the disruption that Trump is causing.

Extreme ideological liberals are probably beside themselves on virtually everything that Donald Trump is doing, but many Democrats should be able to readily see that Donald Trump is getting a lot of good things done. Even after just six months in office, Trump has clearly set the country on a better path that will lead to putting America first and strengthening the United States military. Millions of hard-working Democrats are surely thankful that Donald Trump is working to correct the problem of illegal immigration and is seeking to establish more equitable trade relations with the nations that have been taking unfair advantage of us.

I sure hope that millions of Democrats are paying attention to how Donald Trump has exposed the bias of the media, and that they will invest the time and effort to educate themselves about the issues that our nation faces, and stop allowing the media to spoon-feed them misinformation and fake news. Trump seems to have an incredible talent of using what appears to being thin-skinned on his part to expose the media as being thin-skinned and biased to the extreme. It is so ironic that the media gave Donald Trump perhaps $2 billion worth of free media during his primary campaign with the intention of dismantling him after they propped him up, but then had the tables turned on them in such a dramatic fashion.

Trump Owes Nothing to Anyone

When I say that Donald Trump owes nothing to anyone, I am not speaking about the business debt that Trump's businesses owe, I am referring to political debts that most elected officials owe to donors and lobbyists.

The businesses that are owned by Donald Trump certainly have a significant amount of debt on the books, given that most of his business interests are properties that typically involve significant leverage. Although Trump has had a few businesses fail, it appears that he has had very good success at developing a significant net worth. Many will argue about just how many billions of dollars Donald Trump is worth, but it seems that few people would disagree that his business assets are much more valuable than the total debt that is owed.

Most people, including hard-working Democrats, would rather see an independent businessman as president instead of a political operative that is indebted to and controlled by the entrenched establishment political class. What Trump lacks in political skill he can more than make up for with business skills and experience that help him to be very flexible and nimble in navigating the shark infested waters of Washington DC.

God Can Use Donald Trump

There is great hope that God can use Donald Trump to lead our nation in the direction that God would have us to go. It is God that sets up leaders and takes them down, and He is more than capable of using Donald Trump for His purposes. God chooses the foolish things to confound the wise; He chooses the most unlikely vessels to accomplish His purposes. Donald Trump is a man of great pride, but he has also shown brief flashes of humility that give me hope that God is working in his heart. We can be thankful for good people like Vice President Mike Pence that Donald Trump has chosen to surround himself with that we can hope will have a positive influence on Donald Trump and his presidency.

Whether we like it or not, American citizens are now living at the speed of Trump. Despite his age, Donald Trump seems to have boundless energy. If the first six months of the presidency of Donald Trump is any indication, we should buckle in and hang onto our hats, for we are embarking on a wild ride. For better or worse, Donald Trump is an inpatient man of action that is getting things done at a pace that we have never seen before. Trump is trying to turn our country around at a faster pace than Barack Obama tried to dismantle, undermine and destroy our nation. Good things will certainly come of it, and I am sure that each of us will be able to point to many things that we disapprove of personally. My hope and expectation is that, after we arrive at the destination of what seems to be a wild roller coaster ride, we will find ourselves in a much better America.

THE THREAT OF IMPEACHMENT

Democrats would love to impeach President Trump, and notwithstanding any statements of public support, there are many Republicans in Congress that would jump at the opportunity to impeach President Trump. The only thing that will keep Donald Trump from being impeached is if he manages to not betray We the People by failing to keep his promises.

We the People must get on the same page and clamor for President Trump and Congress to take the actions called for in this plan or one of similar magnitude to save our country from the distress that we are in. We must vigorously oppose actions or inaction that jeopardize any chance of saving our nation, but we must also vigorously oppose efforts by Democrats and the entrenched establishment political class and their globalist puppet masters to remove Donald Trump from the office of president without having first persuaded We the People that such action is justified.

The greatest promise of Donald Trump is that there is a strong possibility that he will awaken to the truth of constitutional conservatism and all that it entails. We the People must not permit those that seem to believe that Donald Trump can do no wrong or those that seem to believe that Donald Trump can do no right to distract us from having a balanced view of the promise and perils of President Donald J. Trump.

FIVE

Clear and Present Danger

WE THE PEOPLE MUST RECOGNIZE THAT OUR NATION IS IN DISTRESS

I believe there are more instances of the abridgment of the freedom of the people by gradual and silent encroachments of those in power than by violent and sudden usurpations.

– James Madison

Of the many forces at work to damage, undermine or destroy our nation, there are some that pose an imminent threat to our country. Some threats pose a clear and present danger to our sovereignty, security or economy. Until We the People successfully identify and neutralize these threats, the United States continues to be a nation in distress.

GLOBAL FINANCIAL CRISIS

The stage is set for globalists to use the impending collapse of the global financial markets as an excuse to introduce their plan to rescue the global markets and to usher in the New World Order that they have been dreaming of for decades. In the summer of 2017, Fed Chairman Janet Yellen stated that she was confident that we would not see another financial crisis in our lifetime. When we hear such foolishness from the chairman of the entity that has virtually assured that we will see a global financial collapse soon, we can be confident that the collapse is close at hand.

The Trump administration has been singing from the same song book as prior administrations that a strong stock market is indicative of a healthy or recovering economy. The stock market setting record highs when our nation has such significant economic problems is indicative to me that we have seen the inflation of the most significant stock market bubble of all time. Housing prices are skyrocketing because of government policies that lead to housing bubbles. Worldwide debt is at record highs and growing. Yes Virginia, there is a collapse coming!

Governments and central banks have recognized that it will be impossible for governments to bail out banks and other sectors of the economy when the next collapse comes. Preparations have been made by the International Monetary Fund for Special Drawing Rights to be granted to countries based upon the size of their economies. They are ready to introduce a new, global currency to usher in a new global economy. We hear talk of negative interest rates, a cashless financial system, and bail-ins, where banks are bailed out by appropriating depositor funds.

There is an unholy alliance of big government statists, big banks, big business, big insurance, big tech, big media, big energy, big pharma and any other sector that has been consolidated for the purpose of establishing a New World Order under a single global government. American businesses that have become multinational conglomerates are no longer loyal to the United States. In the old days it used to be said that what was good for General Motors was good for America, what was good for United States business was good for America. That is no longer true. What is good for small businesses in America is good for America, but what is good for big business is no longer necessarily good for America.

Brexit and other nationalist movements among European Union nations that are seeking independence from the EU, as well as the anti-globalist, anti-establishment liberty movement that is afoot in the United States is an existential threat to the globalist New World Order agenda. These movements could prompt the early implementation of the globalist plan of triggering a collapse of the global financial system. Europe is in the process of committing suicide, so the United States is the greatest obstacle to the globalist agenda to form a New World Order.

If globalists see the United States moving rapidly to restore United States sovereignty and prosperity, they may have no other choice but to collapse the global financial system as their only hope to salvage their agenda.

ELECTION RIGGING, ELECTION FRAUD

Many patriotic Americans believe as I do, that we no longer have election integrity in this country. Furthermore, I believe that we may be one election away from losing our ability to restore integrity to our elections. Republicans certainly have had problems with election fraud, but when it comes to rigging elections and election fraud, Democrats use an "all of the above" strategy. They will stop at nothing to obtain and retain power, and it seems that they are becoming progressively more shameless in their efforts to control the outcome of elections.

The 2016 Democrat primary is a case study in election rigging and fraud. The puppet masters chose Hillary Clinton as their nominee before the first ballot was cast, and Bernie Sanders went along with the show, promising to not be critical of Clinton. With all of the super-delegates in her corner from the start, Bernie didn't stand a chance, even though he was racking up victory after victory. As a WikiLeaks release of documents would later reveal, the Democrat National Committee and the media were in the tank for Hillary.

Hillary Clinton won seven straight coin toss or 50-50 proposition tiebreakers during seven closely contested primaries or caucuses that were decided by a flip of the coin. Seven straight wins! What a lucky gal Hillary was! She won seven out of seven, which is quite remarkable, given that there is less than a 1% chance of that happening. I don't accept that Hillary Clinton was lucky. I firmly believe that the outcome of the seven elections determined by coin toss was rigged in her favor. To me, that is pretty blatant and shameless behavior by Democrats. Their voters wanted Bernie Sanders, and the powers that be said "no way, we're with her."

There is much soft rigging of elections that happens with the media bias, fraudulent polling designed to lead public opinion, the clustering of illegals to pad electoral votes in sanctuary cities and sanctuary states, federal courts denying states the right to assure election integrity in their state, coordinated daily messaging through talking points of media lapdogs, open primaries and caucuses, social media censorship and manipulation and lying by government about the problems of underemployment, illegal aliens, radical Islamic terrorism and the failure of Obamacare.

The most alarming opportunities for election fraud exist in the technology and methods used in implementing electronic voting in this country. At blackboxvoting.org, Bev Harris exposes the means by which nefarious actors can change election results during the counting and tabulation process. Through her *Fraction Magic* videos, Bev demonstrates how over 5000 subcontractors and middlemen that have access to real-time voting databases can manipulate the voting results to change the results of elections in mere seconds over multiple jurisdictions without a trace, like when consultants adjust malfunctioning voting machines during an election.

This is scary stuff. Add to this potential for fraud the fact that Democrats would like to make it easy for anyone to vote electronically, perhaps from anywhere, and we have the makings for losing any remaining integrity over our elections and any possibility of restoring election integrity.

The preponderance of the evidence clearly establishes that there are huge problems with election fraud, and that Democrats are the primary beneficiaries of that election fraud. Democrats will want to argue the point until the cows come home, as that is part of their game to distract from the real issues, but We the People must simply insist that we restore the integrity of our elections, for we are one election away from losing our Republic.

EMP THREAT TO OUR POWER GRID

Although there is not much discussion about it in the daily news cycle, there seems to be a consensus among experts that the electric power grid that supplies electricity throughout the United States is very vulnerable to several threats that could cripple the power grid for a significant period of time. It seems that, over time, electric power generation and distribution in the United States developed into only three independent power grids. One grid could go down and the other two could still operate, or two could go down and the third could still continue to operate.

Establishing vast power grids may have led to efficiencies in the generation and distribution of electricity, but in doing so, the vulnerability of losing the entire grid was built in as an inherent weakness. This vulnerability requires immediate attention.

The threat of an electromagnetic pulse is the scariest threat to our power grid that we could contemplate, as it is estimated that an EMP or several EMP's that completely knocked out the United States power grid would result in the deaths of 90% of our population within one year. The reason for this is that an electromagnetic pulse would not only knock out electric power generation and distribution, it would fry the circuitry of most electronic devices within line of sight of the EMP.

The doomsday scenario that is the subject of several fictional novels on the subject is that nuclear devices are detonated at an altitude of about 250 miles above strategic locations around the country. The detonation of as few as three nuclear devices would completely knock out our power grid and most electronic devices, setting us back technologically about 200 years.

Try to imagine the chaos that would ensue if our nation of 320 million people suddenly lost electric power, communications and the means of producing and transporting the food, medicine and other critical supplies that we need for daily life. Add to that the challenges of losing our supply of clean water and sanitary sewer systems that we have come to rely on. If you consider the famine, disease and lawlessness that would prevail, it is not far-fetched that we could lose 90% of our population within one year.

The threat of an EMP attack is well known to our adversaries, and we can be certain that there are many that would delight to see such a disaster strike the United States. Many evil people, and some rogue nations, would love to have an active role in taking down our nation. Iran and North Korea are two nations that have repeatedly asserted such a desire. It doesn't take an intercontinental ballistic missile to deliver a nuclear device, as one can be delivered by what has been referred to as a "scud in a bucket," which is simply a nuclear device on a short range missile fired from a container ship off one of our coasts.

Another way that an EMP or EMP's could be detonated above the United States is through the use of satellites. This is one reason why we should be greatly concerned that North Korea has put their first satellites into orbit. All North Korea or any other nation has to do is strategically place several satellites with nuclear devices aboard into synchronous orbit over the United States and simultaneously detonate them without warning. In February, 2017, India launched 104 satellites into orbit with a single rocket. In addition to three larger satellites, 101 nano-satellites were launched. I don't know how small a satellite can be and still be capable of holding a nuclear device, and I don't know how difficult it would be to hide the launch of a nuclear device, but I certainly don't want to find out.

OPEN BORDERS, REFUGEES AND RADICAL ISLAMIC JIHAD

The lax enforcement of our national borders, especially the porous southern border with Mexico, has permitted dramatic inflows of illegal immigrants and dangerous illegal drugs. Through the United Nations Refugee Resettlement Program, the United States continues to permit tens of thousands of poorly vetted refugees from countries that are known for generating radical Islamic terrorists to enter the United States each year. The combination of open borders and the refugee program has contributed to an ever-increasing threat of radical Islamic jihad attacks in the United States.

The 9/11 commission report suggested that the most important failure leading to the attacks was a failure of imagination. Those entrusted with the defense of our nation failed to imagine and to prepare for an attack such as the one that happened on that fateful day. You would think that the events of 9/11 and subsequent attacks in the United States and around the world would have our agencies charged with law enforcement and anti-terrorism preparedness working very hard to imagine every possible scenario for terrorist attack.

Occasionally We the People are suddenly confronted with a set of circumstances that make us realize that we were spared from mass casualties that could have resulted from a vulnerability that was not identified as a result of another failure of imagination. This happened again in June 2017, when a lone gunman opened fire on congressmen and staff practicing for a baseball game the next day. Were it not for the presence of Congressman Steve Scalise at the practice that morning, there would have been mass casualties.

Steve Scalise, as majority whip of the House of Representatives had with him at the baseball practice a Capital Police protective detail assigned to him. These two brave officers pinned down the assailant until additional officers arrived to assist in neutralizing the assailant, saving many lives that day.

The failure of imagination comes into play when you consider the fact that, given the elevated terrorist threat that we have lived with for sixteen years, congressmen should never have been gathering for that practice without at least a dozen Secret Service agents forming a perimeter. Someone dropped the ball, including our congressmen and their staff. Since the cat is now out of the bag on this vulnerability, we can discuss what could have happened.

What would have happened if radical Islamic jihadists in the United States had learned that congressmen, senators and their staff were practicing every morning at the same time and in the same place for a baseball game that was to occur at the end of the week? What if three or four, or even a dozen heavily armed jihadists had arrived at multiple points on the perimeter of the baseball field, and after surprising the security detail, proceeded to massacre twenty or thirty congressmen and their staff?

I'm sure that jihadists in this country and around the world are kicking themselves for not being aware of the opportunity to take out a couple dozen United States congressmen and senators. This was just the kind of opportunity that jihadists in our country are looking for to cause maximum damage with minimal risk in soft venues that are relatively unprotected and unprepared.

I trust that this was a wake-up call to our elected officials and the law enforcement and counterterrorism personnel that are charged with protecting them and our country, but I wonder what other risks we face because of a failure of imagination.

We are certainly grateful that the situation did not turn out as badly as it could have, but what We the People should take away from this tragedy is that the failure of imagination persists, that there is a failure among our leaders to recognize the threat, and that our nation is very vulnerable to a continuing threat from radical Islamic terrorists.

TYRANNY OF TECHNOLOGY

The rapid advancement of technology has the potential to bring greater liberty to all of humanity, but it also has the potential to enslave all of humanity. The concentration of the power of technology into the hands of a few is a threat to our liberty. Many of my libertarian friends that believe that we should not fear the establishment of monopolies seem to also believe that man is inherently good. History has shown that man too often yields to his sin nature, seeking to oppress his fellow man through the monopolization of various levers of control, including technology.

Surveillance State

A government by the people, of the people and for the people will not use its power and authority to exploit and oppress its own citizens. Those governing by the consent of the governed would not dare lie to and betray the trust of the citizens that it serves. Our federal government has strayed so far from that designed by our founders, that we cannot trust our government to refrain from using technology to conduct ever increasing surveillance on We the People in order to protect its growing power and authority.

We live in a digital world, and everything that we do that is connected to that digital world can potentially be recorded for future use or abuse. All communications to or from our cell phone number, email address, IP address of any computer or digital device that we use, browser history on Google, Yahoo or Chrome, our social media activity on Facebook, YouTube, LinkedIn, Twitter or other such accounts, and any other imaginable digital activity can be recorded and stored.

Just as our fingerprints are unique to each of us, and can be used to identify us, our digital activity creates digital fingerprints that can be used to identify us with a high level of accuracy. All of the digital information that is collected in the massive NSA storage facilities that we hear about need not be collected in one big bucket, for the vast majority of the digital information can be collected in very discrete, individualized buckets.

Ownership of each individualized bucket could change, such as when someone changes their cell phone number and someone else picks it up, but it wouldn't be difficult for an individualized bucket like a cell phone number to be broken into separate buckets based upon timeframe of ownership. A copy of every email sent could be placed into the bucket of the sender and each recipient.

Location services using GPS coordinates and metadata in pictures or videos that we send out offer the surveillance state much more information about where we are at any particular moment without our direct participation or awareness. Our mobile devices can be used as electronic leashes by simply recording our location in whatever increment of time is appropriate and recording those breadcrumbs that reveal where we were at each increment in time, or at least where our devices were. If every time we were to unlock our devices the digital network was pinged, those breadcrumbs could be recorded in order to establish our whereabouts. Voice recognition of recorded conversations could establish that we were connected to our devices during certain periods of time.

In the old days, when a government agency like the FBI, state or local law enforcement, or other entity with proper authorization from a court secured permission to conduct surveillance upon a United States citizen, it was conducted only with probable cause, and was granted with specific particularity as to what was being sought and the timeframe for which permission for surveillance was granted. The general surveillance of anyone in order to collect information to use in the future was never granted by any court.

In this digital world that we live in, we are being used to conduct surveillance on ourselves. By accepting and using technology such as Google, Verizon and Facebook, and doing so under their terms of use and privacy policies, we have effectively granted the power to conduct surveillance on us without having a viable free-market alternative. Until such time as the federal government passes useful regulation to limit the encroachments on our privacy by these big tech companies, We the People run the risk of completely losing our privacy. Indeed, some involved in big tech companies have effectively told us that we no longer have a right to privacy, and that we should just get used to it.

It is curious to me that our federal government has established the Department of Homeland Security, consolidated and coordinated the sharing of information among various federal agencies and, through the Patriot Act, has encroached upon our liberties, especially our right to privacy, but they have done nothing to secure our borders to staunch the flow of illegal immigrants and refugees that are pouring into our country. Perhaps our government is less interested in national security than it is in controlling every aspect of our lives.

The Threat of Big Tech

The federal government has been more than willing to permit big tech "winner take all" monopolies to be created because, by doing so, the federal government would eventually have access to an unprecedented volume of private information on all Americans. Never before in the history of mankind has it been possible for governments to be empowered with such levers of control over citizens. Our government is not only permissive in this, but is complicit in the use of technology to acquire incredible power over American citizens.

In addition to threats to our privacy, rapidly developing technology that empowers companies like Google, Facebook, YouTube and Twitter to amass huge market shares of billions of people in their market segments has empowered them to individually and collectively control the information that we consume on a daily basis, which gives them the power to censor conservatives and to shape public opinion. Censorship of conservative sites by these and other big tech companies has already begun.

Many that are willing to accept the bread and circuses that the globalist elites want to use to control the masses are also more than willing to be spoon-fed by the liberal propaganda these companies espouse, but We the People must compel our government to use good old-fashioned trust-busting to break up these cartels before it's too late. Big tech has embraced liberalism, globalism and radical environmentalism, posing a threat to all of our liberties.

LAWLESS LIBERALS

The violence that erupted in Charlottesville, Virginia on August 12, 2017 and the resulting deaths of one counter-protester and two law enforcement officers is yet another example of liberal politicians becoming complicit in permitting or even encouraging escalations in violence.

Demonstrators with a valid permit gathered to protest the proposed removal of Confederate monuments. Counter-protesters that did not have permits gathered in greater number. A good number of the permitted demonstrators wearing helmets and equipped with shields were members of deplorable white supremacist or neo-Nazi groups that advertised their participation. Among the permitted demonstrators were ordinary citizens concerned about the effort to revise history by removing monuments.

Some of the counter-protesters were good and decent people exercising their First Amendment right to assemble and protest, but many were members of globalist funded rent-a-riot groups such as Black Lives Matter and Antifa that showed up armed with a battering ram and bottles and cans filled with urine and feces.

State and local officials were well aware of the powder keg that was developing, and instead of diffusing the situation they made tragic decisions that made matters worse, leading to one of the protesters using his vehicle to plow down dozens of counter-protesters. The individual that drove the car through the crowd and rammed into other vehicles is guilty of a heinous crime. Many have laid blame at the feet of the white supremacist or neo-Nazi groups that the perpetrator was alleged to be affiliated with, but little attention has been given to the culpability of Virginia Governor Terry McAuliffe, and other state and local officials.

Shortly before the demonstration was to begin, Governor McAuliffe declared a state of emergency and declared that the assembly was an unlawful assembly, which was a lawless and spineless act on his part. On his orders, law enforcement dispersed the crowd that had permits to demonstrate instead of dispersing the crowd that not only did not have a permit, but was armed with weapons that were clearly intended to cause mischief. To make matters worse, law enforcement forced the protesters to vacate their permitted venue by walking through the crowd of counter-protesters. It was almost as if civil and law enforcement authorities wanted to see violence take place. Numerous reports of law enforcement doing nothing while people were accosted support this view.

Similar failures of civil servants and law enforcement officials to enforce law and order have led to far worse instances of violence causing much bodily harm and property damage in cities like Baltimore and Berkeley. Even in Boston the Saturday after the Charlottesville tragedy, local officials and law enforcement decided to disband a permitted assembly of approximately 300 demonstrators instead of dispersing the 30,000 counter-protesters that did not have permits. In Berkeley a week later, police permitted masked Antifa counter-protesters to assault peaceful demonstrators.

The right to free speech and assembly in the United States is under intense attack by liberal politicians that are in charge of numerous cities plagued by high levels of violence. Many of these cities are also known to be sanctuary cities, and have poor records of maintaining election integrity. These lawless liberals seem to be trying to re-create the 1960s conditions that led to riots all over the country. We the People must recognize this threat and resist all efforts to erode our rights to free speech and assembly and to lay the blame for such displays of violence at the feet of conservatives.

Most Americans, including many decent, law-abiding and hard-working Democrats that are waking up to the tactics of the illiberal left, are well aware of what these lawless liberals are up to. We know that white supremacists and neo-Nazis are deplorable, but we also know that the Black Lives Matter and Antifa groups are as well. We believe that all lives matter, and that all fascists are evil, and we know that some politicians are complicit.

PART II

A CALL TO ACTION

SIX

Cutting the Gordian Knot

THE NEED FOR A BOLD, COMPREHENSIVE, TRANSFORMATIONAL PLAN TO SAVE AMERICA

If the federal government should overpass the just bounds of its authority and make a tyrannical use of its powers, the people, whose creature it is, must appeal to the standard they have formed, and take such measures to redress the injury done to the Constitution as the exigency may suggest and prudence justify.

– Alexander Hamilton, Federalist number 33

The legend of Alexander the Great cutting the Gordian knot is probably not true, but it certainly makes for a great story. It has also given us a wonderful way to summarize a scenario where there are complex and difficult problems that seem to have no solution that calls for an out-of-the-box, bold approach that people describe as "cutting the Gordian knot."

The United States faces many complex and difficult problems that seem impossible to solve. There are so many different issues that have such broad implications that it is difficult to imagine any plan would be comprehensive and bold enough to substantially and simultaneously solve the many problems that we face.

We obviously cannot cut the Gordian knot in one motion in a moment in time and solve the complex problems that we face. What I have put together is a plan that is bold, comprehensive and transformational that we can implement over as long a period of time as it takes to get the job done. Some aspects of the plan, when implemented, will have dramatic immediate effect.

The full, simultaneous implementation of this plan, if it were possible, could certainly be described as cutting the Gordian knot. If we break down the elements of this plan, some elements may only be accomplished by taking a series of steps over a period of time, while other elements are best implemented by decisive action taken at a specific moment in time. In either scenario, implementing a component of this plan should be considered to be cutting the Gordian knot with respect to that component. Cutting the Gordian knot then becomes a matter of cutting a number of smaller Gordian knots. Suddenly the seemingly impossible becomes possible!

CUTTING THE HEALTHCARE GORDIAN KNOT

The opportunity that We the People have to solve the problems created by our government in the health insurance and healthcare markets is the "poster child" of the numerous Gordian knots that we should cut.

We can clearly see that the government isn't the solution to the problem, the government is the problem. We seem to be faced with a problem with no solution, yet the consequences of permitting the status quo to continue would be disastrous. The magnitude of the problem is huge, as it involves one sixth of our economy. Americans are acutely aware of the problem, and are clamoring for our government to provide a solution. Anxious Democrats and Republicans that have played politics with our healthcare system are very nervous about the political repercussions of any action taken.

The solution is very simple and straightforward, but Congressman and Senators will not take necessary action. The need for Americans to organize and speak with one voice in order to compel Congress to do what is necessary could never be more apparent. The reality is that, unless We the People become organized and get behind this solution to our broken healthcare system and compel Congress to cut the Gordian knot, we will be saddled with a single-payer socialized medicine solution.

Only three things are necessary for the federal government to do their part to solve the problem. First, there must be a complete repeal of Obamacare, not a repair or a partial replacement. Second, Congress must outlaw health insurance altogether. And third, Congress must transfer Medicaid and Medicare to the states, completely withdrawing the federal government from any involvement in our healthcare system.

States that follow-up this federal action by eliminating Medicaid, Medicare and any other involvement by the state in healthcare will take the market distorting third-party payments out of the equation, and permit free-market healthcare to thrive.

CUTTING THE GORDIAN KNOT OF BIG GOVERNMENT

The solutions to most of the problems that we face are simple, but the entrenched establishment political class lacks the will or the fortitude to get the job done. The only way we will see the transformative change that we need is if We the People organize and speak with one voice to compel Congress and the president to do what needs to be done to cut a few Gordian knots in order to turn our country around.

Return Power to the States

We the People can restore the federalism intended by our founders by proposing and ratifying several amendments to the Constitution that return power to the states that has been usurped by the federal government. Permitting direct proposal of amendments by the states, repealing the Seventeenth Amendment, permitting states to nullify federal actions, empowering states with the authority to remove federal officers as well as prescribing the manner by which states may exercise their natural right to secede from the union will do much to correct the problem of the usurpation of the rights of states by the federal government.

Return Power to the People

In addition to restoring power to the states that has been stolen by the federal government, We the People can reverse much of the problem of the usurpation of individual liberties by proposing and ratifying seven amendments that will protect life, reaffirm God's definition of marriage, remove infringements on the Second Amendment, restore the integrity of our elections, as well as restore economic liberty with a national right to work amendment, the elimination of taxes on all property and the elimination of federal wage and price controls, including the minimum wage.

Restore Fiscal Sanity

We the People can require fiscal sanity from those that we elect, and repudiate the globalist agenda by proposing and ratifying six amendments to establish a flat income tax, impose a limit on any future national sales tax, limit the quantity of currency issued based upon the quantity of gold held in reserve, eliminate the Federal Reserve and fractional banking, require the federal budget to balance and give the president the power of the line item veto.

Pursue Better Governance

We the People can pursue better governance through the proposal and ratification of several amendments to the Constitution that will impose Congressional term limits, limit the president to a single term of six years and address the problem with entrenched federal employees.

Amendments such as these may seem like common sense proposals to us, but We the People should expect that the entrenched establishment political class will fight tooth and nail over each of my proposed amendments, especially my proposal to make federal workers employees-at-will and to eliminate much of the largess that the entrenched establishment political class has granted to themselves and their minions.

CUTTING THE GORDIAN KNOT OF THE GLOBALIST NEW WORLD ORDER AGENDA

The eminent global financial collapse gives us the opportunity to choose a clearly superior alternative to permitting the globalists to crash the world financial markets and implement their plans to rescue the world from the disaster they create while consolidating power in the hands of a few global elites.

We the People can cut the Gordian knot of the globalist New World Order agenda with several slices at smaller Gordian knots. With one slice we would break the stranglehold that global elites have on our money supply and financial markets by abolishing the Federal Reserve and abolishing fractional banking. Then we can cut the Gordian knot of the debt problem by declaring a Year of Jubilee whereby all debt is eradicated, and perhaps take the additional bold step of outlawing debt altogether.

The next slice at the Gordian knot would be to upend the globalist agenda to undermine the sovereignty of nations and implement global governance by simply withdrawing from the United Nations, securing and defending our borders and also completely banning all immigration to the United States for an indefinite period of time.

CUTTING THE EDUCATION GORDIAN KNOT

Federal and state governments have been throwing more and more money at an education system that has failed to produce satisfactory results. Government isn't the answer to the problem, government is the problem, and we must cut the Gordian knot of education by getting federal and state governments out of education altogether. It will be up to the citizens of each state to determine whether they want to eliminate public education, but We the People can help states make the right decision by compelling our states or the Congress to pass a constitutional amendment that eradicates taxes on all property, including property taxes.

Ratifying a constitutional amendment that eliminates taxes on all property will cut the education Gordian knot, permitting the citizens of each state to pursue twenty-first century free-market education at little or no cost. We the People don't need a failed nanny state education system that primarily serves to indoctrinate our children.

Cutting the Gordian knot requires that We the People reject the axiom promoted by the entrenched establishment political class that politics is the art of the possible, whereby they define possible as what is *politically possible* instead of what is truly possible if We the People become organized and engaged in a coordinated effort to force the federal government and our states to return to government of the people, for the people and by the people. We must think outside the box in order to identify the actions we must take to save our country from the brink of destruction.

Identifying the manner in which We the People can cut the Gordian knot on big problems such as the health insurance crisis and the impending global financial meltdown is fairly easy. Getting enough people to recognize the solutions and clamor for making the bold decisions to implement solutions will be very challenging. We the People must become engaged and organized in advocating for making a series of prudent incremental decisions along with the implementation of big, bold, Gordian knot cutting ideas along the way that will allow us to turn our country around and usher in a new era of American prosperity and exceptionalism. We the People must become community organizers.

SEVEN

Establish or Join Freedom Cells

DEMOCRATS DON'T HAVE A MONOPOLY ON COMMUNITY ORGANIZATION

The strength of the Constitution lies entirely in the determination of each citizen to defend it. Only if every single citizen feels duty-bound to do his share in this defense are the constitutional rights secure.

– Albert Einstein

Perhaps the most important element of this plan is for We the People to form groups of like-minded patriotic Americans through which we may have our collective voices heard and our actions coordinated for maximum impact, so that we can take immediate action to take our country back. We must establish or join what I call "Freedom Cells" in order to do this. It is time that we conservatives try a little community organization.

ORGANIZE INTO FREEDOM CELLS

Establish or join several Freedom Cells of any configuration that makes sense to you. We all belong to various groups, and we should each consider organizing those affinity groups for such a cause as this. Some patriots may form Freedom Cells of immediate or extended family, church groups, friends, neighbors, veterans groups or any other affinity group imaginable. Perhaps the most important Freedom Cell that each and every one of us should establish or join is within our local election precinct.

Hold monthly meetings of Freedom Cells to discuss ideas and to take coordinated action to solve the serious problems that our country faces. If you like the ideas that I have presented in this plan, promote the bold ideas of this plan, or one of similar magnitude and direction to like-minded patriots, encouraging them to form a Freedom Cell with you, or to form Freedom Cells among their other affinity groups. It is important to have a bold, comprehensive and transformational plan of action. Use this plan as a starting point and form Freedom Cells to identify problems, discuss potential solutions and identify specific action steps that can be coordinated to take our country back.

In short, it is what we make of it. Freedom Cells should be established and operate as a network of autonomous, independent units of freedom loving Americans. We the People in each Freedom Cell are the true source of the collective power of the whole, just as it should be with our government. We the People are the Minutemen, and we are served by those who volunteer as Founding Fathers, Sons of Liberty and Patriots to help organize and facilitate communication among our members.

If there is an appetite for freedom loving Americans to get behind this plan to turn our country around and to establish or join Freedom Cells, some Minutemen will become Patriots to provide leadership at the Freedom Cell level. Some will become Sons of Liberty to provide leadership at the county and congressional district level, and some will become Founding Fathers to provide leadership at the state and national level.

There is no need to apologize for the use of Founding Fathers, Sons of Liberty or Minutemen to name the different leadership levels, because strong conservative women know that they are welcome to contribute their leadership skills at any level, and they will not be offended or hesitant to join groups with fathers, sons or men in the names. In this crazy time when a student can receive a lower grade for using mankind in a paper, there are strong conservative women that will enjoy seeing liberal heads explode when they self-identify as Sons of Liberty!

Those that join Freedom Cells as Founding Fathers, Sons of Liberty or Patriots are simply volunteering their time and talent to serve as leaders of the movement to promote this plan or one of similar magnitude and direction to take our country back. The only power that those that volunteer for leadership positions will have to influence or control anything will be earned by effective service to We the People, the Minutemen.

The communication, organization and action of Freedom Cells as a whole should begin at the local level, bubble up and percolate through the network, and result in local action all over the country. My hope is to get enough critical mass that We the People can have a website that will facilitate communications, provide for a method of polling members, and to provide a way to aggregate our voices. We the people must organize a grassroots liberty movement, not a top-down hierarchy. We must guard against establishment types hijacking this movement like they did the Tea Party movement. In the event that the entrenched establishment political class hijacks leadership of Freedom Cells in a congressional district, state or even at the national level, We the People must immediately separate from the wayward leadership and reestablish autonomy.

COMMUNITY ORGANIZATION AND ACTIVISM

With truth on our side, we can beat the liberals at their own game. We the People that seek to repudiate the entrenched establishment political class, restrain an out-of-control federal government and restore the balance of power embedded in the Constitution are more numerous than the extreme liberals that have hijacked our government. We are the truth seekers and the truth speakers. They are the ones that cause division, create victim groups and proceed to exploit those victim groups for their own self-aggrandizement. Their tactics are worn out and tired, and many of those that they have exploited are finally coming to the realization that liberals have used them.

It is time for us to organize the silent majority and transform our nation through a grassroots movement of principled activism. We must seek to speak with one voice and to demonstrate and protest with a frequency and volume that exceeds that of the liberals. We must beat them at their own game, but do so with decency and respect for people, property and authority that will stand in stark contrast to the tactics of the progressive left. When liberals gather at the National Mall, city hall or at state houses and leave a mess when they are finished, We the People that are the true guardians of liberty will not leave a mess when we gather, and will probably even clean up the mess that they leave.

Many conservatives that express concern about the state of our nation do not even make the effort to vote. If we do not vote, we have no right to complain. We the People must do much, much more than simply vote in elections. If we limit our political activity to voting, we seal the fate of our nation as a lost Republic. We the People must organize, we must communicate, we must speak with one voice and we must move as one with purpose and resolve.

It is said that when the people fear the government, there is tyranny, but when the government fears the people, there is liberty. How can We the People instill a proper fear of the people by the government if we continue to allow the voices and actions of the liberal left to drown out the feeble voices and actions of the silent majority?

We the People will have a tremendous impact on all aspects of governance if we organize 30 million patriotic Americans into local Freedom Cells that are organized and coordinated to take the steps set forth in this plan to take our country back. Liberals, statists, globalists and the entrenched establishment political class will have no chance against an educated and committed network of patriots that are clamoring for the federal government, as well as every state government, to restore the United States to a government by the consent of the people.

TRANSFORMATIONAL CONSERVATISM

The terms fiscal conservative, social conservative and national defense conservative are pretty thoroughly understood. We the People must engage in what I call Transformational Conservatism in order to save our Republic.

Barack Obama promised in his campaign for president to fundamentally transform America. He was largely successful in his goal of transforming America through his lawless actions. The goal of Transformational Conservatism is to fundamentally transform the United States, but in the opposite direction of the transformation proposed or accomplished by Barack Obama.

The goals of Transformational Conservatism are to restore the Constitution, restore the balance of power, repudiate the entrenched establishment political class, restore fiscal sanity, restore our national security, restore our national prosperity, restore our national sovereignty, and to humbly ask our Creator to forgive us of our national sins and restore His blessings upon our land.

Prudent Populism

Transformational conservatives recognize the need for a bold, comprehensive and transformational plan to accomplish these goals. We recognize the need to organize and to take action for as long as it takes to save our country. Liberals will describe us as populists and our ideology as populism, which they will use as a derogatory term. We the People must describe our ideology as prudent populism similar to that which led to the birth of our nation.

We the People are simply pursuing the principles laid out by our founding fathers. We do not believe in mob rule, and will not tolerate being described as an angry mob. We believe, as our founding fathers did, that government derives its power from the consent of the governed. We believe in government of the people, by the people and for the people. Prudent populism is how we should describe the necessary organization and activism of We the People in order to take our country back and restore the constitutional republic as our founders intended. We cannot take our country back without populism. We need a movement of patriots to get the job done. Let us not allow liberals to disparage our patriotism.

New American Nationalism

If we are to save our nation from destruction, we must embrace rational and prudent nationalism. We desperately need an era of New American Nationalism. Liberals will have disparaging things to say about any effort advocating for increased nationalism. To them, nationalism is a derogatory term that they equate with isolationism, protectionism and xenophobia. They are entitled to their opinions, but we must push back with the truth.

The truth is that our national security has been compromised by lax border security and immigration policy. We are not xenophobic if we press the pause button on all immigration so that we may have a national discussion about immigration and national security. We are not xenophobic if we deny entry to refugees under the United Nations Refugee Resettlement Program in order to assess the risks. We have been sold a bill of goods by the United Nations and the establishment political class. We should not allow name-calling by liberals to dissuade us from doing what is right for our country, including placing a moratorium on all work visa immigration programs that have been robbing Americans of jobs.

The truth is that we have exported our prosperity along with millions of jobs because the entrenched establishment political class struck an evil bargain with globalists and environmentalists. It is prudent and rational for us to examine our international trade policy and take steps to put America first. We have allowed our generosity as a free people to be taken advantage of to our detriment, and to the detriment of the world. Instead of tying our hands behind our backs, we should insist on secure, strategic trade. We the People must repudiate globalism and put American interests first.

Trade between countries should be win-win. It is not a zero-sum game. There is an abundance of resources for both parties in international trade to be better off. Our trading partners can be better off without making the United States worse off. The United States needs to quickly return to being a net exporting country and repatriate millions of jobs. We will gladly help other nations improve their standards of living, but we do not have to impoverish the American middle class in order to do so.

The Bible says that to whom much has been given, much will be required. I believe that America has been uniquely blessed by God, and that we are the most generous nation the world has ever seen. When we defeat an enemy, we rebuild their nation and require nothing more than enough land to bury our dead. What nation in the history of the world has ever operated that way? We need not apologize for the strength or prosperity of our nation. No president of the United States should ever go out on apology tours like Barack Obama did. We should accept and be grateful for the greatness of our country and acknowledge from Whom our blessings flow. We should also recognize that liberals do not share our values, and that many people around the world despise the United States because of our prosperity and freedom.

We must pursue New American Nationalism by strengthening our military and returning to a policy of speaking softly and carrying a big stick. After the disastrous Obama foreign policy, we must rebuild the trust and confidence of our allies and reestablish fear and respect from our adversaries. The United States must restore its reputation for doing the right thing. We must restore the national sovereignty of the United States.

INDIVIDUAL ACTION

The success of this plan or any plan of similar magnitude and direction hinges upon mobilizing tens of millions of conservative activists to save our Republic and restore liberty. Each and every one of us is responsible for doing our part in this most urgent cause. I have set forth a plan that is bold and comprehensive, and though far from perfect, it is substantially complete and fully adequate to save our country from the perils that we face. If this plan does nothing more than start a conversation that leads to a plan of similar magnitude and direction, I will be happy with that, but we must have the conversation and move decisively and quickly to stop what the entrenched establishment political class, liberals, environmentalists, statists and globalists are doing to our country.

I ask you, dear patriot: who will come to the aid of our country? If not you, who? If not now, when? If you are concerned about the existential threats that our country faces, then I ask you to consider what you will do to help in the cause. Will you establish or join Freedom Cells and be enlisted in the cause as one of 30 million Minutemen that we need to assure victory? If so, make it a priority to join or establish a Freedom Cell for your precinct and encourage others to join. Are you willing to provide leadership at the precinct or county level? If so, promote this plan of transformational change and actively recruit others to join your precinct Freedom Cell or any other Freedom Cell that you establish or join, engaging them in a conversation guided by this plan to save America.

DISPROPORTIONATE SHARE OF INFLUENCE

Politics, by its very nature, is the pursuit of a disproportionate share of influence. Everyone engaged in the political process is trying to magnify their influence in order to accomplish an objective. There are those that seek a disproportionate share of influence for evil purposes, and there are those that seek a disproportionate share of influence for the common good. Ideologues on the left probably earnestly believe that they are seeking the common good, and ideologues on the right believe that they are seeking the common good. The common good, which includes individual liberty, is in the eye of the beholder.

We the People that desire to see our Republic restored must diligently work to secure a disproportionate share of influence so that we may restore the Constitution and set our country on the right path again. We must not be bashful about seeking a disproportionate share of influence, and we must not passively allow ideologues on the left or the entrenched establishment political class of both parties in the vast middle that seek power for their own self-aggrandizement to continue to hold their disproportionate share of influence.

ELECT ADVOCATES OF THIS PLAN

We the People must advocate for a bold, comprehensive, transformational plan to save our country. If a sufficient number of patriots will unite behind my plan, or a plan of similar magnitude and direction, we can turn our country around. We need a grassroots movement that will elect advocates of this plan at all levels of government. We will not be very successful at passing some of the constitutional amendments that we should pass if we do not clean house in the legislatures of enough states. We need to elect representatives that will walk the walk and not just talk the talk.

We must repudiate the entrenched establishment political class at the federal, state and local level. State, county and municipal governments are the farm teams of the federal government, so we must implement some of the same ideas for limited government at the state and local level as well. It is up to the citizens of each state to determine if they will have limited, fiscally responsible government, or if they will permit their state to continue to borrow and spend their state into bankruptcy.

We the People have much work to do to save our Republic. We must repudiate the entrenched establishment political class. We must repudiate the radical environmentalist theology that worships the creation instead of the Creator. We must repudiate the globalists that would submit American sovereignty to global governance by a handful of elites. We must repudiate the liberal policies that are destroying our economy and security. We the People will assure the greatest probability of success by forming Freedom Cells of tens of millions of patriotic Americans that will advocate for this plan or one of similar magnitude and direction.

Transforming and overwhelming the Republican Party through the action of Freedom Cells is a critical step in taking back our country and saving our Republic. We the People can rise up and take back the Republican Party and our nation through the political process if we will simply show up in sufficient numbers. We the People can get the job done if 30 million patriots will join Freedom Cells and work together to implement this plan.

EIGHT

Transform the Republican Party

IT'S TIME TO OVERWHELM AND TAKE BACK THE REPUBLICAN PARTY

"There is nothing which I dread so much as a division of the Republic into two great parties, each arranged under its leader, and concerting measures in opposition to each other. This, in my humble apprehension, is to be dreaded as the greatest political evil under our Constitution."

– John Adams

The GOP establishment political class has failed to recognize that the conservative base is fed up with being taken for granted. The establishment consistently refuses to accept conservative candidates that have the support of the conservative base, while consistently expecting the conservative base to always support every moderate that they put forward. We are tired of being told to sit down and shut up while providing the overwhelming majority of votes needed to elect Republican candidates.

The establishment does not understand that there has been a fundamental shift in the posture and attitude of the conservative base, and that a fundamental change in the posture and attitude of the establishment is necessary in order to maintain party unity. They don't understand that this fundamental shift led to the insurgent candidacies of Donald Trump and Ted Cruz. They don't understand that the change is permanent, and that it is becoming a movement that they cannot control.

Although it is true that the entrenched establishment political class within the Republican Party has consistently ignored, despised and marginalized conservatives, I don't think that the formation of a third-party is the solution. There is nothing wrong with the platform of the Republican Party, as it represents the values and beliefs of the majority of Republicans, and that majority is conservative. By taking control of the leadership and the process of the Republican Party, a minority of establishment political class operatives manage to pay lip service to conservative values in order to gain the support of conservatives while pursuing big government policies that are more in line with liberals, statists and globalists than with the values of the conservative majority of the party they represent.

Conservatives are like the Peanuts character Charlie Brown, and the entrenched establishment political class Republicans are like Lucy, always managing to convince Charlie Brown that, despite the fact that every time she has promised to hold the football for Charlie Brown to kick, she has pulled it away at the last second, that somehow, this time, she will keep her promise and hold the football so that Charlie Brown can kick the ball.

It is time for conservatives to simply take the ball away from the entrenched establishment political class Republicans that have been calling the plays for way too long. We don't have to leave the Republican Party and start a third-party. We the People can start a third-party *within* the Republican Party by organizing Freedom Cells in every precinct that will overwhelm the RINO Republicans at every level of organization of the Republican Party. In order to take back the Republican Party and keep it, it will take the active focused effort of large numbers of conservative activists that will stay in the game year after year.

The fundamental problem that we face as conservatives is the fact that the vast majority of conservatives are too passive. The failure of conservatives to be politically active is the reason why conservatives do not run the Republican Party. Through being more active in the process, RINO Republicans have a disproportionate share of influence, leading to the selection of candidates that do not reflect the majority conservative view of the party.

There is no way that a third-party would ever work unless huge numbers of conservatives become much more active in the political process. If millions of conservatives broke away and started a third-party, it would not be long before the majority of the activists that started the party would become too passive, and the elixir of political power will transform sufficient numbers of the movement into members of the entrenched establishment political class, creating just another vehicle for the establishment to commandeer.

Since the problem is a lack of sufficient activism on the part of conservatives, and starting a third party will go nowhere, We the People should get our act together and implement the very clear solution to the problem by getting tens of millions of conservatives to become sufficiently active in the political process to make a real difference. It makes no sense to pursue activism by large numbers of people within a third-party before we first try activism by large numbers of people within the Republican Party.

One of the key things that concerned patriotic Americans can do to take our country back and restore the liberties and prosperity that we so desperately desire is to become knowledgeable about the process and mechanics of the Republican Party. Acquiring the knowledge and learning the skills to be involved in party politics is the first step of political activism.

Most people think that activism is voting and perhaps showing up at a rally. Most people think that being involved in local party politics is a waste of time, and is something that only entrenched establishment political types engage in. The extent to which entrenched establishment political class types dominate party politics is determined by the extent to which patriotic freedom loving Americans become involved in the process. We the People can take over the Republican Party if enough patriots become active.

DOMINATE PARTY ORGANIZATION, RULES AND STRUCTURE

Through the freedom of association guaranteed to us by the First Amendment, We the People have the liberty of forming political parties, which are in essence clubs. How many of us would join a club without knowing the rules? How many of us would join the club without participating in club activities? How many of us would not participate in any of the club activities all year long and then show up at a Christmas party of the club and complain to every member of the club that we speak to about the leadership of the club, the rules of the club and the decisions made by the club throughout the prior year? That would be kind of silly and wrong to do, wouldn't it?

In a similar way, it is silly and wrong for anyone to be completely disengaged from Republican Party activities, even though a registered member of the Republican Party, and then display some of the ignorance, attitudes and misbehavior that we see on display during primary election season. Rather than complain, and endure unsatisfactory results on the back end of the process, the better path is for We the People, in sufficient numbers, to become knowledgeable of and become engaged in the activities of the Republican Party from the grassroots precinct level all the way up to national committee and convention activities. It really isn't that complicated, and it can actually be fun and enlightening!

Precinct Reorganization

Republican Party activities and organization start at the lowest level at which local elections are organized, which most commonly are election precincts. In my limited experience being involved in Republican Party politics, which has been in Greenville County, South Carolina, the Republican Party has what they call precinct reorganizations every two years. The precinct reorganizations are open to all members of the Republican Party, but the members that actually attend the reorganization meetings have the privilege and responsibility of voting for precinct officers, inviting members in attendance to become candidates for serving as delegates to County, district or state conventions, proposing any resolutions or rules changes to be considered at the county, district, state or national level, and conducting any other business at the precinct level.

It is at the precinct level that We the People must organize ourselves at the grassroots level in order to take back the Republican Party from establishment political class control. Everything else bubbles up from the precinct level, including the advancement of people that may start out with the best of intentions, but eventually become part of the establishment political class. Establishment types are not born that way; they are bred by the system.

The same power that We the People seek in order to transform the Republican Party so that we may take our country back will corrupt the best of us if we are not vigilant in refreshing our members at the grassroots level and implementing the elements of this plan that will remove power from the entrenched establishment political class and make it harder for them to reacquire power.

I was first introduced to my precinct reorganization when, a few days prior to the scheduled reorganization, a friend of mine in another precinct told me about the reorganization and suggested that I participate. There were only about four or five of us that showed up at the meeting, which was a very informal process that followed the protocols contained in a precinct reorganization packet that one of the other gentlemen had picked up from the Greenville County Republican Party. It struck me that there were so few people in attendance that there were more offices to fill than people in attendance.

If We the People will form a Freedom Cell for each precinct, the Freedom Cell can conduct regular meetings as a subset of the precinct similar to the way the Freedom Caucus meets as a subset of the Republican Caucus of the House of Representatives. We the

People should form Freedom Cells for each precinct with such overwhelming numbers that at the time of precinct reorganization, the Freedom Cell for each precinct would effectively become the voice for each precinct. We the People can easily overwhelm the Republican Party at the precinct level by electing like-minded advocates of a plan such as this one to every office and delegate slot available for each precinct.

Of the numerous conceivable affinity groups that transformational conservatives may choose to organize Freedom Cells around, Freedom Cells organized around the local election precinct is one of the most critical ones for Minutemen to participate in. If we are to consolidate and magnify our voice and act as one so that we may take our country back, we must do so at the Republican Party grassroots precinct level. That is where the process starts to elect the right kind of conservative representatives that will stand up to the entrenched establishment political class.

County Meetings and Convention

The next level in the structure and organization of the Republican Party, at least in the state of South Carolina, is at the county level. My precinct, for example, elected a president and an executive committeeman that would attend executive committee meetings of the Greenville County Republican Party every month or two. The executive committeeman had the authority to vote at the meetings on behalf of the precinct, with the president of the precinct voting in the absence of the executive committeeman. Needless to say, if We the People overwhelm the Republican Party at the precinct level and elect representatives to the next level in the organization, we will be able to continue to dominate the process through the election of County officers, delegates to conventions, the process of rulemaking and resolutions that will then bubble up to the next level in the party. The activities of the Greenville County Republican Party, for example, culminate with the county convention.

The county level is where we see establishment political class types in action. We the People will prevail in overwhelming the Republican Party at the county level if we have Patriot members of Freedom Cells that either have experience with the process or quickly learn the process in order to protect the conservative grass-roots movement from being co-opted by entrenched establishment types. We the People must be constantly diligent and observant in identifying those among us that will be tempted by the evil allure of political power. I believe that a very good percentage of the entrenched establishment political class will come back over to the light once we have shone the light brightly on the corrupt system that captivates them.

District and State Conventions

Just as counties are rolled up into congressional districts for the purpose of elections, the Republican Party is organized with sublevels of activity that culminate with the district convention. Populous cities such as Los Angeles, Chicago or New York City obviously have slightly different structures, as one county may have two or more congressional districts. Entire states like Vermont and Alaska have just one congressional district. Regardless of differences in population density, the structure and organization of the Republican Party follows the same pattern of small election precincts, wards, etc. being rolled up into one or more subgroups that culminate with a congressional district.

In South Carolina, the Republican Party wraps things up with a state convention every two years. Along the way, from precinct to state convention, elections are held for offices and delegates, and decisions are made by voice vote or ballot. The process is a very orderly process most of the time, with parliamentary procedure and parliamentarians used to keep order.

If We the People will show up consistently in overwhelming numbers that demonstrate the sincerity of concern that we have for

91

saving our Republic, we will have no problem following the rules of the Republican Party to transform the Republican Party into one of bright colors instead of pale pastels, to use the words of Ronald Reagan.

Republican National Committee

At the top of the food chain of the Republican Party is the Republican National Committee. Predictably, as you go higher up the line from precinct, to county, to congressional district, to state, and then to the national level, the entrenched establishment political class becomes stronger and stronger, and the corruption greater and greater. It will take some time, but if We the People are to dominate the Republican Party, we will have to be very organized, diligent and determined in order to displace and repudiate the entrenched establishment types from the state and national levels of the GOP.

Republican National Convention

During the 2012 and 2016 Republican national conventions, we witnessed examples of the Republican wing of the establishment political class at work. The 2012 convention suppressed the voice of Ron Paul. At one point John Boehner was calling for a voice vote, and ruled that the "chair finds that the ayes have it" when it was obvious that the nays completely overwhelmed the vote. We expect this kind of behavior from Democrats, but we must not tolerate this kind of behavior from leaders of the Republican Party.

There were a lot of shenanigans that took place at the 2016 Republican national convention by the entrenched establishment political class. Instead of letting the grassroots have a greater voice in the process, the establishment again squashed the voice of conservative grassroots delegates. The establishment joined with Trump delegates to preempt efforts by Ted Cruz delegates to seek to allow delegates to vote their conscience during rollcall votes for the presidential nominee. Trump delegates reciprocated by joining with the establishment by prohibiting rules changes that would have brought power in the Republican Party back to the grassroots. The net result was that the entrenched establishment political class was strengthened as a result of the 2016 Republican national convention. The obvious danger is that Donald Trump and his supporters get sucked into the establishment political class instead of remaining anti-establishment. Time will tell if Donald Trump is truly an anti-establishment conservative Republican.

REFORM THE PRIMARY PROCESS

If the 2016 Republican primary process taught us anything, it is that the primary process is quite varied due to the right that each state has to set their own rules about everything from whether the state will hold a caucus, a convention or primary, to the manner in which delegates are allocated.

The Republican Party of each state should retain broad power over the process by which they select a presidential nominee preference for their state. We the People of each state have the liberty to influence not only the Republican Party in each state, but the process by which candidates are selected for national, state and local offices. Having carefully observed the primary process in 2016, it seems to me that there are some beneficial changes that we can make to the primary process.

Closed Caucus or Closed Convention Works Best

When We the People retake the Republican Party in a state, we should advocate for conducting the primary process through a closed caucus or a closed convention. Permitting those that are not registered Republicans to participate in a primary, caucus or convention affords liberals the opportunity to influence the choice of Republican candidates.

When the Republican Party in a state chooses to elect nominees for office by holding a closed caucus or a closed convention, every Republican in the state is afforded the opportunity to participate in the process. Contrary to the contentions of some that do not fully understand the caucus or convention process, there are no disenfranchised voters that result from a state Republican Party choosing that route for selecting nominees for office. There are actually very good reasons that states choose a closed convention or a closed caucus for selecting nominees for office.

A closed caucus that is open to all registered Republicans that is held on a specific day gives everyone a chance to participate under very transparent circumstances. Each voter has the opportunity to consider all information available up to the time of the caucus. Under some caucus rules, time is allotted for candidates or surrogates to make a final pitch for their candidate. Caucus goers seem to enjoy the process of trying to persuade one another to vote for their candidate, and in forming coalitions during the caucus itself. There is great benefit in having a selection process that is time intensive and information intensive to improve the knowledge and awareness of issues by the voters.

A closed convention is a great way for a state Republican Party to choose nominees in a truly Republican manner. State party rules may vary, but if South Carolina, as an example, were to choose nominees by convention, the process would start at the precinct level, where delegates to the county convention are selected who would then vote for the delegates to the district convention. At the district convention, delegates to the district convention would choose the delegates that would attend the state convention, as well as select the Republican nominee for the congressional seat in their district.

Every step along the way, delegates would be selected by popular vote by those with voting rights at the precinct meeting, county convention or district convention. Candidates for delegate at each level would present themselves to those with voting rights by campaigning on any relevant issues that are important to the voting members, including perhaps declarations of support for specific candidates for specific offices.

I don't know if any state that holds a closed convention does so in the manner I described above, but if We the People were involved with this kind of a process whereby the grassroots activists represented by members of Freedom Cells dominating the process, we would be able to assure that the Republican Party would choose nominees that represent our values.

If We the People organize precinct Freedom Cells and remain active all the way up the food chain, we could assure that a majority of those with voting rights every step of the way would be solid advocates of this plan or one of similar magnitude and direction that we must implement to save our country.

The entrenched establishment political class has been using the open primary process to block conservatives from putting forth the candidates that will dismantle the power structure of the entrenched establishment political class. It seems that the RINO wing of the Republican Party would rather see a Democrat win an office than a conservative. We the People need to put an end to this practice by encouraging state Republican parties to adopt a closed caucus or a closed convention as a method for selecting nominees.

Two-Step Process to Select Nominee for President

We can do better than the drama and mayhem that we had to suffer through in the 2016 Republican primary season. Early in the process it was evident that many Republicans would be dissatisfied with the results of the process, and that uniting Republicans for the general election would be a difficult task.

There is a simple way to frustrate the purposes of the entrenched establishment political class, streamline the process for selecting the nominee, assuring conservatives the best opportunity to succeed in choosing the nominee, and even realizing the greatest possible level of unity at the end of the process.

The first step in the process is the "beauty pageant" phase of the primary season. That phase, from early February to early June, can be the free-for-all battle between all candidates seeking the office of president to make their best case to states in groups of five or six states or territories every two weeks or so.

Because of all the wacky methods that states use to allocate delegates to candidates in order to seek a disproportionate share of influence for their respective states in the process, the caveat is that this phase will serve to winnow down the field to the two leading contenders that amass the greatest number of delegates. Even if the leading contender has a majority of delegates at the end of the last primary, a runoff election of the top two candidates should be held to determine the final nominee.

The second step in the process, the runoff election between the two top contenders in the "beauty pageant" phase, will determine the nominee. State Republican parties may choose the manner in which they conduct their runoff election, but the winner of the election will receive all of the delegates for each state. The runoff election can be scheduled for late June, with the National Republican Convention scheduled for late July. This process will eliminate the drama of a brokered or contested convention, and the binary choice presented in the runoff election will assure the greatest level of satisfaction and unity.

Some may think that it is not fair for a candidate to win a majority of delegates in the "beauty contest" phase of the primary process to have to win a majority the second time in a runoff against the second-place candidate. The solution to this issue, if it really is a problem that people that participate in the process have difficulty accepting, is for all state Republican parties to agree to allocate all of their delegates in a proportional fashion.

One way to limit the power of the entrenched establishment political class in the Republican Party of each state is to prohibit any elected official from also holding a Republican Party office, including serving as a delegate at any level. Since elected officials already have enough of a disproportionate share of influence, we must deny them from adding to that influence, or to power that they already have, by not permitting them to become delegates in the process of selecting the presidential nominee.

SAFEGUARD THE REPUBLICAN BRAND AND MESSAGE

The Republican Party continues to make the fatal mistake of permitting the mainstream media to dominate the primary and general election process. This grants too much power to mainstream media to define candidates and issues, and to prioritize the national discussion of the issues and policies being discussed. We the People must use our collective voice with technology and social media to define our candidates and issues for the general population.

The truth is being suppressed by the coordinated effort of the Democrat Party and their mainstream media lapdogs. A good case could be made that the Democrat Party are the lapdogs of the mainstream media and the globalist elites, but the end result is that the truth is being suppressed and twisted. The 2016 election also revealed that the dominant social media and information networks such as Facebook, Twitter and Google are just as biased as the mainstream media, and therefore represent a significant threat to protecting our liberties, especially freedom of speech, association and assembly.

Debates

It is time for the Republican Party to stop submitting to holding debates moderated by extremely biased media types, especially Republican primary debates. Republican primary debates should be moderated by credentialed conservatives that will focus the attention of candidates on the substantive issues that are important to Republican voters. It is truly an embarrassment for the Republican

Party to submit itself to the circus acts that liberal moderators have put together that they package as debates.

Republicans should hold their primary debates in any manner they choose, and Democrats should do likewise. When it comes to the general election, debates should not be conducted by moderators that weigh in with their own opinions and biases, but rather conducted by dispassionate moderators that permit true debate. With rapidly evolving technology that gives access to incredible volumes of information to anyone and everyone, debates should become less important as debates will rage on in real time via social media. Despite some of the outlandish things that Donald Trump has tweeted, I think that he has forever changed the manner in which presidential candidates will campaign in the future.

Repudiate RINOs

Republicans in name only that campaign on the Republican platform and then betray the platform and the promises made during the campaign bring shame and embarrassment to the Republican Party. We the People should repudiate such RINOs and bring greater meaning and clarity to what it means to be a Republican.

One of the benefits of We the People getting behind this plan or one of similar magnitude and direction is that we can properly vet Republican candidates by asking them to make a public commitment to each of fifty points in the plan that 30 million American patriots get behind. We should no longer accept empty promises from moderate Republicans in name only and force them to take a public stand on a whole host of specific action steps that will save our Republic. We should choose candidates that substantially agree with the plan and reject those that don't. It is especially important that we use the primary process to reject existing members of the entrenched establishment political class in favor of candidates that support this plan. The Republican primary is one way that we can drain the swamp of the entrenched establishment types.

NINE

Wake-up Call to Christians for Action and Revival

If my people, which are called by my name, shall humble themselves, and pray, and seek my face, and turn from their wicked ways; then will I hear from heaven, and will forgive their sin, and will heal their land.

    – 2 Chronicles 7:14

The message from God in 2 Chronicles 7:14 was intended for his people, Israel, but Christians in America today are at liberty to claim by faith and believe that if Christians, called by the name of Christ, shall humble themselves, and pray, and seek the face of God, and turn from their wicked ways; that God will hear from heaven, will forgive their sin, and will heal their land.

The Bible teaches us that, to whom much is given, much shall be required. Those of us that profess to be Christians bear a higher level of accountability to God for our stewardship of the liberty and the blessings that he has bestowed upon us. If there was ever a time for American Christians to repent in sackcloth and ashes, now is that time.

Our country needs revival. Our churches need revival. We as individual Christians need revival. The Bible says that in the end times, before Jesus can return, there will first be a falling away. It is quite likely that we are seeing that falling away, but just as Hezekiah prayed for God to give him fifteen more years before God judged Israel, we may see God spare his judgment on the United States a little while longer if we seek revival.

Pastors need to show some leadership and start preaching against the evils of liberalism and big government. Start speaking the truth and forget about the muzzle that has been placed upon you by a tyrannical government. Congregations and their pastors have failed to speak the truth because of the threat of the loss of tax deductibility of contributions. Folks, is there not a cause? Should we have permitted this great evil for the last fifty years? Does not the church in general and pastors in particular bear much responsibility for the current state of our country? We the People are responsible and we must accept that responsibility. We the People that are Christians bear an even greater share of responsibility.

This plan calls for a flat tax with no deductions or exemptions that will completely eliminate charitable deductions, but it also calls for the elimination of property taxes. These changes may offset each other, but even without these potential changes, we should have been doing the right thing all along. We the People that are Christians have shamefully allowed government to place a muzzle upon us, and have allowed political correctness to stop us from speaking the truth, as we are commanded to do by Scripture.

Many Christians have refrained from political activity because they have considered it to be a dirty, tainted business. Our founding fathers were deeply involved in political discourse and action, and did so predominantly as believers. They did not advocate for the separation of church and state, but rather demonstrated that their mandate that government not establish a religion was rooted in the reality that religion absolutely permeated everything that our founders did. The prohibition was against the establishment of a religion by government, not a prohibition of religious conviction of citizens having an impact upon the government.

We must get back to the founding principles of a God fearing people that are intimately involved in political discourse and action. Our nation needs the leadership of Christian men and women that have the backbone to stand up and fight for what is right.

A CHALLENGE TO PASTORS

There is plenty of blame to go around for the current condition of our country politically, economically and spiritually. Liberals are to blame, but Republicans should be held to higher account because of the fact that they were so weak in standing up to liberalism. As a subset of the American citizenry, Christians should be held to a higher account for not taking a stand against the drift toward socialism and secular humanism.

Pastors have permitted their churches to be silenced in the political process by the unconstitutional and un-biblical doctrine of the separation of church and state. It is imperative that pastors take a stand and lead their churches in throwing off the muzzle that has silenced political speech from the pulpit. Is maintaining tax deductibility of donations worth the loss of our nation? It reminds me of the verse that asks what it would profit a man to gain the whole world but lose his own soul.

Pastors should lead their congregations in taking the marriage issue back from government by repudiating all government authority in defining and establishing marriage relationships. Marriage suffered a great loss when churches yielded to government authority dictating that a marriage license was necessary. The right to marry is a natural right, and requires no government approval. Granting authority to government to license marriages put us on the slippery slope that gave government the notion that they could redefine marriage.

Since God defines marriage, and asserts that it is He who joins a man and woman in marriage, the truth is that any person officiating a marriage that says "I now pronounce you man and wife" is making a false claim of authority that he does not have. By adding in the phrase "by the power vested in me by the state of," to that pronouncement, pastors not only usurp God's authority in establishing the covenant of marriage, they grant the state authority over marriage that God did not intend the state to have.

If the state should not have authority in marriage, then the state should have no authority in divorce. Pastors should lead their congregations back to the biblical practice of a husband or wife providing a bill of divorcement to their spouse when they choose to divorce. Marriage is established by public pronouncement by the parties involved, followed by the consummation of the marriage, and divorce is also by public pronouncement. The courts should only get involved in divorce if there is a dispute about the division of assets, or if there are minor children involved.

I truly believe that if you get the government out of marriage and get the government and attorneys out of the divorce business to the greatest extent possible, marriages will actually be strengthened. Lawyers are famous for causing great acrimony in divorces, and it is big business for them.

A SPECIAL CALLING FOR BLACK CHRISTIANS

I can think of no group of Americans that will receive greater benefit from the implementation of this plan than black Americans. It is time for black America to break the shackles of the Democrat Party, which treats black Americans like they are owned by the Democrat Party. Democrat leaders and their cheerleaders from the black community that feign efforts to benefit the black community while exploiting the black community treat black conservatives like they are Uncle Tom's, or not truly black. It is time for this to come to an end, and black Christians have the opportunity to lead the way in the effort to bring this practice to an end.

Black conservative Christians must stand up to the accusations of being traitors to black America, or Uncle Tom's and simply preach the truth to our black brothers and sisters that the Democrat Party is the party of tyranny and oppression, and that true liberty is available to those who break free of the shackles placed upon them by Democrat leaders and race baiting black leaders. Teach the truth of the history of the Republican Party versus the Democrat Party from the days of the Civil War through the civil rights movement. Republicans wanted to abolish slavery, while Democrats resisted. Republicans were leaders in the civil rights movement while Democrats sought to block the civil rights movement. The first blacks elected to Congress were elected as Republicans. Black conservative leaders like Walter Williams have written much about such well documented truth.

As black Christian leaders, advocate for the elimination of all race-based criteria for education and employment. Applications should be free of any indication of what a person's race is, and race should not play a factor at all in education or employment. There is no reason to continue the NAACP, for there should be no national association for the advancement of any race. Tear down all of the victim group distinctions that give the Democrat Party power and control over millions of Americans.

Repudiate the race baiting black leaders that constantly remind black Americans of the former sin of slavery and the oppression that took place in the 1960s as America took additional steps to treat black Americans equally. Reject their calls for punishing all of America today by granting extra rights to black Americans in order to make reparations for sins committed by people long gone against victims that are also long gone. We the People need to rise up and take our country back, and we need black Christian leaders to take the lead in converting the hearts and minds of black Americans that have been victimized by the Democrat Party.

IS THERE NOT A CAUSE?

Christians must reject the passive approach that Christians have taken in the past that has accelerated the downward spiral of our nation and become active in advocating for truth and righteousness in the political process. Is there not a cause? Are we to sit back and do nothing, allowing evil to prevail in the world because we are eagerly awaiting the return of the Lord? We as Christians must recognize that simply voting in elections is not enough. As in the days of the founders of this nation, we must actively resist tyranny and promote liberty.

May we as Christians in this country restore our nation to the Judeo-Christian values that our nation was founded upon so that our nation may once again be blessed by God as no other nation has. I believe that we are in the last days, and are witnessing the falling away that was prophesied, but God's strength is made perfect in weakness, so let us not allow our weakness to hold us back from taking our country back.

A CALL TO ACTION

We the People that are Christians must rally behind this plan or one of similar magnitude and direction. We must organize and form Freedom Cells, which can come in any form that you can imagine, so it includes anything that you might do to organize. We must find a way to make our voices heard by speaking as one and moving as one. We must take the time to show up in person every time the call goes out for feet on the street to show support for something that we believe in.

We must transform government at the federal, state and local level. Those that have the skills and intestinal fortitude and are committed to this plan or one of similar magnitude and direction must seek elected office. We must support such candidates with our time, talent and treasure. We the People must hold government at all levels accountable. We must repudiate the entrenched establishment political class. We must repudiate radical environmentalism. We must repudiate globalism and secular humanism.

We the People that are Christians must seek revival, we must seek to win the lost and we must tear down the idols that keep us from doing what we should be doing. As we seek to win the souls of men, we should also seek to win the hearts and minds of the millions that have been deceived by liberalism, globalism, radical environmentalism and secular humanism. We must declare a Great Emancipation Proclamation that all those that have been enslaved by the lies of the Democrat Party can be freed of those shackles and enjoy the spiritual and economic liberty that God intended all men to enjoy.

PART III

AMEND THE CONSTITUTION

TEN

Convention of States to Propose Amendments

WE THE PEOPLE MUST COMPEL OUR STATES TO PROPOSE THOUGHTFUL AMENDMENTS TO SAVE OUR CONSTITUTIONAL REPUBLIC

The Congress, whenever two thirds of both Houses shall deem it necessary, shall propose Amendments to this Constitution, or, on the Application of the Legislatures of two thirds of the several States, shall call a Convention for proposing Amendments, which, in either Case, shall be valid to all Intents and Purposes, as Part of this Constitution, when ratified by the Legislatures of three fourths of the several States, or by Conventions in three fourths thereof, as the one or the other Mode of Ratification may be proposed by the Congress...

– United States Constitution, Article V

The Framers of the Constitution provided for two mechanisms by which amendments to the Constitution may be proposed. The first mechanism, which requires a two thirds vote by both houses of Congress, is not likely to be used anytime soon to propose amendments to limit the powers of the federal government.

The second mechanism for proposing amendments to the Constitution, which is initiated by the states, was designed by the framers to give the states equal opportunity to propose amendments to the Constitution. This mechanism was designed to protect us from a federal government that would be reluctant to introduce amendments limiting the power of that federal government.

In Federalist number forty-three, James Madison addressed the balance between the ease and difficulty of amendment, and the intention the framers had of providing equal ability to the federal and state governments to propose amendments to the Constitution. Madison had the following to say about the necessity of a method to amend the Constitution:

That useful alterations will be suggested by experience, could not but be foreseen. It was requisite, therefore, that a mode for introducing them should be provided. The mode preferred by the convention seems to be stamped with every mark of propriety. It guards equally against that extreme facility, which would render the Constitution too mutable; and that extreme difficulty, which might perpetuate its discovered faults. It, moreover, equally enables the general and the State governments to originate the amendment of errors, as they may be pointed out by the experience on the one side, or on the other.

Through wisdom and prudence, the framers recognized that there would be a future need to amend the Constitution. By design, they provided a means by which the federal government, or the states, could propose amendments to the Constitution. The framers intentionally designed the process to be difficult enough that the Constitution would not be too easily changed, yet not so difficult that its imperfections could not be corrected. According to James Madison, the framers intended to equally enable both the federal government and the states to propose amendments.

Regardless of the method used for proposing an amendment, the framers set a high bar for ratification of a proposed amendment by requiring the ratification of three fourths of the states. Once Congress determined whether the ratification process by the states for amendments would be by vote of each state legislature or by conventions held by each state, the ratification of an amendment is determined by the states. The framers appropriately determined that the true power and authority to amend the Constitution belonged with the states, with no power granted to the federal government in the ratification process.

Many of the serious problems that beset our nation can be fixed by amending the Constitution. We the People should work diligently to repudiate the establishment political class by electing state and federal representatives that will follow the Constitution, and that will propose amendments that are needed. As experience has taught us, we cannot rely solely upon this first mode of proposing amendments by electing representatives and trying to hold them accountable. Since Congress is a big part of the problems we now face, the best path for us to propose amendments is by the citizens of each state demanding that their legislatures call for a Convention of States for Proposing Amendments. Once thirty-four states make application to Congress to call a Convention of States, Congress must do so. Article V of the Constitution plainly states that Congress "shall call a Convention for proposing Amendments." Congress has no option in the matter.

From the plain language of Article V of the Constitution, it seems straightforward that the purpose of calling for a Convention of States is for the delegates of the states in attendance to propose amendments to the Constitution during the assembly. Some argue that the application that the states make to Congress to call a Convention of States must have identical language stipulating a narrow range of subject matter to be taken up by the Convention of States for Proposing Amendments. This seems to be more limiting than the Framers of the Constitution intended by the plain language of Article V.

If thirty-four states informed Congress that they are making application to Congress to call for a Convention of States for the purpose of proposing amendments to the Constitution, Congress is constitutionally bound to call a Convention of States to Propose Amendments. It is not complicated, although many attorneys will try to make it complicated in myriad ways. If thirty-four states communicate to Congress that they are calling for an Article V Convention of States to Propose Amendments using different language to do so, Congress has no authority to mince words and debate the matter so long as the intent is clear that each state is calling for a convention to propose amendments.

The language of Article V is clear that the convention that Congress shall call is one for proposing amendments. Any attempt to limit a Convention to a specific amendment or topic of amendments, or to require that all thirty-four states make one application or make individual applications with exactly the same language would be unconstitutional, and subject to challenge. An application by a state for Congress to call a Convention of States is simply a request by a state that Congress call a convention.

Some fear that calling for a Convention of States to Propose Amendments without limiting the scope of such a convention would risk what they call a "runaway" convention that would exceed the intended scope of the convention. The Constitution broadly defines the scope as a "Convention for proposing Amendments." The scope is necessarily limited strictly to proposing amendments to the Constitution, but there is no intended limitation on the subject matter or number of proposed amendments. The Constitution prescribes the process by which the states may compel Congress to call a convention, but entrusts the representatives of the states in attendance at such a convention with the details of the number and subject matter of amendments proposed. There can be no runaway Convention so long as the Convention limits itself to proposing amendments.

The concern is that if such a convention were called for by thirty-four states, that all manner of amendments could be proposed at such a convention, or that the Constitution could somehow be rewritten entirely. The framers wisely bifurcated the amendment process by separating the proposal of amendments from the ratification of amendments.

An amendment proposed at a time of high emotion or without all of the pertinent facts would be ratified only after the passage of sufficient time for an even greater number of states to carefully consider facts and circumstances with an opportunity for cooler heads to prevail. We also have the added protection that any amendment proposed by Congress or a Convention of States will be ratified by different bodies, regardless of whether the mode of ratification is by state legislatures or by state conventions.

If there is a legitimate fear of a "runaway" convention, there should be an even greater fear of a runaway Congress proposing all manner of amendments as it is much easier for Congress to propose amendments. We don't see that happening because Congress knows that they would not get away with it. The notion of a wacky amendment by a "runaway" convention having any more success getting through the ratification process is only possible if the establishment political class somehow rigs the process to further enslave all Americans. God help us if we are at that point.

The tyranny of the federal government necessitates that we consider quite a few amendments in order to restore the balance of power. We the People desperately need to compel thirty-four of our state legislatures to put Congress on notice that we are calling for a Convention of States to Propose Amendments. The States should not tolerate any delay by Congress or any attempt by Congress to control the process. If Congress does not comply with their constitutional duty to call a Convention of States to Propose Amendments, which is a strong possibility given the behavior of Congress in recent decades, then the states have the liberty and the constitutional authority to proceed without Congress.

We the People, as citizens of our respective states, must engage our state legislators in discussing any and all amendments that should be considered. We should direct our legislatures to engage in discussions with other states about any and all amendments that should be considered. We the People must demand that our legislatures force the hand of Congress and give Congress no option but to call a Convention of States to Propose Amendments.

We the People must become organized and active in order to take our country back. We must repudiate the entrenched establishment political class by simultaneously pursuing both methods of proposing amendments to the Constitution. It is doubtful that, with the current makeup of our state legislatures, we would be successful in securing the affirmative votes of thirty-eight states to propose and ratify the amendments necessary to restore our lost liberties, so We the People must also become organized and active in electing constitutional conservatives to all state and local elected offices in our respective states.

In the following chapters I propose several amendments and the rationale for each. Through dialogue and debate, We the People and our elected legislatures are capable of proposing numerous amendments to restore the balance of power wisely intended by the framers, to rein in out-of-control federal spending, to restore our national security and national sovereignty and to restore liberty to the citizens and to the states.

ELEVEN

Direct Proposal of Amendment by the States Amendment

PERMIT STATES TO DIRECTLY PROPOSE AMENDMENTS TO THE CONSTITUTION

Upon receipt of notification of the affirmative vote of the legislatures of two thirds of the several States adopting the identical language of a proposed Amendment, Congress shall immediately submit said proposed Amendment to the States for Ratification. Any State may rescind its notification of affirmative vote on a proposed Amendment prior to the receipt by Congress of affirmative votes from two thirds of the States.

– Proposed Constitutional Amendment Language

Congress can easily propose amendments to the Constitution by a simple joint resolution of both houses that is approved by two thirds of the members of each house. Congress may or may not have the necessary votes, but the process is very simple, as both chambers are in session for much of the year, are in very close proximity and are in constant communication.

The framers may have intended to "equally enable" Congress and the states to propose amendments, but as a practical matter, the process for proposing amendments is far more difficult for the states than it is for Congress. There have been many applications by states for Congress to call a Convention of States for Proposing Amendments, but Congress has never called such a Convention. We the People should advocate for a method by which states may propose amendments to the Constitution without the necessity of calling for a Convention of States for Proposing Amendments.

The above proposed language would make the process easier for the states to propose amendments to the Constitution, but by no means would the process be as easy as it is for Congress. The option of calling for a Convention of States for Proposing Amendments is one that we would retain, but by permitting states to form a consensus by discussing proposed amendments using twenty-first century technology in order to promulgate draft amendments that would have a chance of adoption by two thirds of the states will level the playing field somewhat. If two thirds of the state legislatures vote affirmatively on identical language for a proposed amendment, and each state notifies Congress of the vote of their respective state, the proposed amendment would be submitted to all of the states for ratification just as it would if it had been adopted as a proposed amendment by a Convention of States for Proposing Amendments.

The ratification process by three quarters of the states would not change, but by empowering states to more easily propose amendments to the Constitution, we would see much improvement to the imbalance of power that now exists between the states and the federal government.

RESCISSION OF RATIFICATION OF PROPOSED AMENDMENTS BY STATES

There has been some controversy over whether or not a state that has ratified a proposed amendment may rescind that vote of ratification. Unless a proposed amendment has a deadline for ratification, it continues to exist as a proposed amendment for decades, or even sometimes for centuries. Over the many years that a proposed amendment continues to be viable, states have voted to rescind their prior ratification and other states have voted to ratify an amendment that they previously rejected.

A number of states that had previously ratified the Equal Rights Amendment voted to rescind their ratification of the proposed amendment prior to the expiration date set by Congress. Proponents of the Equal Rights Amendment maintain that a state may not rescind their ratification of a proposed amendment, while maintaining that states that vote to reject proposed amendments may change their decision and ratify the proposed amendment that they previously rejected.

Given the long life of a proposed amendment, and given that over a long period of time political winds change within each state, it seems reasonable and logical that any state may change its vote to ratify or reject a proposed amendment prior to the threshold of ratification by three fourths of the several states being met, or prior to a ratification deadline. It is not equitable or wise to permit states to change their vote in one direction but not the other. The following proposed language would clarify this matter in an equitable manner and allow us to avoid the inevitable battle that we will have over this issue if we fail to clarify it:

Prior to the Ratification of a proposed Amendment by three fourths of the several States, any State that has ratified said proposed Amendment may rescind its Ratification of said proposed Amendment. Likewise, any state that has previously rejected a proposed Amendment may vote for Ratification of said proposed Amendment.

–Proposed Constitutional Amendment Language

The language confirming the right of states to ratify an amendment that they previously rejected should be unnecessary, but it doesn't hurt to make it crystal clear. The right that states have, prior to any deadline imposed, to ratify amendments that they previously rejected has long been recognized. The prudence and necessity of recognizing the right of a state to rescind its prior ratification of a proposed amendment prior to the ratification of the proposed amendment by three fourths of the states can be demonstrated by considering the proposed Child Labor Amendment, which is still pending before the states.

The Child Labor Amendment, introduced in 1924, has been ratified by twenty-eight states, and will become effective upon ratification by ten additional states. Twelve of the states that have ratified the amendment did so years after they previously rejected the amendment, which they had every right to do. Kansas was the last state to ratify the amendment in 1937, after rejecting it in 1925.

The Child Labor Amendment would give Congress the power to limit, regulate or prohibit the labor of persons under eighteen years of age. The ratification of this amendment by ten additional states would transfer power that belongs to the states to the federal government, which would be going in the opposite direction of where we need to take this country. Clearly, it would be equitable and desirable to recognize the right of the twenty-eight states that have ratified an amendment like this to rescind their ratification of the amendment, especially if there was a movement to get ten more states to ratify. As inconceivable as it is that ten more states would ratify the Child Labor Amendment, it should alert us to the need for making it crystal clear that states have the right to rescind the prior ratification of proposed amendments that have not yet been ratified by three fourths of the states.

PROHIBIT EXTENSION OF RATIFICATION DEADLINES FOR PROPOSED AMENDMENTS

Congress, or a Convention of States for Proposing Amendments, may impose deadlines on the ratification of proposed amendments, but those deadlines should not be permitted to be extended. In the case of the Equal Rights Amendment, Congress extended the deadline for ratification after states had voted to ratify or reject the proposed amendment. The vote of two thirds of both houses to submit the language of a proposed amendment to the states for ratification would most certainly be influenced by the imposition of a deadline for ratification. Once a vote has been taken with a deadline imposed, no change to that deadline should be permitted. The following language should be adequate for addressing this concern:

No deadline for Ratification of any proposed Amendment, whether proposed by Congress, or the several States, may be extended once said proposed Amendment has been submitted to the several States for Ratification.

–Proposed Constitutional Amendment Language

Congress, or a Convention of States for Proposing Amendments, may impose any deadline for ratification that they choose to impose. Eliminating the possibility of extension of any deadline imposed will simply force Congress or the states to be very thoughtful in imposing any deadline for ratification. Any amendment that is ratified after being submitted to the states with a deadline for ratification imposed that was later extended will certainly invite a challenge before the Supreme Court if ratification happens after the initial deadline imposed. Minor changes like this may seem too trivial to add proposed language to proposed amendments, but by doing so we will avoid future problems.

CONGRESSIONAL INTERFERENCE

We can expect Congress to be tempted to interfere with, hinder or obstruct the effort by We the People, through our states, to call for a Convention of States for Proposing Amendments. Just as Congress has failed to respect the balance of power imposed by the framers in other ways, Congress is likely to try to overreach their enumerated powers in any Constitutional amendment process initiated by the states. This is especially true in light of the fact that the primary purpose in calling for a convention will be to limit the powers of an out of control federal government. We the People must guard against interference in this process by Congress.

119

We may not be able to cut off every conceivable opportunity for congressional overreach, but when we go through the process of compelling Congress to call a Convention of States for Proposing Amendments, and we have had the experience of battling Congress for control of the process prescribed by Article V, we may find that the following language will be good to have for the next time around:

> *The method of selection of delegates to any Convention for proposing Amendments or any Ratification Convention, the rules and procedures of said conventions, or the method by which any State shall choose to prescribe that the legislature or convention follow for the proposal or Ratification of Amendments shall be in accordance with the laws of each State or the vote of the delegates permitted by the laws of each State, without input or interference from Congress.*

–Proposed Constitutional Amendment Language

The anticipatory language above will certainly be expanded or contracted based upon our experience. We can be sure that the entrenched establishment political class will work hard to derail our efforts to restore the balance of power and end their spending spree. Some would argue that Congress should have already called a Convention of States for Proposing Amendments, as scores of applications by the states have been made.

States should be at liberty to use any language that they choose to communicate a request that Congress call a Convention of States for Proposing Amendments. States should refrain from limiting the scope of their "application" for a Convention in order to not give Congress the opportunity to deny that two thirds of the states have called for a Convention due to differing scopes. States should recognize that a convention with limited scope may not be constitutional anyway, and should therefore ask for a Convention of States for Proposing Amendments using the same words used in Article V in order to eliminate any excuse Congress has for not calling for a convention. Once we go through the gauntlet and have our first Convention of States for Proposing Amendments, we can consider language such as the following that will make it harder for Congress to discount legitimate "applications" by states to call for a Convention of states:

Any language used by a state making application to Congress to call a Convention for proposing Amendments that may be plainly construed as an application or request to Congress to call said Convention shall satisfy for that state the provision for the Application of the Legislatures of two thirds of the several States. Upon the receipt of requests or applications from two thirds of the several States, Congress shall immediately call a Convention for proposing Amendments. The time, place and duration of any Convention for proposing Amendments shall be at the discretion of a majority of the States. Any request or application for Congress to call a Convention for proposing Amendments made by any State shall be a continuing request until such time as the two thirds threshold is met, or until such time as such State rescinds its request or application.

–Proposed Constitutional Amendment Language

It is important that Congress recognize that a request for a convention is the same as an application for a convention. Congress must also recognize that an application by a state for Congress to call a convention is a continuing request unless rescinded by the state. Congress should be compelled to follow the Constitution and immediately call a Convention of States, and the States should control the process from that point forward.

If we propose and ratify an amendment that permits states to directly propose Amendments, states would be able to collaborate on a single amendment such as a balanced budget amendment without the need for calling for a Convention of States to Propose Amendments. At times like this, when there are many amendments that We the People believe should be considered in order to rein in the numerous and egregious usurpations of power by a tyrannical federal government, a Convention of States to Propose Amendments is necessary.

TWELVE

Repeal the Seventeenth Amendment

RETURN AUTHORITY TO SELECT SENATORS TO STATE LEGISLATURES AND AFFIRM THE AUTHORITY OF STATE LEGISLATURES TO REMOVE SENATORS FROM OFFICE

The seventeenth Amendment to the Constitution of the United States is hereby repealed. The authority of the legislatures of the several States to remove Senators from office is hereby affirmed.

– Proposed Constitutional Amendment Language

The Framers of the Constitution wisely designed the bicameral legislative branch as part of a carefully designed system of checks and balances of power between the states and the federal government. Senators, chosen by state legislatures, represented the interests of each state. Members of the House of Representatives were elected by popular vote of congressional districts to represent the interests of the people.

The Seventeenth Amendment, which provided for the direct election of Senators by the general population of each state, may have sounded like a good idea at the time, but has turned out to be very damaging to our country.

As representative bodies elected by the citizens of each state, state legislatures are in the best position to advocate for the interests of each individual state and to defend the collective rights of all states from encroachments by the federal government. By taking away the power of state legislatures to select and remove Senators, the Seventeenth Amendment has diminished the power of states that the framers intended to safeguard against the very encroachments by the federal government that we see today.

The Senate has become an exclusive club with far too much power, little transparency and virtually no accountability. Senators are not accountable enough to the people of the states they are supposed to represent, and are very difficult to remove from office. They are more concerned about preserving their own power and prospects for reelection than they are about the interests of the states that they represent. They have become the very core of the entrenched establishment political class, thumbing their noses with impunity at the people that they represent.

Repealing the Seventeenth Amendment and restoring the power to select Senators to the state legislatures will do much to restore power to the states that has been usurped by the federal government. The Constitution did not explicitly address the removal or recall of Senators chosen by state legislatures, but it appears self-evident that state legislatures had the authority to remove or recall senators chosen. Experience has shown us that we cannot always rely upon common sense in acknowledging something that appears to be self-evident, so I am proposing that, in addition to repealing the Seventeenth Amendment, we affirm the authority of state legislatures to remove or recall senators.

Until such time that we repeal the Seventeenth Amendment, the citizens of each state should take immediate action to compel the legislatures of their state to establish a means by which senators may be quickly and decisively removed from office. Any and all means by which senators may be removed should be immediately pursued, whether removal is by vote of the legislature of each state, by popular referendum, or any other lawful means. We the People must work diligently to transform the United States Senate from the seat of power of the entrenched establishment political class to a chamber that once again represents the interests of each state.

THIRTEEN

Nullification by the States Amendment

PERMIT STATES TO NULLIFY LAWS,
EXECUTIVE ORDERS OR SUPREME COURT
DECISIONS BY THE AFFIRMATIVE VOTE OF
TWO THIRDS OF THE STATES

"...In cases of abuse of the delegated powers, the members of the general government, being chosen by the people, a change by the people would be the constitutional remedy; but, where powers are assumed which have not been delegated, a nullification of the act is the rightful remedy: that every State has a natural right in cases not within the compact, (casus non-foederis) to nullify of their own authority all assumptions of power by others within their limits: that without this right, they would be under the dominion, absolute and unlimited, of whosoever might exercise this right of judgment for them..."

– Thomas Jefferson, Kentucky Resolutions of 1798

States should be collectively empowered with the ability to nullify any law, executive order or Supreme Court decision that two thirds of the states find to be objectionable. This will serve as an additional safeguard against overreach by the federal government. The assertion by many advocates of states' rights that states have the right of nullification of federal laws has not been tested by the Supreme Court. My view is that nullification of federal law by an individual state will not be supported by a Supreme Court decision. A sure way to give the states collectively the right of nullification of federal actions is to do so by constitutional amendment.

FOURTEEN

Amendment to Permit States to Remove Federal Officers

Any federal officer may be removed from office for any reason by the affirmative vote of the legislatures of two thirds of the several States.

– Proposed Constitutional Amendment Language

We the People need a mechanism by which we can remove any federal officer from office. Tyranny and lawlessness in the executive and judicial branches cannot be permitted to continue. The legislatures of two thirds of the states voting to remove a federal officer from office would be a very compelling justification for removal from office under any circumstances. The need for states to have a means by which they can remove federal officers is so great that we should probably set the threshold for removal at sixty percent of the states instead of two thirds.

The current means and method of impeachment as the only means for removal from office is completely inadequate for We the People to check the tyranny that we have witnessed in recent years. We must no longer put our trust in congressmen and senators to do the right thing, as they have demonstrated time and time again that they are incapable of doing the right thing.

The threat of removal from office by the states should keep our federal officeholders in line, so we should rarely ever have to use such an extreme measure.

FIFTEEN

Right of Secession Amendment

PRESCRIBE THE MEANS BY WHICH A STATE MAY EXERCISE ITS RIGHT TO SECEDE FROM THE UNION

Governments are instituted among Men, deriving their just Powers from the Consent of the Governed, that whenever any Form of Government becomes destructive of these Ends, it is the Right of the People to alter or to abolish it, and to institute new Government, laying its Foundation on such Principles, and organizing its Powers in such Form, as to them shall seem most likely to effect their Safety and Happiness.

...it is their Right, it is their Duty, to throw off such Government, and to provide new Guards for their future Security.

– Declaration of Independence

We will make great progress in restoring the balance of power if we pass an amendment that clearly recognizes the right of a state to secede from the union. I am not advocating that any state secede from the union, I am simply advocating for recognition of the right that states have to secede from the union.

I believe that if we can restore the balance of power established by the Constitution, we can save the union from dissolution or civil war. I firmly believe that if we do not rein in the tyranny of the federal government, and that if the federal government does not recognize the right of states to secede, we may once again see a civil war in this country.

127

The big argument is whether a state can secede from the union or not. The manner by which a state may secede is the smaller of the two arguments. The reasonable and prudent thing to do is to have discussion about this and, ideally, to amend the Constitution to remove all doubt. I fear that the federal government and liberal states take the view that a state may not secede, whereas freedom loving people in the majority hold to the view that our founders would hold to, that it is preposterous to expect us to be held against our will. Those of you that would have your will imposed upon us do not want to permit us to secede, and those of us that know better than to try to impose our will upon you are happy to allow you to secede.

The same effect would be realized if we appropriately weaken the federal government vis-à-vis the states and permit roughly the same differentiation between states that we would have as separate nations. We can work out our differences best by allowing states that want to be liberal to be liberal to their hearts content and those of us that want to espouse freedom can have it and live in peace. The problem that liberal states will have is that they will tax themselves to death and drive good people move away. You can't have freedom and control. If a state considers it tyranny to live in a land where abortion is illegal, they should be free to secede from the union. Likewise, if a state considers it tyranny to live in a land where abortion is legal, they should be free to secede from the union.

The founders of our nation never intended that states be prohibited from leaving the union. The Declaration of Independence quite clearly established the right of the governed to throw off a tyrannical government, so it is highly improbable that they intended their states to be permanently bound to the union if the citizens of a state chose to sever the tie.

Are we less free as Americans than the citizens of the USSR in the 1970s? Article 72 of the USSR Constitution, adopted in 1977, stated: "Each union Republic shall retain the right freely to secede from the USSR." The words "shall retain" in this article indicates that the several nations that formed the Russian Federation had a right of secession that preceded the article adopted in 1977. I don't know whether Article 72 of the USSR Constitution was intended to confirm in writing a pre-existing right, or if it was merely restating a right that had been previously stated in writing, but I marvel that the right of secession was not only confirmed, but was successfully used by the nations comprising the Russian Federation to dismantle the USSR within fifteen years.

Are we less free as Americans than the citizens of Great Britain that put a referendum before its citizens to determine whether Great Britain would remain in the European Union or exit the European Union? As the world watched to see if Brexit would succeed or fail, other members of the European Union were debating whether they would follow in the footsteps of Brexit, and some Texans were asking "if Brexit, why not Texit?"

Fellow patriots, we need not look to the examples of Great Britain putting the choice before their citizens of whether to exercise their right to exit the European Union, or to the USSR Constitution affirming the rights of the member states of the Russian Federation to secede in order to assert precedents in allowing any of the United States to secede from the union.

Each state in the union has the right to secede from the union. We would be simply prudent if we affirm the right of secession by constitutional amendment. It may not make intuitive sense, but by making it clear by constitutional amendment that states have the right to secede, and prescribing the means by which they may do so, we will strengthen the union. A clear path for states to secede will do much to correct the imbalance of power between the federal government and the states. Tyranny by the federal government will be checked by the very real possibility that states will secede. The notion that states cannot secede without a fight only encourages tyranny by the federal government.

The federal government exists to serve the people and the States, not the other way around. Our founders devised a brilliant system of checks and balances with a weak federal government with enumerated powers, with all other powers reserved to the states or to the people. We the People have the right and authority to restore the balance of power instituted by our founders, and to take our country back by any and all means necessary.

Recognizing the right of states to secede from the union and prescribing the manner in which a state may exercise its right to secede from the union will do much to restore power that rightfully belongs to states that has been usurped by the federal government, and will hopefully help us to preserve our union.

SIXTEEN

Life Amendment

WE MUST PROTECT LIFE FROM CONCEPTION TO NATURAL DEATH

Recognizing that life begins at conception, the individual rights of each person, from conception to natural death, shall be afforded equal protection under the law.

– Proposed Constitutional Amendment Language

We must amend the Constitution to recognize that life begins at conception, and that each life is entitled to protection from the moment of conception until the moment of death from natural causes. Abortion, assisted suicide and euthanasia should be illegal in this country, just as murder is illegal. All life is precious, and should be protected. The strong should protect the weak. The healthy should protect the infirm. The living should protect the unborn.

To my pro-life friends that condone exceptions to abortion in the case of perceived endangerment to the life of the mother, rape or incest, I ask you to reconsider your position. The argument for allowing abortion for certain exceptions only undermines the value of life. If the life of the mother is at risk, doctors can use continuously improving technology to try to save both mother and child. In the case of incest, the rights of the child should prevail and the child should be permitted to live, even with likely health problems. In the case of rape, the rights of the child should prevail, for the mother could give the child up for adoption if she chooses. In the case of a child that has Down's syndrome or other birth defect, that child should not be deprived of the right to life.

To my friends that are pro-choice, I ask you to re-examine the arguments for abortion that are rooted in the alleged right of a woman to choose what to do with her body. Do we really believe that anyone has the absolute right to do absolutely anything they want to do with their own body? Of course we don't believe that, nor should we. Furthermore, the argument fails because abortion involves more than just a woman's body, for it involves terminating the life of another human being.

Anyone that argues the pro-choice position should have no problem with establishing life termination clinics where people can walk in off the street, sign some paperwork, go back into a room and lay down beneath a guillotine that will promptly behead them. I choose this gruesome scenario instead of a lethal injection because it is closer to the barbaric act of abortion. The decapitated body or the body made still by the lethal injection could both be disposed of in a manner similar to the way aborted babies are. It would make the process easier and more efficient if such a clinic was connected to a crematorium to finish the job.

The truth is that abortion was embraced as a means of population control by eugenicists like Margaret Sanger. There are people that still believe that it is desirable to limit the population growth of certain segments of the population. Even a sitting justice on the United States Supreme Court once spoke of the desirability of limiting the growth of certain populations.

As a nation, we must deal with the national sin of abortion, a silent holocaust that has claimed almost sixty million lives. If our nation does not end abortion by constitutional amendment, we should divide our nation into two nations and allow people to choose whether to live in a nation that allows the slaughter of the unborn, or to live in a nation that values all life. Our nation cannot expect to continue to enjoy the blessings of God if we do not bring an end to abortion.

SEVENTEEN

Marriage Amendment

REAFFIRM THAT MARRIAGE IS BETWEEN ONE MAN AND ONE WOMAN

Therefore shall a man leave his father and his mother, and shall cleave unto his wife: and they shall be one flesh.

– Genesis 2:24

God created the institution of marriage before he established any government, so no government has the right to try to redefine marriage as anything other than a union of a man and woman. Government can restrict marriage to a union of one man and one woman, but the attempt to redefine marriage to include same-sex unions is simply another blatant attempt to deny the very existence and authority of God.

It is shameful that we must amend the Constitution to reestablish what God ordained to be the bedrock of civilization. If liberals will not acquiesce to the national consensus of defining marriage as between one man and one woman, we should not continue to expose all citizens of all states to the judgment of God for the national sin of validating same-sex marriage. We the People are at liberty to peacefully divide our nation into two nations, one that validates same-sex marriage, inviting the judgment of God, and another that reaffirms God's definition of marriage and seeks God's blessing.

As a nation, we cannot expect to continue to enjoy the blessings of God or escape His judgment if we do not correct the shameful act of the United States Supreme Court. We will soon see that the 2015 decision by the Supreme Court to redefine marriage is not the fulfillment of the LGBT agenda; it is just the beginning of their agenda. We have witnessed early indications that the LGBT community will not rest until they have destroyed our culture and denied us of our right to religious liberty.

LGBT activists and their liberal allies have launched a full frontal assault on the religious liberties that we have enjoyed in our nation since its founding. A bakery may not refuse to sell products from their storefront to people because of their sexual orientation, but no bakery should be forced to bake and decorate a wedding cake with two grooms or two brides on the cake if it violates their conscience to do so. Bakeries, photographers, caterers, florists, and any other businesses or professionals that cater to people that are getting married should not be threatened by costly lawsuits if they refuse to participate in a same-sex wedding. Our religious liberty and freedom of association guarantees us the constitutional right to conduct business with whom we wish to conduct business.

LGBT activist Barack Obama issued an edict that all public schools were to submit to the LGBT agenda by requiring them to permit transgender students to use bathrooms and locker rooms of their choice. Liberal states and cities gleefully complied with this edict, and the battle has only just begun for the rest of us to beat back the insanity.

The LGBT community has given us a hint about where they are going next with their agenda, as they have started referring to themselves as the LGBTQ community. The Q stands for queer, which I always thought referred to homosexual, which they replaced with gay. It seems that they will be introducing us to a new definition of queer, which raises the question of what other sexual perversions they will try to impose upon us with their agenda.

We must tirelessly fight to regain the lost ground given up by the shameful, unconstitutional action of the Supreme Court, which is not settled law, and stop the LGBT agenda dead in its tracks by passing a marriage amendment and fighting their agenda every step of the way.

EIGHTEEN

Open or Concealed-Carry Amendment

ELIMINATE GUN-FREE ZONES THAT ARE NOT ADEQUATELY SECURED WITH ARMED LAW ENFORCEMENT

The individual right to keep and bear arms, whether openly or concealed, shall not be infringed except in venues, established by Congress, which are adequately secured and protected by sufficient armed law enforcement personnel. The individual right to keep and bear arms, whether openly or concealed, shall not be infringed by the imposition of any tax, limit on quantity, permit, license or registration.

– Proposed Constitutional Amendment Language

Liberals will never stop trying to take away our constitutional right to keep and bear arms. They cannot consolidate power if the general population is armed. Although their arguments for gun control contradict the truth, they will be unrelenting until they succeed in confiscating weapons from all ordinary citizens.

Having just become free of the tyrannical rule of Great Britain, the founding fathers were keenly aware of the need to protect the right of ordinary citizens to keep and bear arms so that we could protect ourselves from a tyrannical government. They knew that if the federal government that they were creating were to infringe upon our right to keep and bear arms, that the freedoms that they had won would be lost.

The founding fathers recognized and sought to preserve the right of ordinary citizens to keep and bear arms, and to be trained,

135

organized and capable of repelling invading forces, or God forbid, even a tyrannical federal government. I believe that this is what they meant by a "well regulated" militia. Our founding fathers intended that the armed ordinary citizens of our nation would be the militia. It seems very obvious that even today, well-armed ordinary citizens capable of forming militias are necessary to protect our nation from foreign invasion and from a tyrannical federal government. The liberal wing of the entrenched establishment political class is chomping at the bit to dramatically infringe upon our Second Amendment rights so that they can consolidate power.

We must be steadfast in our defense of this fundamental con-stitutional right. Our right as citizens to keep and bear arms has been eroded, and has indeed been infringed. In order to reverse the damage done, we should add clarifying language by amending the Constitution to recognize the right of citizens to carry weapons, except in venues where adequate security barriers are established where sufficient numbers of armed law enforcement personnel are present to protect the unarmed citizens within the venue.

Restrictions on guns by liberals have created gun free zones that attract mass shooters. The best way to defend against a mass shooter is to allow citizens to open or concealed carry to all venues that are not adequately secured and protected by armed personnel. When mass shootings happen, liberals double down and call for stricter gun laws when the opposite course of action is needed.

If ten to twenty percent of people in a public place were typi-cally carrying a firearm, there would be a small increase in accidental shootings, but there would also be a dramatic reduction in the op-portunity for mass shootings and other crimes. With the increased likelihood of organized terrorist attacks, we need to encourage Americans to arm up and to be vigilant in identifying potential threats. The day may also soon come when coordinated terrorist attacks will take place with such ferocity that they will overwhelm local law enforcement, if not supported by armed citizens.

The Orlando Islamic terrorist attack on the Pulse nightclub should be a wake-up call to the urgent need to eliminate gun free zones in this country. A single terrorist with two weapons was able to lay siege to the nightclub for several hours, and because it was a gun free zone, the terrorist was at liberty to massacre forty-nine souls that were made in the image of God. Had Florida law permitted the concealed carry or open carry in the nightclub, the attack would have resulted in far fewer casualties.

The state of South Carolina quickly responded two days after the Orlando terrorist attack by passing legislation that allows the concealed carry in bars by concealed carry permit holders, provided that they do not drink while carrying. Concealed carry, permitted in restaurants that serve alcohol, was prohibited if the primary business of an establishment was to serve alcohol. It made perfect sense for South Carolina to pass such a law in response to the Orlando massacre. It makes no sense to argue for stricter gun laws when the truth is that the right response is to remove infringements on the right to keep and bear arms so that people may exercise their right to defend themselves.

After Orlando, Barack Obama, Hillary Clinton, the liberal media and the gun control lobby redoubled their efforts to attack the Second Amendment rights of American citizens, while trying to suppress the truth that the Orlando attack was perpetrated by a radical Islamic terrorist that pledged allegiance to ISIS and to his god Allah. When the president of the United States and the Democrat candidate for president fail to name the true enemy that we are facing while attacking our Second Amendment rights, we should not be surprised by the surge in gun sales that result. They may stick their heads in the sand, but Americans are waking up to the clear and present dangers that we face.

One of the greatest threats to our Second Amendment right to keep and bear arms comes from the spineless Republicans in Congress that cannot be relied upon to fight for conservative principles.

In the wake of the Orlando terrorist attack, establishment Republicans permitted the gun grabbing lobby to focus attention on gun control legislation instead of forcing Barack Obama, Hillary Clinton and the entire Democrat Party to face the compelling truth about radical Islamic terrorism and the dangers of continuing to legislate gun free zones.

We the People must drown out the liberal drumbeat to further infringe upon our Second Amendment rights by vociferously demanding that our state and federal governments remove infringements upon our right to keep and bear arms that have been incrementally imposed upon us over the years. The Second Amendment alone should have been adequate to keep states from infringing upon our right to keep and bear arms, but many liberal states have been successful in infringing upon those rights.

The language of my proposed amendment is intended to permit citizens to keep and bear arms uniformly throughout the country. Anyone traveling from state to state should not have to worry about whether they are violating restrictive gun laws in the states through which they travel. There should be no license, registration or tax imposed on guns and ammunition. The right to keep and bear arms, just like the right to vote, should be limited to United States citizens only.

Our veterans should not be deprived of their Second Amendment rights without due process. A diagnosis of PTSD should not bar any veteran from the right to keep and bear arms. The mentally ill should not lose their right to keep and bear arms; they should be institutionalized if they are a danger to themselves or others. Even criminals that have been deemed to have paid their debt to society should not be deprived of their Second Amendment rights after serving their time and being released from prison.

NINETEEN

Security of the Vote Amendment

WE MUST RESTORE THE INTEGRITY OF OUR ELECTIONS

Each citizen, having been lawfully registered to vote, shall personally present themselves to their assigned polling place on election-day, with verifiable photographic identification, and shall affix their right thumbprint to a paper ballot, which shall be retained for one year.

– Proposed Constitutional Amendment Language

Our Republic will be lost if We the People do not take decisive, immediate action to restore the integrity of our elections. Liberals can and will use every means available to them to commit election fraud. They do all they can to grant voting rights to non-citizens, they make sure that cities are not required to clean up their voting rolls so that fraudulent votes may be cast, and they advocate for every mechanism that will give them additional opportunities to commit election fraud, such as motor voter registration, same-day registration, absentee voting, early voting, electronic voting and electronic vote tabulation. Liberals have institutionalized election fraud, and they have stacked the courts with liberal judges that are successful in stopping virtually all efforts by states to restore the integrity of elections.

There will always be potential for isolated and limited cases of voter fraud, even after we have made all diligent effort and used every means possible to eliminate all forms of election fraud. How can we be assured that only eligible citizens vote, that each citizen votes only once, and that counts are accurate? We presently have a crisis of confidence in the legitimacy and accuracy of our elections.

VOTER REGISTRATION OF CITIZENS ONLY

There has been much controversy over the registration of voters, and the concern about people that are ineligible to vote becoming registered. The so-called "motor voter" registration efforts in some states have allegedly granted voting rights to illegal aliens that have obtained drivers licenses in those states. People that have been deceased have somehow managed to vote, and some people manage to vote multiple times in more than one jurisdiction.

People should not be allowed to vote unless they can prove that they are citizens, and that they are lawfully registered. The problems that we face of noncitizens voting, the proliferation of fraudulent voting in our elections, as well as the resistance we face in taking corrective action to solve these problems directly result from the strategy of liberals to commit election fraud.

ELIMINATE EARLY VOTING AND VOTING BY ABSENTEE BALLOT

Voting by absentee ballot might sound like a good idea, but it presents too much opportunity for election fraud to make it worthwhile. If someone cannot present themselves to their assigned polling location personally on election-day, they should not have the opportunity to vote by absentee ballot.

Early voting creates opportunity for election fraud, and also skews election results by eliminating the opportunity for people to make a final decision based upon candidates that have continued to seek office as opposed to those that may have suspended their campaigns, or to adjust their vote based upon information that becomes public in the days and hours prior to election day. It is also impossible to be assured that the votes of dead people are not counted if we continue to permit early or absentee voting.

The right to vote is a precious right, perhaps our most valuable right, and is worthy of special effort to arrange our schedules to show up to vote. It is also worth standing in line to vote, even in inclement weather. The natural progression of the concept of absentee voting will lead to a point where everyone would simply vote electronically from wherever they are. Liberal politicians have hinted that this is their ultimate objective. God help us if we see the day when unseen masses vote electronically! We would then see election fraud like we have never seen before.

NO PHOTO ID, NO VOTE

Liberals are so adamantly opposed to requiring a photo ID to vote because they know that the vast majority of fraudulent votes cast are for liberal candidates. They know that many of their candidates would not win without all of the voter fraud that they can possibly get away with. We must make the presentation of a valid photo ID mandatory in order to vote.

RETURN TO THE PAPER BALLOT

We should not trust electronic voting machines, and we should not entrust the counting of electronic votes to anybody. Even without all of the stories of machines changing votes cast, just the potential for that to happen should make us reject electronic voting. It is certainly easy to imagine that smart programmers could create programs that would change votes and then erase the program from existence on the machine. We know beyond a shadow of a doubt that, if given the opportunity, liberals would use such a program to rig elections. Sure, some conservatives would from time to time be tempted by such opportunities, but it is in the liberal DNA to do such things on a massive scale.

Who gets to tabulate the votes when electronic voting is used? Is there opportunity for fraud? After votes are cast on machines that could possibly change votes in accordance with hidden programs, there is additional opportunity for fraud in the tabulation process that should make electronic voting unacceptable. The only secure alternative we have is to return to good old-fashioned paper ballots. Election fraud will be easier to identify and control if we use paper ballots in conjunction with the other measures that we can use to restore the integrity of our elections.

Liberals will argue that it makes absolutely no sense to go back to paper ballots in the twenty-first century. While observing the process by which the United Kingdom voted to remain in or leave the European Union, I was delighted to see the stacks of paper ballots that were binder clipped in stacks of 100 votes with a half page of colored paper that stated "leave" or "remain." The British had the good common sense to realize that they could tabulate votes on such an important matter by counting paper ballots into groups of 100 that were easy to tabulate. I can imagine each side of the Brexit decision had precinct monitors to make sure that the votes were accurately tabulated.

Since it is the only decision that is voted upon nationally, it would be incredibly easy to immediately return to choosing our president and vice president by paper ballot. Each state would have a potentially different ballot to distribute, as not all political parties are successful in placing their candidates for president and vice president on the ballot of every state. Each state would distribute sufficient paper ballots to every precinct, and the votes of each precinct could be quickly tabulated under the close scrutiny of monitors for each political party, making it very difficult for voter fraud to occur. In order to maintain the highest level of integrity, it is important that all tabulating of votes take place at the precinct where the votes are cast under the watchful eye of representatives of the various interested parties, as well as by streaming video.

Although it was reported that no credible threats to the electoral system were identified during the 2016 election, Obama administration DHS Secretary Jeh Johnson indicated that DHS was considering the designation of certain electoral systems as "critical infrastructure," which could give the federal government unprecedented access and control over state and local elections. Rather than permit the federal government to become entrenched in the electoral process due to a potential cyber security threat, We the People should insist upon returning to the use of paper ballots.

FINGERPRINTS TO THE RESCUE

We can nail the coffin shut on 99% of voter fraud by adding the use of fingerprints to the other measures above. I know it might sound blasphemous for a conservative to speak of requiring voters to put a thumbprint on a ballot, but we can assure maximum integrity of our elections while also substantially preserving the anonymity of the individual vote.

When someone lawfully registers to vote, and shows up on election-day with photo ID in hand, and the poll worker confirms that he is on the role of registered voters, he could then place his thumbprint on the ballot. Indelible ink on our right thumbs would not only reduce the possibility of voting more than once on election day, it would serve as a substitute for the "I voted" stickers given to us by poll workers when we vote.

What better way to assure that a person is a lawfully registered citizen voting at the proper location than to use fingerprints to confirm this at polling locations on election-day? Instead of having poll workers sit at tables with registration rolls at the entrance to each polling location, they could verify each voter with a fingerprint scanner that would pull up the voter information and photograph on a computer screen that the poll worker and election monitors could verify by looking at the person in front of them.

By placing a thumbprint on each page in a package of ballots presented to each voter at a polling location prior to the voter entering the voting booth, we would have a secure way to audit the voting results of each precinct by scanning all of the paper ballots and matching the fingerprints of all of the votes tabulated to the electronic record of fingerprints of those that actually showed up to vote at the polling location. There should be no discrepancy between the inbound data tabulated on voters that were verified and given ballots when compared to the electronic record of fingerprints scanned from ballots cast. There should also be no discrepancy between the numbers of votes cast and the numbers of voters that entered and exited the polling location.

Paper ballots would be easy to tabulate if each decision for which a voter was casting a vote was printed on a separate single page so that the ballots could be sorted and counted quickly and easily in a fashion similar to that used to count Brexit votes. Since each ballot page would have the thumbprint of the voter affixed to the page, it would be feasible to scan all of the fingerprints at any point in the tabulation process, or for any future audit of the results. The scanning of fingerprints would be for authentication and audit purposes to prevent election fraud, not for tabulation purposes, as the tabulation of votes would be done the old-fashioned way by simply having real people count paper ballots by hand.

I realize that we would be giving up our fingerprints at the point of voter registration and at the polling place, but we are seeing our right to privacy completely obliterated in this modern technological age, so it seems like a very small price to pay in order to be sure that we are doing everything possible to prevent election fraud. Liberals have slowly and steadily undermined the integrity of our elections, and they will fight us to the death in order to preserve the ground that they have taken. If we are to take our country back, we must prevail on this issue.

TWENTY

Right to Work Amendment

ABOLISH COMPULSORY UNION MEMBERSHIP AND COMPULSORY UNION DUES AS A REQUIREMENT TO WORK

Every man also to whom God hath given riches and wealth, and hath given him power to eat thereof, and to take his portion, and to rejoice in his labour; this is the gift of God.

– Ecclesiastes 5:19

Unions were instrumental in addressing many problems created by big business at the turn of the twentieth century, but they have changed from advocating for the working man to exploiting the working man. The Constitution grants Americans the right to assemble, which includes the right to associate with unions for collective bargaining purposes. Each worker should be free to choose whether to join a union or not, whether to associate with a union or to not associate with a union. Compulsory union membership and compulsory union dues should be banned by constitutional amendment.

There is a right to work movement that is slowly spreading across the nation, state by state. States are passing right to work laws that effectively end compulsory union membership or dues. States that have passed right to work laws and are permitting the free market to function more freely in other ways are seeing their economies improve. We should accelerate the process and give workers in all states the freedom to work without being compelled to join unions and pay dues that support activities that are contrary to their values and beliefs.

All Americans currently in the workforce, and those desiring to be in the workforce, including union workers, will benefit from a dramatic reduction in federal government interference with a free market economy. Instead of trusting in a monopoly whereby coercion is used to extract dues from workers that are used to support pro-union liberal candidates, union members may find it more beneficial to support this plan to take our country back and reinvigorate our economy with free market principles and the pursuit of secure, strategic trade that will bring jobs back to America.

As is the case with conflicting interests between the entrenched establishment political class and the American people, the conflicting interests between the union bosses and the workers they purport to represent should be highlighted. When forced to participate in a free market economy, big labor will have to demonstrate value to their members if they want to continue to be relevant and have a role to play in the future.

TWENTY-ONE

Amendment to Abolish Taxes on all Property

WE THE PEOPLE SHOULD BE FREE TO ACCUMULATE WEALTH AND TO PASS IT ON TO OUR POSTERITY

No tax shall be levied or collected against any real, personal or financial property, or against the estate of any individual upon death.

– Proposed Constitutional Amendment Language

The right to own private property is essential to the existence and continuation of a free society. Property is not truly owned if government has the authority to tax that property. The right of citizens to own property is a fundamental God-given and constitutional right that has been infringed upon by all levels of government through the taxation of property.

The proper function of government at any level should be funded by a combination of user fees, reasonable taxation of income or by transaction taxes such as the gas tax or a sales tax. All taxes on property should be rendered unlawful by constitutional amendment.

The assessment and collection of real estate taxes renders property owners as tenants, and not true property owners. If you think that you own your house, refrain from paying property taxes and see how long you get to stay in your home. We are really just renting from the government empowered to tax our property, and we effectively become slaves to the taxing authority, deprived of the economic freedom intended by God and our founding fathers.

We should have the freedom to give away our property without being required to pay a gift tax or declare to the government that we are making a gift of our property. We should likewise have the freedom to receive a gift or gifts of property without having to declare anything to the government or to pay a tax. Estate taxes should be abolished.

Personal property taxes on such things as machinery, equipment and inventory should be eliminated. The mere ownership of property should not trigger taxation. We should also eliminate the temptation for government to impose a wealth tax.

Eliminating the authority for government at any level to tax property in any form, and limiting the federal government to raising revenue by taxing income and transactions at reasonable levels will unleash a period of unprecedented economic growth.

TWENTY-TWO

Amendment Prohibiting Wage or Price Controls

WE MUST ELIMINATE THE MINIMUM WAGE

Congress shall pass no law establishing wages or prices.

– Proposed Constitutional Amendment Language

Liberals always seem to advocate for increasing the minimum wage in order to help the poor. The truth is that the minimum wage actually hurts poor people and young people by killing jobs. As is often the case with government policy, the actual impact of the policy is the opposite of the stated intent. The federal government has no business tinkering with wages and prices. Even if it was a permissible function of the federal government, the free market is more reliable in establishing appropriate prices and wages than any level of government is capable of doing. Individual states will also do well to respect the free market system by refraining from establishing minimum wages or controlling prices.

Full employment and a vibrant economy are most easily achieved and sustained when wages and prices are established by a free market that is permitted to function freely. More jobs would be created if buyers and sellers of labor hours were permitted to make mutually agreeable arrangements without government interference. The ugly truth is that there are influential groups that have a vested interest in advocating for government policy aimed at suppressing the supply of labor in the economy. Permitting the free market to function in a manner that creates jobs for unemployed and under-employed people would be in conflict with the perceived self-interests or objectives of these groups.

149

Groups that advocate for inflation must advocate for policies that suppress the natural deflationary forces at work in the free market driven real economy. One way to pursue the inflation objective is to artificially suppress the supply of goods by reducing employment. The minimum wage is a very useful tool that is used to reduce employment, thereby reducing real output.

Radical environmentalists that hold to the view that the environment is fragile, the earth is endangered and humans are killing the planet are not very bashful about wanting to curtail economic activity by any and all means possible. The most radical adherents of environmentalist theology believe that unless we depopulate the earth by about ninety percent, we will destroy the planet. Theirs is the ultimate game of winners and losers. They hold to the scarcity mentality, denying the truth that there is an abundance of resources for the human race to go forth and replenish the earth, as God commanded Noah after the flood. Full employment and a vibrant economy is the last thing they want to see. They advocate for less output, lower employment and less economic activity.

Big labor loves to see increases in the minimum wage, as an increasing minimum wage protects union jobs and justifies increasing wages of union members. Higher wages, after all, will bring in more union dues, which will permit higher contributions to liberal politicians, which they hope will lead to more pro-union policies.

The Democrat Party has a vested interest in increasing membership in their various constituent victim groups. They are deathly afraid of dramatic decreases in membership of these victim groups that would result from the implementation of the ideas put forth in this plan. They need unemployed, underemployed and poor people to sell their lies to. They know that increasing minimum wages will lead to increased unemployment and underemployment, which they think helps their cause. My hope is that there will be an awakening of members of these victim groups that will throw off the yoke of the Democrat Party.

TWENTY-THREE

Income Tax Amendment

TAX ALL PERSONAL AND CORPORATE INCOME AT THE SAME FLAT RATE, NOT TO EXCEED 15%

All personal and corporate income shall be taxed at the same rate, not to exceed fifteen percent.

– Proposed Constitutional Amendment Language

They say that "ignorance of the law is no excuse", but when it comes to the tens of thousands of pages of the Internal Revenue Code, we should more accurately say that ignorance of the law should be expected. It seems that, somewhere along the way, Congress decided that its primary function was to identify every conceivable way to extract the greatest level of taxes from the economy. It seems that Congress believes that every dollar in the economy belongs to the federal government, and it is up to them to decide how much, in their wisdom and magnanimity, that We the People are entitled to keep from the fruit of our labor.

Congress also realized that they could determine winners and losers through taxation and spending, which permitted our elected officials to raise campaign cash from lobbyists and special interest groups and to buy favors, loyalty and votes from their peers and constituents. This gave rise to the era of big government dominated by liberal tax-and-spend policies controlled by the entrenched establishment political class at the helm. Nothing will cause the establishment politicians to squeal more than losing their authority to tax-and-spend without any accountability or fear of consequences, so we can expect them to fight this plan tooth and nail.

151

By restricting the federal government to activities enumerated in the Constitution, we will be able to limit federal government spending to a level of taxation that We the People can bear. A progressive tax structure where higher levels of income pay higher rates is unjust. Every person that receives income should pay federal income tax so that they can feel the pain of taxation and have an interest in limiting federal government activity to only constitutionally permitted and necessary activities.

Even proponents of so-called "flat tax" proposals provide for exclusions from taxation of individuals earning less than some arbitrary threshold amount. We the People need to stop buying into the argument that there is some level of income under which people should be exempt from paying federal income tax. We should abolish the practice of exempting people from paying federal income tax, and we should stop subsidizing able-bodied people that do not work with funds from the United States treasury.

We will be committing national suicide if we continue to institutionalize two groups of citizens with opposing interests. We have one group of taxpayers and another group that does not pay federal income tax. The second group even has a subset that not only does not pay taxes, but receives payments from the federal government to boot. We have created a class of voters that are incentivized to vote themselves a paycheck from the national treasury or to vote to exempt themselves from paying federal income tax, and the percentage of that class of voters is approaching fifty percent of the population. We need to correct this very dangerous situation.

ELIMINATE DEDUCTIONS AND EXEMPTIONS

It will probably be most prudent to go straight to the maximum flat income tax rate of 15% initially and maintain that rate through a transition period in order to get to a new equilibrium where we could allow surplus revenue to accumulate in a rainy day fund before reducing the tax rate.

The dramatic reduction in federal spending envisioned by this plan will permit a corresponding dramatic reduction in federal taxes. The greatest benefit of tax reduction will necessarily accrue to taxpayers. The greatest impact of tax relief will be felt by the middle class, which is appropriate because the middle class bears the greatest burden of taxation in this country.

Along with the implementation of the lower, flat tax, we should eliminate all deductions and exemptions, taking away from Congress one of the opportunities they have to pick winners and losers. Less time and effort will be wasted by Congress inventing new ways to buy votes and redistribute income, and filing tax returns will be simple and straightforward.

A simple flat tax requires that we deny all tax preference items to everyone. It means the end of marital status having any impact on taxes. It eliminates deductions and exemptions for items like the child tax credit, the earned income tax credit, mortgage interest, education expenses, healthcare expenses and charitable deductions. To file a tax return all taxpayers would have to do is fill out a postcard-sized tax return showing total income and the income tax due.

A flat tax with no preferences will permit us to eradicate all nanny state accounts like health savings accounts, IRAs, 401(k)s and any other concoctions that the federal government has come up with to complicate our lives and cause us to unnecessarily expend time and resources to figure out how to comply with the law and minimize our tax liability. Congress could simply legislate these complexities out of existence by immediately imposing an income tax at the 15% rate and permit Americans to keep the rest of their money.

ELIMINATE PAYROLL TAXES

It is important to make a distinction between earned income, which is subject to payroll taxes, and unearned income, which is not subject to payroll taxes. Since the employer and employee shares of payroll taxes add up to about 15% of wages, it is clearly better to have unearned income instead of earned income. This is why you'll find that people that typically earn large amounts of money will try to have most of their income classified as unearned income. This is perfectly legitimate by law, and anyone that did not take advantage of this distinction would be foolish. The elimination of payroll taxes and the introduction of a flat tax on all income, regardless of source, will effectively eliminate the distinction between earned income and unearned income.

Later in this book, I will present my plan for the elimination of entitlements from the federal budget, which will result in the elimination of payroll taxes for Social Security, Medicaid and Medicare. Payroll taxes should be eliminated simultaneously with the imposition of a 15% federal income tax rate on all income so that workers with earned income will see a negligible change in their net pay.

CORPORATE TAXES

All corporate income should be taxed at the same rate as personal income. In order to encourage corporations to reinvest income into the economy, and to more closely align income recognition with cash flow, corporations should be permitted to deduct 100% of capital expenditures from current income. The double taxation of all corporate dividends should be eliminated. Corporate dividends paid to shareholders out of corporate income that has already been taxed should flow through to shareholders as tax-free income.

Corporate income that is earned outside the United States should be permitted and encouraged to return to the United States economy to be employed in our economy at a tax rate no greater than 15%. Not only do we need to encourage the repatriation of income to be employed in this country, we need to encourage the repatriation of jobs to this country.

TWENTY-FOUR

Sales Tax Amendment

Any national sales tax, if implemented, shall not exceed 5%, and no value added tax shall be imposed without amendment.

– Proposed Constitutional Amendment Language

When the Sixteenth Amendment to the Constitution regarding the income tax was proposed, it is my understanding that there was great opposition to setting a cap of 15%. It was argued that the federal government would gravitate quickly to that level, as Congress would interpret the cap as permission to elevate the tax rate to that level. If only they had included the provision for a maximum rate in the amendment!

Many have argued for the implementation of a national sales tax as part of a plan for tax reform. It would be an excellent way to simplify tax policy in an efficient, equitable manner, so long as there is a limit to all tax rates and the overall federal tax burden. My proposal for a simple flat tax on all income at a maximum rate of 15% coupled with a maximum national sales tax of 5% would provide adequate revenue to a properly functioning federal government. The only way to assure that maximum rates are established is to do so by constitutional amendment. It is important to note that this proposed amendment does not establish a national sales tax; it simply sets an upper limit on any potential future national sales tax.

If we restore the power to the states and to the people that has been usurped by the federal government, and if we limit the role of the federal government to the activities prescribed by the Constitution, the federal government should be able to function effectively with revenue at well below the total of the maximum permitted income tax rate of 15% and the maximum permitted sales tax rate of 5%. The full implementation of this plan should result in a dramatic reduction in federal expenditures, and a doubling of real GDP within ten years. The federal government should eventually be able to function with a flat income tax rate of 12%, using a national sales tax sparingly in order to balance the budget.

The beauty of incorporating the use of a national sales tax with a low flat tax on income is that the sales tax rate can be immediately adjusted as needed with instantaneous results, and little or no administrative cost. A disciplined Congress that is accountable to the people would be able to adjust the sales tax upwards as needed and then quickly reduce the rate when the need has been met. We the People need to be diligent in holding Congress accountable and making our voices heard when they are slow to make appropriate changes to taxes, spending or policy.

One of the big benefits of having a flat tax coupled with a sales tax is that any change in the income tax rate or the sales tax rate will be equitable. We will remove the opportunity for the entrenched establishment political class to use revenue as a mechanism for the redistribution of wealth. Many of the other elements of this plan, when implemented, will dismantle the expenditure side of the redistribution of wealth scheme that the entrenched establishment political class has used for decades to acquire power and control.

When We the People make revenue generation at the federal level simple and equitable, and we eliminate federal spending that the federal government should not be engaged in, sad establishment types that have lost their levers of control will flock to state and local governments. We the People must also make diligent effort to take our state and local governments back from the entrenched establishment political class, and make changes of similar magnitude and direction as those that I propose in this plan that we make with the federal government.

TWENTY-FIVE

Sound Money Amendment

AMEND THE CONSTITUTION TO REQUIRE CURRENCY ISSUED TO BE LIMITED BY GOLD RESERVES

Congress shall issue no more than $2000 in coin, paper or electronic currency for every ounce of gold held in reserve, and shall not redeem currency for gold or deplete reserves of gold for any reason.

– Proposed Constitutional Amendment Language

Money in various forms has been around for millennia. There are many Bible references to money, and much wisdom can be gained by taking out a Bible concordance and looking up all of the Bible references to money. Money can be used for both good and evil purposes. Perhaps the most often quoted Bible verse about money states that "the love of money is the root of all evil." This verse is often misquoted by people who omit the first three words. Money is not inherently evil. If used properly, money is a very good and useful thing.

THE NECESSITY OF MONEY

Money has several important uses in economic activity. Money is used as a medium of exchange in order to facilitate transactions. Money is used as a unit of account in accounting for transactions, and for maintaining records of values of assets and liabilities. Money is used for paying taxes. Money is also used as a store of value. Without money, our economy would grind to a halt. Barter transactions would certainly support some level of economic activity, but the size of the economy would dramatically shrink.

DEMAND FOR MONEY

Currency is needed as a medium of exchange for transactions in our economy, and to satisfy the desire that people have for maintaining a store of value buffer for potential transactions. Greater levels of economic activity generally lead to an increase in demand for greater quantities of currency. Changes in circumstances and perceptions will lead to adjustments in the buffer of currency people require for anticipated transactions. We need an adequate supply of money to meet these demands for currency.

GOVERNMENT ABUSE OF MONEY

The issuance of money is one of the legitimate functions of government. Even the simple function of coining fixed quantities of gold as money is one that a government can best engage in, as there is a need for engendering trust that the currency is valid and is what it purports to be. As long as there are governments issuing money, there will be counterfeiters trying to pass bogus reproductions off as real. One of the roles governments must serve is to identify and eliminate counterfeit operations.

All governments are comprised of people who sometimes yield to the temptation to defraud others. Throughout history, governments have become notorious for the dilution of their currencies, either by reducing the quantity of precious metal in their coinage, or by firing up the printing presses. In recent years, the problem has become exponentially worse, as those controlling the printing presses realized that they could create electronic money without even having to run the presses. Central banks refer to this practice as "quantitative easing."

The most egregious example of government abuse of money is the quantitative easing that was introduced by Japan and expanded dramatically by the Obama administration and the current Federal Reserve, which created about $4.5 trillion in new money through QE1, QE2 and QE3. We must hold our federal government and the Federal Reserve accountable for their actions. The leadership of the United States in this foolishness has led many other nations to use quantitative easing, which has resulted in a dramatic increase in worldwide debt.

Government has the responsibility to provide its citizens with sound money that is of stable value and has integrity. Governments that do not fulfill this responsibility put their citizens and nation at risk. Government should supply adequate currency, whether physical or electronic, to support the level of economic activity that the free market generates. Government should not use money or monetary policy to control interest rates, inflation rates or the availability of credit. The free market is more efficient and more equitable in these matters, and has no political agenda.

Government would do well to bear in mind that if maintaining sound money is not a priority, the very tax base upon which government relies is threatened. If money becomes unstable and unreliable, people will transact business through barter, which makes it more difficult for government to derive tax revenue. If one receives currency in exchange for labor or goods, income is derived that government may then tax. In a barter transaction, there is no financial transaction whereby income may be recognized. The economic and political survival of government is only possible if government fulfills its responsibility to provide sound money.

THE GLITTER OF GOLD

Many commodities have been used as money, but gold is perhaps the most enduring commodity that has been used for transactions and a store of value over millennia. The supply of gold has been very stable over many centuries, as mining has added modest amounts to the supply over the years, and there has not been substantial demand for gold for industrial consumption, as is the case with silver. It is a good thing that alchemists failed in their attempts to turn lead into gold, as they would have ruined a good thing.

159

Instead of returning to a gold standard, as some advocate, I propose that we use the supply of gold held in reserve to limit the supply of currency that Congress may authorize. If we peg the quantity of currency permitted to be in circulation to a fixed ratio of dollars per ounce of gold held in reserve, we may thereby restrict our government from creating money out of thin air.

It is very important to make the distinction between pegging the value of the dollar to a quantity of gold and limiting the quantity of dollars permitted in circulation to the supply of gold reserves on hand. We must permit the free market to establish the price of gold as a commodity. There are many factors that influence the market price for gold. Establishing an artificial rate of exchange between dollars and gold will tie the value of the dollar to a commodity that is quite volatile when the free market is permitted to set the price without government intervention.

Using gold coins as a store of value and in transactions is still a good idea, and We the People should be vigilant in protecting our right to own gold and to transact business with gold, cash or barter. We must never return to a time when the federal government makes it illegal for ordinary citizens to own gold, and we should never yield to globalists that will want to convert us to a cashless economy. Although Utah has minted gold coins, and other states are considering doing the same, it is unclear to me that states are permitted by the Constitution to mint gold coins. This may soon become an issue, so we may need to fight for a constitutional amendment that permits states to mint gold or silver coins.

No matter how popular gold coins may become in transacting business, there is a need for a United States paper currency that has stable and predictable value that can also be used in electronic transactions as well as serve as a world reserve currency. There is no going back to a gold standard with redeemable currency fixed to a specific quantity of gold, so the next best thing is to issue currency based upon the quantity of gold reserves on hand.

We should not issue currency that is redeemable in gold, and we should not permit an outflow of our gold reserves. Maintaining the security of our gold reserve, protecting our currency against counterfeit, the cost of printing or minting our currency and replacing worn out currency is a cost of doing business. The benefits of supplying a sound, stable currency to our economy far exceed those costs.

THE DOLLAR AS RESERVE CURRENCY

If we fix the problems that have been created by an irresponsible Congress and a Federal Reserve that has been reckless and lacking in transparency and accountability, then we may see the continuation of the US dollar as the world reserve currency. The demand for US dollars may balloon because much of the rest of the world finds the US dollar to be the most appropriate form of money to use as their currency, or to peg their currency to, or to use as a store of value. To the extent that this happens, the United States will have to expand the supply of dollars in order to avoid having foreign demand for dollars deprive the United States economy of the currency needed to conduct business. This will be accomplished by Congress authorizing the purchase of more gold to hold in reserve.

If Congress believes that it is beneficial to have the latitude to increase the supply of money from time to time, then Congress should use the tools that it has in its toolbox to do that. If we pass a sound money amendment in the manner that I propose, Congress would still have the means to make adjustments to the supply of currency. Congress could target a normal supply of currency that is less than the supply permitted by the quantity of gold held in reserve. This will give Congress the latitude to issue more currency if circumstances warrant. Congress could authorize the purchase of additional gold if the price of gold is below the limit authorized. This would not only permit an increase in the supply of currency, it would build our reserves of gold.

The freedom and security enjoyed by the United States created the most robust economy the world has ever seen. By securing and maintaining our liberties that permitted the United States to enjoy a robust economy for decades and showing reasonable fiscal responsibility, the US dollar became the world reserve currency. If We the People dramatically change the path that the United States is on, work diligently to assure the security and liberty of our nation, and restore fiscal and financial responsibility, our economy will surge and we will have no problem seeing the US dollar continue as the world reserve currency.

TWENTY-SIX

Amendment to Abolish the Fed and Fractional Banking

IT'S TIME TO DRIVE A STAKE INTO THE HEART OF THE GLOBALIST AGENDA

I believe that banking institutions are more dangerous to our liberties than standing armies.

– Thomas Jefferson

History records that the money changers have used every form of abuse, intrigue, deceit, and violent means possible to maintain their control over governments by controlling money and its issuance.

– James Madison

For years, some in Congress have tried in vain to assemble enough support to pass legislation to audit the Federal Reserve. Although those efforts have enjoyed much popular support, and make good sense, defenders of the Fed have succeeded in derailing all efforts to audit the Fed, despite the significant impact that the Fed has on our economy, and the fact that it is an unaccountable non-government entity.

My view is that we should stop trying to audit the Fed, and simply eliminate the Fed by abolishing the central bank altogether by constitutional amendment. The founding fathers argued against and resisted efforts to establish a central bank, warning us that the control of money by a central bank would lead to tyranny. A United States central bank was established and disbanded several times prior to the twentieth century. In 1913, which was a very bad year

163

for our Republic, we saw the Federal Reserve established, along with the passage of the Sixteenth and Seventeenth Amendments.

The Federal Reserve was established as a lender of last resort in order to avoid bank panics and the resulting damage to the United States economy. Actions of the Fed led to more bank failures and created the circumstances that led to the Great Depression. The FDIC was created to protect deposits in order to avoid a similar set of circumstances from occurring in the future. Although there have been bank failures along the way, the combination of the Fed and the FDIC has been successful in avoiding bank panics.

A FOOL'S ERRAND

The mandate given by Congress to the Federal Reserve was modified by the Federal Reserve act of 1977, which charged the Fed with the dual role of seeking maximum employment while maintaining stable prices and moderate long-term interest rates. Instead of trusting the free market to create jobs, establish prices and set interest rates, Congress entrusted the Fed with somewhat dubious monetary policy tools to pursue sometimes conflicting goals of maximum employment and low inflation.

Full Employment

Giving the Fed a mandate to pursue full employment while the federal government pursues policies that suppress employment is essentially sending the Fed on a fool's errand. The federal government can claim that unemployment is around five percent, but the reality is that almost 95 million Americans of working age do not participate in the labor market. If you consider that many of the people that are currently employed would desire to work more hours, or work a second job, it is easy to conclude that the citizens of the United States are dramatically under-employed.

I don't think that the current level of underemployment in the United States is accidental, or that it is the "new normal" that we simply have to adjust to. I sincerely believe that the dramatic under-employment of American citizens is a result of statists, globalists and environmentalists pursuing their goals of population control, the suppression of economic activity, and the political and financial enslavement of all people under a New World Order led by the privileged few. As treasonous co-conspirators with the globalists, the entrenched establishment political class has treacherously used crony capitalism to enrich global elitists and to assure themselves seats at the table of the ruling class.

If federal government policy is to pursue full employment, then the best way to pursue that goal would be to eliminate the Federal Reserve, eliminate most federal regulations and permit the free market to operate. It is not the function of federal, state or local government to create jobs. The best that any government can do is to minimize the impediments to the proper functioning of free-market capitalism.

Target Inflation Rate

The current Federal Reserve policy regarding inflation is to target an average two percent annual rate of inflation. The justification given for this policy is that the economy works best when there is a modest escalation in prices, as opposed to high rates of inflation or sustained deflation. History has shown that high rates of inflation are bad for the economy, and economists assert that the deflation experienced during the Great Depression is something that we should avoid at all costs.

There are two types of deflation, one that is good for the economy and one that is bad for the economy. Bad deflation results from a dramatic and sustained drop in demand. The deflation experienced during the Great Depression was an example of bad deflation. Good deflation results from the gradual, steady increase in production relative to consumption, which increases supply relative to demand, thereby reducing prices. Bad deflation will generally

165

result in the decline of the average standard of living, while good deflation will generally result in an increase in the average standard of living.

Economists employed by the federal government and at the Federal Reserve have erroneously chosen to pursue a policy of modest inflation instead of differentiating between good deflation and bad deflation and pursuing a policy of permitting the free market to produce full employment, stable prices and modest interest rates of its own accord. At best, economists have concluded that all deflation is bad, and that extreme measures by central banks are justified in order to combat deflation. In all probability, popular economic theory has been used to support the notions of the issuance of currency by central banks, the control of credit and interest rates as well as policies that promote sustained inflation as a means to concentrate worldwide wealth in the hands of elite globalists.

Deflation as the Natural Force of the Free Market

The laws of supply and demand and the corresponding impact upon prices is one of the most basic, yet one of the most powerful concepts in economics. Most people can easily grasp the concept that an increase in supply of a commodity, while holding demand constant, will lead to a reduction in price of that commodity. Likewise, an increase in demand for a commodity, while holding supply constant, will lead to an increase in price of that commodity. We don't live our lives in constant awareness of these laws and concern ourselves about whether people around us are obeying the laws of supply and demand, or whether supply, demand and prices are in equilibrium. Economic concepts don't drive human behavior; they merely attempt to explain human behavior. They are simply common sense expressions of how rational people behave.

In a free market that is substantially unfettered from government intervention, most people will work and contribute to real economic output because God wired us to work. God instructed man to work and to have dominion over the world that we live in. The Bible also instructs us to provide for our own needs and the needs of others, and admonishes that those capable of working that will not work should not eat. If everyone that is capable of working was free to work and was also deprived of any opportunity to enjoy having their living expenses met by the labor of other hard-working people, we would see aggregate production increase substantially. Good deflation would occur, resulting in an improvement in the average standard of living.

The reason that our economy does not enjoy an increasing average standard of living and enjoy the benefits of good deflation is because government policy restricts the opportunity of Americans to freely produce more output and enjoy the fruit of their labor, and because government policy has created the opportunity for tens of millions of American citizens and millions of illegal immigrants to consume far more than they produce. The flawed economic policy of the federal government has negated the natural deflationary force of the free market to the detriment of most Americans.

DUBIOUS TOOLS OF MONETARY POLICY

As I previously stated, it is improper for the federal government to attempt to directly impact employment in the private sector, and it is foolish to expect the Fed to pursue the goal of full employment while the federal government policy runs contrary to that goal. It is also inappropriate for the federal government to attempt to control prices or interest rates instead of permitting the operation of the free market to accomplish what is best for the economy. It truly is a marvelous thing that the invisible hand described by Adam Smith seamlessly orders the economic affairs of a free people without cost, and with such efficiency.

The Fed has dubious tools at its disposal with which it may meddle with the free market in pursuit of the dubious mandates given to it by Congress. For decades, the Fed has used three con-

ventional tools with which it influences credit, the money supply
and interest rates. The first tool the Fed uses is the Discount Rate,
the interest rate at which the Fed lends funds to member banks
overnight. The second tool that the Fed uses is Reserve Require-
ments, which is the percentage of deposits outstanding that member banks must maintain in reserve with the Federal Reserve. The
third tool that the Fed uses is Open Market Operations, which is
when the Federal Reserve buys or sells government securities.

The reason that these tools that the Fed has at its disposal are
dubious is that, although these tools provide the Fed with limited
direct influence over credit, the money supply and interest rates, the
use of these tools of monetary policy by the Fed has a more indirect
impact on inflation, output and employment.

If the economy was a car, and the Federal Reserve the driver,
driving the car would be straightforward if the tools that the Federal
Reserve has to influence the economy would work like a steering
wheel, accelerator and brake. The driver of the car can turn left or
right, accelerate or brake with a very high level of predictability of
what the car will do when the tools are used. The tools that the Fed
has to work with would be like driving a car using a bunch of
knobs, switches and buttons on the dashboard of the car that indi-
rectly influence, but do not directly correlate to steering, accelerating or braking. Driving a car would be very difficult and dangerous
if the impact of using the knobs, switches and buttons did not bring
immediate, predictable results, but rather brought unpredictable
results over uncertain and variable periods of time.

THE FAILURE OF MONETARY POLICY

Instead of enhancing the performance of the free market economy,
the Federal Reserve and fractional banking brought about the Great
Depression as well as numerous asset bubbles, market collapses and
recessions over the last century, causing massive redistribution of
wealth, suppression of employment and reduced productivity. The

creation of the subprime mortgage crisis that resulted from fault, federal government policy, bailouts that have created new asset bubbles as well as new winners and losers, and the great evil experiment of quantitative easing all combine to make the collapse of the global financial system inevitable. Whether this problem has been created intentionally or not, the solution is the same.

Since the Fed has failed miserably in using the dubious tools it has available to it to accomplish the conflicting goals of full employment, stable prices and meeting their target rate of inflation of two percent, we must conclude that monetary policy is a failure at best, and at worst a nefarious plot to subjugate the population to a New World Order.

Quantitative Easing: The Largest and Most Risky Monetary Experiment in History

When we consider the quantitative easing implemented by the Fed, we have to wonder why they would make such a risky move with no apparent rational objective for upside. What on earth were they thinking? Were they forced to use such a destructive tool in order to purchase mortgage-backed securities held by banks caught up in the subprime mortgage debacle? Did they have such fear of deflation that they felt the need to pump trillions of new dollars into the system? Were they seeking to create asset bubbles in the equity, bond and real estate markets in order to make it appear that the Obama economy was actually moving in a positive direction, hiding the reality that the Obama economy was a dismal failure? Is there a nefarious intent to collapse the global financial system so that the very perpetrators of the collapse will arrive just in time to implement a New World Order solution?

If there is a rational reason for the Fed to implement three rounds of quantitative easing, creating approximately $4.5 trillion out of thin air, I don't see it. What I believe, is that the Fed has made a bad situation far worse, and created a set of circumstances that makes the collapse of the global financial system inevitable. As with so many problems created by the federal government, the circumstances created by the problem reveal an opportunity that we may not have recognized otherwise. The more significant and complex the problem, and the more impossible a solution seems, the easier it will be to find the path that cuts the Gordian knot.

RESET OF THE GLOBAL FINANCIAL SYSTEM

According to a McKinsey study, from the financial collapse of 2007-2008 to the end of 2014, total global debt had increased by forty percent. You would think that governments and their central banks would have learned the lesson of excessive debt from the collapse, but the addiction to debt just grew stronger. The global financial system seems to be operating like a heroin addict that needs larger and larger doses, leading to death by overdose. Central banks led the way with quantitative easing measures that created vast amounts of new credit. Corporations gobbled up their own shares or acquired other companies, and despite an incredibly weak economy, stock markets soared.

The asset bubbles created by reckless action by governments and their central banks create the circumstances for an imminent global financial meltdown that seems unavoidable. Whether intended or not, the stage has been set for those that created the coming global financial crisis to present themselves as the saviors of the world from impending global financial calamity. Rahm Emanuel famously said to "never let a good crisis go to waste," and there are many times when predictable crises have occurred when the very culprits that created a crisis were entrusted with proposing and implementing solutions to the crisis.

We the People have a choice to make. We can wait until the statists and globalists eventually collapse the world financial system and impose a New World Order upon us with a new currency and financial system, or we can choose the path of freedom whereby we eliminate fractional banking, eliminate the Fed and perhaps even go so far as to declare a Year of Jubilee and not only wipe away all debts, but actually outlaw all debt. Because of the mess that statists and globalists have created, there is no easy solution. We simply have the choice of choosing which tumultuous path to take. One path will lead to totalitarianism and tyranny, and the other path will lead to freedom and renewed opportunity for prosperity.

The Day After the Reset

The day after the United Kingdom voted to exit the European Union, headlines reported that the world financial markets lost $2 trillion, followed by another trillion dollar loss the next day. There may have been winners and losers on paper, but there was no net loss of tangible wealth as a result of Brexit. There was no loss in the value of physical assets; there was simply an adjustment to the market valuation of intangible assets created to represent the value of tangible assets.

In the event of a global financial collapse of asset values that leads to a reset of the global financial system, or in the event that We the People proactively initiate the global reset and collapse of asset values by taking the actions I have prescribed, there will be no net loss of tangible wealth overnight. The critical difference between these two scenarios of the collapse of asset values lies in the psychology that will prevail under each scenario. If the globalists have their way in establishing their New World Order, they will impose tyranny and mitigate the effect by continuing to offer bread and circuses to the masses. If We the People succeed in throwing off the yoke of servitude under an economic system driven by debt by embracing economic freedom, we will again find the path to prosperity.

Regardless of what the stated purpose was for establishing the Federal Reserve in 1913, or in re-tasking the Fed in 1977, there is much support for the widespread belief that the Fed, and all central banks worldwide, share the common goal of establishing a New World Order governed by a central authority and under a single currency and unified financial system. We the People can drive a stake in the heart of the globalist agenda by eliminating the Fed and encouraging all other nations that desire freedom to eliminate their central banks as well.

TWENTY-SEVEN

Balanced Budget Amendment

IT'S TIME TO FORCE FISCAL DISCIPLINE UPON OUR SPENDTHRIFT CONGRESS

Federal expenditures shall not exceed revenue unless approved by a two-thirds vote of both houses of Congress, and in all such cases, deficit spending shall be funded by the accumulated surplus.

– Proposed Constitutional Amendment Language

Congress has shown no restraint in spending historically, and has irresponsibly permitted the national debt to escalate to very dangerous levels. If the other measures presented in this plan are implemented, a balanced budget amendment to the Constitution may not be necessary, but given the track record of Congress, it is in the best interest of our nation to force Congress to balance the budget by constitutional amendment.

It may be inconceivable, but imagine that We the People have succeeded in restoring the balance of power, limiting the federal government to those activities intended by our founders, limiting federal taxes to a maximum of fifteen percent of income and a maximum five percent sales tax, and somehow eradicating the national debt. In short, assume that we are successful in implementing this plan, or a plan of similar magnitude and direction.

Such unimaginable success in repudiating the entrenched establishment political class and properly restructuring our federal government would unleash the American economic engine that has been artificially restrained by oppressive liberal policy for so long that we have lost any memory of what a robust economy looks like. In time, the liberated American economy would generate enough tax revenue for Congress to properly fund appropriate activities of the federal government at well below my proposed maximum sales and income tax rates.

Removing the governor from the economic engine would permit us to really see what we are capable of as Americans again. By placing the governor on Congress, the courts, the president and the dramatically reduced regulatory system, We the People will be capable of holding the federal government accountable so that they don't automatically spend more money than is taken in. The new paradigm would permit the federal government to actually run a surplus in most years, which will allow surplus funds to accumulate for a rainy day.

It would be reasonable to target the operation of all federal government activities at eighty percent of the maximum tax rates, which will allow for some breathing room for variations in revenue and expenditures, as well as the potential for building an accumulated surplus. If over the years, we discover that we can run the federal government for less, while still building a surplus, we can force Congress to have the discipline to reduce taxes instead of spending the surplus revenue. With only two tax rates to adjust, and little opportunity for pork-barrel spending or for buying votes, We the People will finally be able to hold Congress accountable.

Having a balanced budget amendment that permits deficit spending by Congress for good reason will provide a path for making an exception to balancing the budget when deemed necessary by a vote of two thirds of the members of both houses of Congress. The only good reasons for deficit spending, in my opinion, are times of national emergency such as calamity or war. In such circumstances, Congress would have no problem meeting the two thirds threshold, provided that there is an accumulated surplus to work with. Building an accumulated surplus should be a national priority.

TWENTY-EIGHT

Line-item Veto Amendment

EMPOWER THE PRESIDENT TO VETO ANY PART OF ANY SPENDING BILL, WHICH THE CONGRESS MAY OVERRIDE

The President may veto any provision of any spending Bill presented for signature by the Congress.

– Proposed Constitutional Amendment Language

Congress gave the line item veto power to the president back in the 1990s and the Supreme Court struck it down, doing a great disservice to our nation. We the People can reverse the Supreme Court decision by compelling Congress or the states to propose and ratify a constitutional amendment giving the president the line-item veto. The president would then be able to veto specific spending provisions from an omnibus spending bill without derailing the bill entirely. Limits on the length of bills should also be imposed upon Congress in order to eliminate bills that our representatives cannot even read before being required to vote on them.

Giving the president the opportunity to eliminate pork from spending bills makes too much sense to be acceptable to the establishment political class. Or perhaps they simply don't want to give up the power to buy each other off with the promise of votes in favor of ridiculous spending proposals. If Congress chooses to override a line item veto spending proposal, they should do so on the record so that voters at home could hold them accountable. We the People should also hold Congress accountable by requiring that all votes are conducted as rollcall votes and that sufficient time for public comment is given to all bills prior to a vote.

TWENTY-NINE

Congressional Term Limits Amendment

LIMIT SENATORS TO TWO TERMS, AND CONGRESSMAN TO FOUR TERMS, INCLUDING PARTIAL TERMS SERVED

Senators shall serve no more than two terms, and congressmen shall serve no more than four terms, including partial terms served.

– Proposed Constitutional Amendment Language

One of the things that We the People must do in order to break the stranglehold that the entrenched establishment political class has on the power of the federal government is to impose term limits on congressmen and senators. Limiting the time that congressmen and senators can serve will go a long way to stripping the political class of the power that they hold. By limiting the power that individual congressmen and senators may accrue, we will limit the potential for abuse of that power.

I believe that the founding fathers intended that members of Congress function as public servants, not lords and masters over the citizens. We need to reinvent and redefine the term "public servant" to actually mean what it very plainly says. We the People need to elect a new wave of public servants instead of new recruits to the political class. Most members of the establishment political class got started at the local and state level. We the People must also root out the entrenched establishment political class from local and state government and implement elements of this plan such as term limits at the state and local level as well.

THIRTY

Presidential Term Limit Amendment

LIMIT THE POWER AND POLITICS OF THE PRESIDENCY BY LIMITING THE OFFICE OF PRESIDENT TO ONE TERM OF SIX YEARS

Election of any person to the office of President shall be limited to one term of six years. No person who has acted as President for more than two years of the term to which another person was elected President shall be elected to the office of President.

– Proposed Constitutional Amendment Language

More power resides in the office of President of the United States than the Framers of the Constitution ever intended. One of the ways that We the People can reduce the power that has accrued to the office of president is to advocate for the passage of a constitutional amendment that limits anyone elected to the most powerful office in the world to just one term in office. We could keep the length of that one term at four years, but I am suggesting six years in order to mollify the folks that will object to cutting in half the potential time someone can serve as President.

This proposed amendment would allow anyone that served less than two years of the term of someone else that was elected to the office of President to seek election to one full term of office. Only this scenario would permit a sitting President to seek reelection to the office of President, which would be of immense benefit to our nation, as the attention of the President will be focused on leading our nation instead of being distracted by reelection. It seems that before a newly elected President has been sworn in or completed his or her first month in office, plans for reelection of the president are already being formulated by the political team that managed the election that just ended.

It would be a wonderful thing if a newly elected President could simply focus on doing the best job possible instead of thinking about how decisions will affect prospects for reelection. It would also be a tremendous benefit to the party in power to liberate other leaders of that party, including the Vice President, to lay the groundwork for potential campaigns for the office of President during the last two years of an administration instead of deferring to the current president, who may not be the best choice for the party or the country.

The opposition party would benefit, as they will have a better shot at having their candidate elected President during the next election. We the People benefit, because we know that we will not be stuck with the person just elected president for more than one term.

We can really bring dramatic change to our political process by holding the national election for the offices of President and Vice President at a time that is completely disconnected from state and local elections. Imagine what it would be like if the only national election were to take place every six years on the first Tuesday in May, instead of November. We could shake things up even more by holding the national election during odd-numbered years! No one is compelling us to continue to allow the election of the President of the United States to have such a profound influence on all other elected offices.

We the People will benefit greatly by transferring power from the federal government back to the states and substantially reducing the power of the office of the President. Doing so will benefit all Americans except for those in the establishment political class. We the People are limited only by our own creativity and commitment to saving our Republic.

THIRTY-ONE

Federal Employment Amendment

DRAIN THE SWAMP OF ENTRENCHED EMPLOYEES OF THE FEDERAL BUREAUCRACY

All federal employees shall be employed at will, shall be prohibited from collective bargaining activities, and shall receive no pension or other promise of future compensation for past services rendered.

– Proposed Constitutional Amendment Language

When campaigning for president, Donald Trump frequently used the term "drain the swamp" to characterize his commitment to presumably dismantle the entrenched establishment political class, which transformational conservatives have been clamoring for with increasing volume and passion. We the People have simply become fed up with business as usual in Washington, and expect President Donald Trump or any other future Republican president to take decisive action to "drain the swamp" as we would define it, and We the People will accept nothing less.

The most obvious and visible opposition to any efforts made to dramatically reduce the power and influence of the entrenched establishment political class will come from the vigorous and vocal resistance from Democrat senators and congressmen. Less visible will be the creative and dubious ways that some Republicans in the House and Senate will find to undermine, impede and dilute efforts by President Trump or any other anti-establishment president that comes along. Far less visible and more dangerous is the opposition that will come from entrenched, unelected employees of the federal bureaucracy.

What has become known as the "fourth branch" of the federal government is where the fiercest battles will take place to effect change that will allow us to dramatically reduce federal spending. The true cost of the federal bureaucratic overreach and overregulation is far greater than the expenditures in personnel and other hard costs. The loss of liberty, the barriers that make it difficult or impossible for citizens to live productive lives and the demoralization of a people oppressed by a tyrannical federal government result in incalculable financial and intangible costs to American citizens.

To successfully cut the Gordian knot that will restore personal and economic liberty to American citizens, We the People must be unrelenting in our quest to disgorge all federal employees that are bitterly clinging to the special rights and entitlements granted to them by the entrenched establishment political class to which they belong. Those federal employees that see the necessity of stripping the special rights and entitlements from the federal bureaucracy will not find continued employment difficult as long as they are productive and cooperative employees. The bitter clingers will have to go, just as air traffic controllers that did not obey the directives of Ronald Reagan lost their jobs.

STRIP FEDERAL EMPLOYEES OF COLLECTIVE BARGAINING RIGHTS

Federal employees should have never been granted collective bargaining rights, as there is an inherent conflict of interest in granting collective bargaining rights to people that also have the opportunity to vote themselves a paycheck.

The appropriateness of denying collective bargaining rights to federal employees should be obvious under normal circumstances, but if We the People are to restore personal and economic liberty to all Americans by taking the dramatic action set forth in this plan, we must sever all of the cords that bind us as a nation from pursuing the right path before us to free ourselves and our posterity.

Congress has the power through simple legislation to strip collective bargaining rights from federal employees. Although it has been asserted that 95% of federal employees cast their votes for Democrat candidates, I have to believe that the majority of federal employees are patriotic Americans that will recognize the wisdom and prudence of doing their part to save our Republic.

STRIP FEDERAL EMPLOYEES OF PENSIONS

As set forth earlier in this book, the reset brought about by a global financial collapse whereby the New World Order imposes a new global financial system to "rescue" the broken, debt laden global financial system, or a reset that We the People initiate ourselves by the implementation of this plan or one of similar magnitude and direction, will result in a complete reset of commodity and asset prices, as well as a reset of all debt.

Under either reset scenario, the pension liabilities of the federal government will either be revalued under the new paradigm or will be completely wiped out. Under either scenario, it will be necessary to establish an equitable way to provide some relief to all groups that are vested with some form of federal retirement income, whether federal pensions, or Social Security retirement income. Any equitable relief provided to retirees by the federal government in the context of a reset would have to be based upon need, indexed for significant adjustments to price levels during the transition to a new equilibrium established by the free market.

Since I would argue that American citizens would be far better off under a reset scenario that we initiate than a reset brought about by the collapse of the global financial system by globalists, I would also argue that it will be easier for us to provide relief to retirees based upon need if we initiate the reset. We the People will not initiate a reset without taking proper care of citizens too old or too feeble to work through the transition that we will all be going through together as a nation. Any reset will produce winners and losers on a massive scale, but we will fare better as a sovereign nation if we are free to pursue our personal and economic liberty in a way that creates prosperity that our country has not seen in decades. The renewal of American prosperity will permit states to provide sustenance to those that are incapable of participating fully in the revived American economy.

Since the pensions afforded to federal employees were much more lucrative than Social Security, providing equitable relief to retired federal employees at the same level as that provided to Social Security recipients may not sit well with retired federal employees, but given the manner in which such lucrative pensions were granted by the establishment political class to themselves, it is only right to use the same need-based criteria for all retirees, including those not covered by federal pensions or Social Security.

MERIT-BASED EMPLOYMENT-AT-WILL

If we are to have any chance to dramatically reduce the federal budget and the overreach of the federal bureaucracy in our daily lives, we must strip federal employees of the job security that they presently enjoy. It seems that federal employees are almost impervious to termination for what are sometimes very egregious actions that would never be tolerated in the private sector. As we seek to eliminate entire departments and bring dramatic reductions to other departments, it is imperative that we are able to retain the best and brightest federal employees, not necessarily those with the most seniority or connections.

Federal workers must be transformed into employees-at-will that are hired, compensated, retained and promoted based upon merit and job performance. There will be a lot of kicking and screaming as We the People compel Congress to legislate such dramatic changes to federal employment, but our nation will be far better off if we can make it happen. Displaced federal workers will find new job opportunities in a reviving economy.

As We the People are successfully downsizing the federal government, the new American economy will add jobs at a pace that will absorb displaced federal workers that are flexible and willing to work. Hard times can be good times, and through the turmoil many federal workers that have been suddenly introduced to the pain that bureaucratic overreach brought to displaced private sector workers over the last few decades will perhaps find private sector opportunities in the reviving economy that will bring them greater satisfaction than their government jobs ever could.

PART IV

NATIONAL SECURITY

THIRTY-TWO

Provide for the Common Defense

Restore National Security as the First Priority of the Federal Government

We the People of the United States, in Order to form a more perfect Union, establish Justice, insure domestic Tranquility, provide for the common defence, promote the general Welfare, and secure the Blessings of Liberty to ourselves and our Posterity, do ordain and establish this Constitution for the United States of America.

– Preamble to the United States Constitution

The single most important function of the federal government that is prescribed by the Constitution is to provide for the common defense. The federal government has been wayward in the execution of this duty, erroneously pursuing redistribution of wealth, social engineering and economic malfeasance instead of performing the single duty that it must not shirk.

One of the biggest benefits that we will see from getting the federal government out of entitlements and other functions not authorized by the Constitution is that our nation can then focus the federal government on the all-important responsibility of national defense. When the states and the private sector are permitted to function as the founders envisioned when they established the separation of powers, the federal government is liberated to focus on the common defense instead of being constantly distracted by pork-barrel spending and disputes about where the federal government should spend money that the federal government should not even collect in the first place.

If the federal government will simply get out of the way, the free enterprise system will create the strong economy that is essential to a strong defense. This will free up the federal government to focus on national defense. By withdrawing from activities that properly belong to the states or to the people, and providing for a strong national defense, the federal government will also simultaneously secure the blessings of liberty, which is another mandate given to the federal government by the Framers of the Constitution.

REBUILD OUR MILITARY

Our military was significantly degraded during the administration of Barack Obama, and we must make it a national priority to rebuild our military as well as all other facets of our national defense. The world became a much more dangerous place as a result of the policies of Barack Obama. His actions emboldened the enemies of freedom and created distrust and uncertainty among our allies. The world is a much safer place when America is strong, so we must quickly restore international stability through the leadership of a strong America.

Great prosperity will result from the economic liberty that we will obtain by implementing this plan or something of similar magnitude and direction. Under the New American economy that puts underemployed Americans to work, American citizens will be free to enjoy a much higher standard of living while also providing the resources to rebuild our military and national defense infrastructure to the point where we are out front and pulling ahead again. We don't have to choose between guns and butter, for we can have both in abundance.

American military might is a strategic advantage that we should build upon by racing down the learning curve ahead of all other nations. We can provide the majority of security for NATO if other member nations pay their fair share. Aggregating the production of military equipment and technology will allow us to exploit the advantage of the sheer volume of production to the benefit of the United States and our allies. I am not advocating that the United States function as the world's policeman, I am simply stressing the point that the more accumulated experience we have in the development and production of military assets, the further ahead of the competition we will be.

An important part of being strategic in approaching national security is the integration of clandestine services, cyber security, drones, robots and all other emerging technologies that will contribute to the capacity of the United States to fight conventional and asymmetric wars, as well as to defend our nation against all current and emerging threats.

As an integral part of our strategy to rebuild our military, the primary mission of NASA should be to contribute to our national defense. The "Star Wars" defense system envisioned by Ronald Reagan should be pursued. Any and all prospects for improving our national defense should be considered in order that we may stay significantly ahead of all other nations.

DECLARE WAR ON RADICAL ISLAMIC TERRORISM

Whether we choose to face the reality or not, the truth is that Radical Islam has declared war on the United States and all of Western Civilization. There are two kinds of Muslims, those that rejoice when they hear of terrorist attacks such as 9/11, and those that are abhorred by such attacks. All Muslims that rejoice when they hear of terrorist attacks are Radical Islamists at heart. It doesn't matter if the attack is on the United States, London, Paris, Kenya, Yemen, Lebanon or Mali. Those that rejoice at such attacks are evil.

We should give no place to the argument that liberals make that Western Civilization is somehow at fault and has called for these attacks by our actions. Radical Islam hates the very existence of free societies that are prosperous. Radical Islamic Terrorism is a wake-up call to Muslims everywhere to examine the Koran and the Muslim faith to see if it lines up with truth and righteousness. Many Muslims have converted from Islam to Christianity and have paid for it with their lives. But for the fact that, in many Muslim countries, conversions from Islam result in execution, there would not be 1.6 billion Muslims on earth.

We should declare war on Radical Islam and ask other free nations to do the same. Radical Islam has declared war on Western Civilization and called for the annihilation of the United States and Israel. The Islamic State of Iraq and Syria, or ISIS, has declared itself to be the revived caliphate of Islam. Their objective is to consolidate Islam and to impose sharia law on the rest of the world. They seek to prepare the way for their Twelfth Imam, or Messiah, and in order to do so they must destroy Israel and the United States. We are not at war with all of Islam or with peaceful Muslims, but we should not trust any Muslim that will not denounce and condemn all acts of terrorism.

Joel Rosenberg has written extensively on what he calls the Radicals, Reformers and Revivalists among Islam. He has correctly identified the theology, objectives and strategy of radical Islam and has also written some chilling works of fiction that are so close to reality that it will make your blood run cold. Rosenberg suggests that Islamic radicals are followers of Jihad, Islamic reformers are followers of Jefferson and Islamic revivalists are followers of Jesus. Rosenberg's book, *Inside the Revolution*, provides a good framework for understanding the different factions of Islam. In his book, *The Epicenter*, Rosenberg argues that, in order to truly understand what is going on in the world today, one must view the world not just through the lens of politics and the lens of economics, but also through what he calls the third lens of Scripture. When pressed for how he could be so prescient in the writing of his books, Rosenberg asserts that he simply views world events through the third lens of Scripture.

THIRTY-THREE

Secure Our Borders

WE MUST BE FULLY COMMITTED TO USING
ALL AVAILABLE MEANS TO IMMEDIATELY
SECURE OUR BORDERS

*The United States shall guarantee to every State in this Union a
Republican Form of Government, and shall protect each of them
against invasion.*

– United States Constitution, Article IV, Section 4

We will not continue to exist as a sovereign nation if we don't have secure borders, and have knowledge of and control over the people and goods that enter our country. One of the grave mistakes made by President George W. Bush after 9/11 was his failure to secure our borders. Congress and the Obama administration continued to fail to take this most basic step toward securing our nation. Under the leadership of President Trump, securing our borders seems more likely to happen, but there is still much resistance by Congress and the establishment political class.

It seems that the establishment political class has been invested in maintaining the status quo in permitting massive illegal immigration into our country. Democrats have seen our open border policy as a means of increasing their constituency base, and the Republican establishment has not had the backbone to deal with the problem for fear of political repercussions. Our national security has suffered as a result of playing politics with illegal immigration.

Border security is not just about controlling illegal immigration. Our insecure, open borders have been very inviting to radical Islamic terrorists, drug cartels and those engaged in human trafficking.

191

The actions and statements of the Obama administration effectively advertised that the back door of America had been left open. At best, this was naïve and stupid. At worst, it was a malevolent act of treason intended by evil people to destroy our nation.

We the People must insist upon immediate and decisive action to secure our borders. We must hold our federal and state governments accountable to addressing this most urgent need. Where there has been no political will to deal with the problem, we must rise up and use our collective voice to compel corrective action. We must insist upon our state and federal governments using all means possible to immediately secure our borders. If Donald Trump is serious about securing our borders, he will need our voice to help persuade Congress to take action. If he isn't committed to securing our borders, then it will be even more imperative that we speak with one voice about this important issue.

BUILD A WALL/FENCE ON OUR SOUTHERN BORDER

Building a wall, fence or some other barrier to keep people from illegally crossing our southern border will take some time. We have about 2000 miles of border to secure, and only a small portion of it is presently secure. Congress appropriated the money to secure our border with Mexico shortly after 9/11, yet the job has not been done. Even if President Trump is fully committed to securing the border, there is much inertia to overcome in getting the job done. It would make sense to use a design-build approach to segment and prioritize portions of the border and solicit bids from numerous design build firms that can simultaneously work on the entire length of our southern border.

We don't have to wait for construction to begin to secure our border, because we presently have the ability to use the National Guard, an augmented border control force and even citizen volunteers to provide security along the entire length of our border with

Mexico. Our nation is being invaded. Political correctness will not change that reality. Our nation is being invaded, and it is the duty of the federal government to immediately secure our borders, and if the federal government fails to secure the border, We the People should demand that our states fill the gap.

Our border with Canada does not represent anywhere near the immediate threat of the flow of illegal persons and material over the border with Mexico, but we must also come up with a plan for greater security of our border with Canada before it becomes a problem. Our border with Canada is longer, is more desolate and less secure than our border with Mexico, and once we secure our border with Mexico, there will be more incentive for illegal entry from our neighbor to the north.

If instead of advertising that our back door is open, we advertised that anyone illegally entering our country would be subject to being shot, we would quickly eliminate the vast majority of the illegal immigration that is happening for economic reasons. The drug cartels and terrorists entering our country illegally would not be so easily dissuaded, but at least we would be able to concentrate our efforts on these most dangerous elements. In the short term, we might need to deploy the National Guard along unprotected segments of the border. Sniper teams every 500 yards backed up by quick reaction teams would stop 99% of the flow of people and material that is illegally crossing our border between ports of entry, giving us time to build more permanent, cost effective barriers.

We must not allow the implementation of environmental laws on federal lands or litigation over eminent domain to impede our efforts to secure the border with a wall or other barrier. We must also reverse the damage caused by the creation of national monuments and wildlife areas along the border with Mexico, to which our border patrol agents are denied unfettered access. Bad Federal government policy effectively created corridors of safe passage for Mexican drug cartels to move illegals and drugs with impunity. This is a huge security breach that is not very well publicized outside of the immediate areas affected.

SECURE PORTS OF ENTRY

We should immediately institute a policy of 100% inspection of all shipments into our ports of entry. We compromise our national security if we fail to inspect 100% of incoming people and material because we don't have the resources for full inspection. The cost of inspection should be levied against imported goods so that the free market can take the true cost of imported goods into account when determining the supply and demand of those products.

There has been much debate over the years about free trade vs fair trade. Perhaps it is time that we have a debate about secure trade. Perhaps we should limit ourselves to international trade that can be conducted fairly and securely.

PROTECT OUR COASTS WITH MISSILE DEFENSE SYSTEMS

The United States has deployed missile defense systems in other parts of the world, but what do we have for missile defense along our vulnerable coastlines? What protection do we have from a rogue nation launching nuclear missiles against our country using what has been described as a "scud in a bucket," a missile launched from one of countless ocean freighters within range of our coast? The threat of an electromagnetic pulse attack is very real, and the potential for devastating our country is well known.

We need to take a hard look at the security of our coastlines, which could be just as vulnerable as our land borders with Mexico and Canada. I recall an incident a few years ago when a small craft came ashore in a coastal California town and perhaps a dozen men exited the vessel, walked up the beach into town and disappeared. Our efforts to secure our borders must be as imaginative as the efforts of our enemies to infiltrate our nation.

THIRTY-FOUR

Immigration Moratorium

Stop Illegal Immigration and Immediately Impose a Moratorium on All Legal Immigration

Are there no inconveniences to be thrown into the scale against the advantage expected by a multiplication of numbers by the importation of foreigners?

– Thomas Jefferson

We are a nation of immigrants, but we are also a nation of laws. We undermine our security as a nation if we permit lawlessness, including lawless immigration. We endanger our liberties and our economy if we encourage people from other nations to enter our country illegally in search of jobs, free education and free healthcare.

Those that are seeking to change our nation into one that is not defined by common culture with shared values knowingly or unwittingly seek the destruction of our nation as we know it. Those that want to permit illegal immigration or to allow legal immigration by immigrants that are not likely to assimilate into or enrich our culture do the same.

ILLEGAL IMMIGRATION

When Democrats and RINO Republicans speak of "immigration reform," they are advocating for amnesty for millions of illegal immigrants instead of simply enforcing the immigration laws that are already on the books. It is time for We the People to say enough is enough, and to insist upon securing our borders and enforcing our immigration laws. When Ronald Reagan agreed in 1986 to grant amnesty to several million illegal immigrants, it was with the promise that the flow of illegal immigration would end, and that our border would be secured. Democrats and RINO Republicans did not keep their promise, yet they are again seeking to grant amnesty to millions of additional illegal immigrants.

Remove the Incentives

If we eliminate the incentives for people to immigrate to our country illegally, fewer people will try to enter our country and many of those that are here illegally will self deport by returning home. Employers that knowingly employ illegal immigrants should be penalized. Welfare, the license to drive and other privileges should be denied to illegal immigrants.

Removing the incentives will result in the self-deportation of millions of illegal immigrants, as they will no longer be able to easily find work and send money back home. Mass deportation will not be necessary. Deportations of illegal immigrants that do not self-deport will happen in an orderly manner over several years. The state and federal governments just need to do their jobs.

Americans Will Work

The argument that we need illegal immigrants to do work that Americans refuse to do is not based in reality and runs contrary to the principles of the free market. Without government constraint or intervention, the free market will get the job done.

It is true that many jobs that involve hard work are performed by illegal immigrants, but only because the free market was not permitted to set the price for the services without the outside force of illegal immigration intervening. Illegal immigration creates a pool of labor that is unskilled, undocumented, hamstrung by a language barrier and education deficiency, and therefore willing to work for less. This pool of labor is enslaved by working illegally.

We will free up and incentivize the labor pool of legal United States citizens by removing all disincentives to work. How can we expect Americans to work in low-paying jobs when welfare or unemployment will pay them more? Eliminating all federal and state entitlements and eliminating the minimum wage while permitting the free market to operate will create an abundance of good paying jobs and motivate people to work. It's a simple matter of structuring incentives appropriately and creating an environment that encourages people to work.

Enforce Current Law

We don't need immigration reform; we just need to enforce the immigration laws that are currently on the books. The federal government has been the leading lawbreaker, followed by sanctuary states and sanctuary cities. It is shameful, and We the People must stop it. How can we expect lawful behavior from people that come to this country unlawfully? How can citizens be expected to obey the law if elected officials will not obey the law? We face a serious crisis if we don't fix this problem.

By imposing a temporary moratorium on legal immigration, shutting down illegal immigration, and figuring out how to get the federal government, sanctuary states, and sanctuary cities to enforce the law, we will force the debate of the issues of immigration so that we may pursue a course that consistently applies the principles of freedom and security while preserving the uniqueness of American exceptionalism.

We need a national dialogue about anchor babies. Given the mobility of people in the twenty-first century, and the intent by some to give birth to their children in the United States in order to acquire for their children the status of natural born citizen, we need to reevaluate that practice to see if it is in our national interest. Even if we conclude that we will continue to extend the privilege of United States citizenship to babies born in the United States regardless of the status of their parents, we can certainly recognize the fact that granting the infant citizenship does not grant any rights to the parents.

The noncitizen parents of a child born in the United States that is granted the privilege of natural born citizenship have no right to continue to be in the United States beyond any permission granted to them. If the parents are here on a visa, or illegally, they have no right to stay in the United States beyond the period granted by a visa. Those parents simply must leave the country and take their child with them. If the child becomes a natural born citizen, then the child could return to the United States when they become a legal adult.

Since we have learned that the couple that perpetrated the San Bernardino terrorist attack used the United States immigration and citizenship laws to entitle the jihadist wife of a United States citizen to gain entry and citizenship to our country, we need a national dialogue about the merits of changing those aspects of the immigration and citizenship laws. Should we make it so easy for someone to become a United States citizen by marriage, and does reciprocity by the country of citizenship of the noncitizen matter?

Whether through legislation or executive order, the United States should immediately implement a policy that requires the immediate deportation of any illegal immigrant that does not register their presence in this country and maintain a record of their whereabouts and contact information, if any. Any illegal immigrant that does not register after the effective date of such a policy would be justifiably deported in an expedited manner. Criminal illegal immigrants, whether registered or not, should also be deported without delay.

Illegal immigrants that register their presence in this country and maintain contact with Immigration and Naturalization Services will be dealt with in a manner prescribed by the conclusion of the national discussion we must have regarding how we should deal with noncriminal illegal aliens that are already here. If someone is in this country illegally, they have obviously broken the law, but we can distinguish between that infraction and other criminal activity. If we stanch the flow of new illegal immigrants and encourage the self-deportation of those that will leave voluntarily, the number of illegal immigrants that we must figure out what to do with will diminish over time.

MORATORIUM ON ALL LEGAL IMMIGRATION

It is true that the United States is a nation of immigrants, but there is a big difference between the immigration that built our country and the immigration that we have seen in the last fifty years since the passage of the 1965 Immigration Act. Immigrants that helped build our nation moved to this country in search of freedom and assimilated into the melting pot that America has been known to be. They became Americans.

We need to return to a policy of limited, legal immigration of people that are yearning to be free and that are willing to assimilate into our culture. Our national motto, "*E Pluribus Unum*" is translated "out of many, one." Multiculturalism runs contrary to our motto, as the celebration of cultural differences is valued more highly than the assimilation of many cultures into one. The uniqueness of America can be traced, in part, to the special quality of the melting pot that we are.

Work Visa Programs like H-1b and H-2b

Decades of massive European immigration to the United States came to an abrupt end at the start of World War I. The reality of the war depriving the United States of cheap labor from Europe forced American employers to hire American workers. The black community in America was the primary beneficiary of this renewed interest in American workers, and millions of blacks were added to the middle class over more than four decades of restricted immigration to the United States that came to an end with the 1965 Immigration Act.

The last fifty years of immigration has seen the restriction of immigrants from Europe in favor of immigrants from countries all over the world that don't espouse the values of Western civilization. Whereas in the past, immigrants quickly assimilated into American culture, we have seen a wave of almost two million immigrants per year that have no desire to assimilate.

Large American employers continue to push incessantly to admit additional immigrants under worker visa programs that have notoriously displaced American workers, particularly in technology fields. We the People must clamor for an immediate end to not only the worker visa programs, but to all legal immigration currently permitted. With over 100 million Americans out of the workforce or underemployed, it is obvious what the entrenched establishment political class and globalist leaders of big business are doing to our country. The middle-class will shrink away to nothing if we don't bring a stop to the insanity.

United Nations Refugee Resettlement Program

The United Nations refugee resettlement program, and specifically the resettlement of Syrian refugees with the threat of embedded jihadists, gives us good reason to immediately cease taking any refugees under the United Nations program. We the People must clamor with one voice until we overcome the resistance of the entrenched establishment political class and the judicial tyranny that is perpetuating this suicidal United Nations program.

Americans have compassion for hurting and displaced people from all over the world, but that doesn't mean that we have to accept the United Nations refugee resettlement program as the solution. There are many other ways to offer temporary assistance, and just because we accept refugees into our country doesn't mean that we have to let them stay if they don't assimilate.

THIRTY-FIVE

Withdraw From the United Nations

RESTORE UNITED STATES SOVEREIGNTY AND EXPEL THE UNITED NATIONS FROM AMERICAN SOIL

Frankly I had thought at the time Roe was decided, there was concern about population growth and particularly growth in populations that we don't want to have too many of.

– Ruth Bader Ginsburg

The United States will not continue to be a sovereign nation if we continue to participate as a member of the United Nations. We must reassert our national sovereignty and reject all efforts by globalists to establish global governance.

The globalist agenda of the United Nations is incompatible with the Constitution of the United States, and the Judeo-Christian values upon which our nation was founded. The freedoms that we enjoy in our constitutional Republic stand in the way of the tyranny of the New World Order that the United Nations globalists seek to establish. The only way that our nation can escape the current globalist path that we are on is if We the People clamor for Congress and our president to completely repudiate the United Nations agenda by immediately withdrawing from the United Nations and expelling them from American soil.

REJECT THE UNITED NATIONS AGENDA

Notwithstanding the lofty language of the United Nations charter and the stated commitment to respect the sovereignty of nations,

201

there is no doubt that the true intentions of the globalist leaders of the United Nations are to usurp the sovereignty of nations and to subject the citizens of all nations to the common governance of the United Nations. The goals of the United Nations will be impossible to achieve without consolidating power over member nations and imposing their restrictive globalist agenda.

I believe that the United Nations is anti-American, anti-Israel, anti-capitalist, anti-Christian and anti-growth. The United Nations advocates for the control of population growth, if not for the outright depopulation of the planet, the restriction of the sovereign right of nations to use their own land and natural resources for economic development, and for picking winners and losers through the global redistribution of wealth.

We the People don't need another layer of government that works to deprive us of our liberties, as we already face significant challenges in repudiating the entrenched establishment political class in our state and federal governments. There is no need to conduct an exhaustive analysis of all United Nations programs and initiatives, as it will only take the brief consideration of several key elements of the United Nations agenda in order to see the necessity of the United States withdrawing from the United Nations.

UN ANTI-ISRAEL RESOLUTIONS

According to an article by Jonathan Wachtel published at FoxNews.com on December 27, 2016, the United Nations General Assembly adopted twenty anti-Israel resolutions in 2016, while only passing four such resolutions for the rest of the world combined, one each for Syria, Iran, North Korea and Russia.

The extreme bias of the United Nations against Israel culminated on December 23, 2016, when the United States failed to veto United Nations Security Council Resolution 2334, which declared that the establishment of settlements by Israel, including those in East Jerusalem, has "no legal validity and constitutes a flagrant violation under international law." Interference by the United Nations in the affairs of Israel as a sovereign nation is a huge obstacle to the resolution of the Israeli-Palestinian conflict.

In his last parting shot to Israel before leaving office, Barack Obama coordinated the attack on Israel in order to try to set the stage for the United Nations to prescribe the terms of a two state solution to the Israeli-Palestinian conflict. Israel has long been open to a two state solution, and has been more than willing to make sacrifices of land and national security in order to appease the demands of the Palestinians and their United Nations cheerleaders.

It has become abundantly clear that it is the Palestinians that have no interest in a two state solution, since they refuse to acknowledge the right of Israel to exist and thereby provide a path for the state of Israel to peacefully exist alongside a Palestinian state. The United Nations, and at times the United States, has been wrong in trying to pressure Israel to make unilateral concessions to adversaries that have no interest in peace with Israel.

God promised to bless those that bless Israel, and to curse those that curse Israel. It is a time of choosing for the United States. Will we choose to bless Israel, or will we choose to curse Israel? It is time for us to leave the anti-Israel United Nations and choose to stand unequivocally with Israel as a friend and ally. The fact that the United Nations is so anti-Israel is reason enough for the United States to withdraw from the United Nations, but there are other equally compelling reasons to do so.

AGENDA 21/AGENDA 2030

At the United Nations Sustainable Development Summit on September 25, 2015, the United Nations adopted what they call the "2030 Agenda for Sustainable Development," which replaced the controversial United Nations Agenda 21 program with an enhanced version. Agenda 2030 sets forth seventeen "Sustainable Development Goals," or SDG's. When I Googled "Agenda 2030," the first item that pops up leads to a United Nations Department of Economic and Social Affairs webpage entitled *Transforming our world: the 2030 Agenda for Sustainable Development.*

A review of the UN Agenda 2030 reveals the comprehensive plan that the United Nations has to fundamentally transform our world. The plan is so ambitious and so inclusive that it could only possibly be realized under the direction and control of one central government, so the only conclusion a reasonable person can draw is that it is a globalist plan to establish global governance under the United Nations.

The United Nations is using a call to action for nations to jointly combat the mythical dangers of climate change, through the pursuit of sustainable development goals, as another means to pursue the UN goals of population control, limits on property rights and economic freedom as well as the redistribution of wealth among nations. Sustainable Development Goals will be used to coerce all nations to submit to the global governance of the United Nations. Although the plan claims to reaffirm the autonomy and control of individual nations, it appears that autonomy and control will only truly be possible if each nation conforms to the mandates of the United Nations.

CONTROL OF POPULATION GROWTH

The United Nations has aggressively pursued an agenda of limiting global population growth through advocating for abortion, sterilization and contraception. Not all of the estimated 1.4 billion abortions performed worldwide directly result from the efforts of the United Nations, but the UN has much blood on its hands from the global sin of abortion.

The United Nations obsession with controlling the growth of population is based upon the false notion that our world is fragile, with limited resources that will be depleted if we permit the global population to increase much more. That view is driven by a scarcity mentality that sees the birth of each newborn as another mouth to feed, even referring to them as "eaters."

The truth is that the earth is very resilient, with an abundance of resources for humans, the image bearers of God, to be fruitful and multiply as God commanded us to do. The truth is that each person that is born has enormous capacity to contribute many times more than they consume in their lifetime. Through good steward-ship of the resources that God has given to us, humanity has the capacity to develop the means and methods by which we could see a tenfold increase in the population on the earth without depleting natural resources or destroying the planet.

The primary cause of poverty in the world today is not the sheer number of people, but rather the lack of freedom and security needed for people to live productive lives. American citizens should reject the United Nations plan to curtail population growth, and instead work cooperatively with other free nations to assist other nations in establishing the freedom and security by which they can enjoy free market economic growth and prosperity. We the People should not be in league with tyrannical nations that suppress the economic freedom of their own people.

REFUGEE RESETTLEMENT PROGRAM

The United Nations Refugee Resettlement Program is the greatest threat that Western civilization has ever faced. There is a coordinat-ed effort to use the program to force the migration of millions of refugees with political views that are incompatible with Western civilization, and with no will to assimilate into the culture of West-ern nations. It is quite possible that Europe has reached the point of no return, unless millions of refugees are returned to their countries of origin, or to countries with more compatible political views. The United States is on the same path as Europe, and will face the same perils, if we do not immediately withdraw from the Refugee Reset-tlement Program.

Conflicts in Muslim majority nations in the Middle East have created a refugee crisis that is being used to overrun Western nations with adherents of Sharia law. Some of the conflicts were started or intensified by the decision by the Obama administration to support the Arab spring, and the flow of refugees into Europe has been encouraged by elitists and globalists that are concealing or minimizing the problems created by the flow of migrants. In short, it appears that there is a coordinated effort between globalists and Islamists to fundamentally transform Western civilization at a pace that is just overwhelming. The good news is that it seems that Western civilization has been awakened to the threat.

There are many Muslim majority nations that for some reason have not participated in accepting Muslim refugees since the crisis intensified several years ago. Some of those nations are rich, oil-producing states, and it seems unreasonable that rich Sunni nations would not take in Sunni refugees or that rich Shiite nations would not take in Shiite refugees. It also seems unreasonable that the United States should be expected to take in large numbers of sharia law adherents when there are large numbers of Christian, Kurdish and Yazidi refugees that are more compatible with Western values. There seems to be a coordinated strategy being implemented by globalists and Islamists to overwhelm and transform Western civilization through civilization jihad.

STRONG CITIES NETWORK

According to their website, strongcitiesnetwork.org, the Strong Cities Network is "designed for policy-makers and practitioners operating at city, municipal or sub-national level." According to their website, the stated purpose is to "facilitate systematic sharing of knowledge, expertise and lessons learned on building social cohesion and community resilience to prevent violent extremism across cities on an international basis, through both regional workshops and international conferences."

A press release by the Department of Justice Office of Public Affairs on September 28, 2015, the day before the keynote address given by Attorney General Loretta Lynch introducing the new initiative by the United Nations, had this to say about the Strong Cities Network (SCN):

The SCN will strengthen strategic planning and practices to address violent extremism in all its forms by fostering collaboration among cities, municipalities and other subnational authorities.

So many threats to our constitutional Republic are embedded in this statement. Strengthening strategic planning and practices as well as fostering collaboration are globalist code words for the global government that they intend to impose upon all nations, especially the United States, which is the greatest threat to their agenda. Establishing an alliance of cities, municipalities and other "subnational authorities" is also a direct threat to the national sovereignty of the United States, and undermines our Constitution. The Strong Cities Network invites our cities to potentially form alliances with foreign nations, which the Constitution prohibits the states from doing.

The use of the term "violent extremism in all its forms" is just one more instance of the refusal of globalists and our weak-kneed political leaders to identify the real threat of radical Islamic terrorism. More insidious was the intent of globalists and our treasonous leaders at the time to target conservative activists that oppose the Islamization of America as violent extremists.

Through their attacks on our law enforcement community, Barack Obama, Eric Holder and Loretta Lynch made significant inroads in establishing federal involvement in local law enforcement in numerous cities across the country. Their desire to nationalize law enforcement, to effectively nationalize a police force, has simply taken a new form in the initial steps toward the establishment of a global police force that circumvents national governments by the direct involvement of the United Nations. Like most UN initiatives, the establishment of the Strong Cities Network using innocuous, nonthreatening language will turn into an insidious force used to undermine the sovereignty of nations if the initiative is permitted to gain traction.

We the People must never permit the nationalization or globalization of law enforcement. Cities, municipalities, counties and states will be strengthened by dramatically reducing the power of the federal government and by immediately withdrawing from the United Nations.

SMALL ARMS TREATY

The United Nations Arms Trade Treaty, commonly known as the UN Small Arms Treaty, is another insidious attempt by the United Nations to undermine national sovereignty and establish global governance. Barack Obama signed this nonbinding treaty, and the United States Senate blocked its ratification, but the efforts of the liberal left and the United Nations globalists to disarm ordinary American citizens will not stop. Protecting our natural right to keep and bear arms, as affirmed by the Second Amendment, is one of the most compelling reasons for We the People to insist that the United States immediately withdraw from the United Nations.

THIRTY-SIX

Foreign Policy

SPEAK SOFTLY AND CARRY A BIG STICK; PROMOTE FREEDOM AND RESIST TYRANNY

We maintain the peace through our strength; weakness only invites aggression.

– Ronald Reagan

The United States has a special obligation to use its economic and military power to promote freedom and resist tyranny throughout the world. We should not seek to be the world's policeman, but we must get back to a policy of speaking softly and carrying a big stick and making it clear to the world that we will use our might to make right. We need to get back to where we once were when our allies trusted us and our enemies feared us.

If there was a freedom scale by which we could measure where nations were on a scale from absolute freedom to absolute tyranny, all nations could be placed somewhere on that freedom scale. It is true that no nation enjoys absolute freedom, and although no nation is beset by absolute tyranny, it seems that the natural tendency for all governments is to slip down the scale toward tyranny.

We the People must be diligent in restoring and retaining the liberty that we once had as a nation. Since we have slipped way down the freedom scale ourselves, we must patiently coax, and not hypocritically badger, other nations to move up the freedom scale with us toward greater liberty. We cannot invade a sovereign nation and impose liberty upon them, but we can use our economic and military power to encourage other nations to grant more of the blessings of liberty to their citizens.

We the People can likewise use our economic and military power to resist nations that seek to impose greater tyranny upon their citizens, and we can enlist the support and participation of other friends and allies of liberty to collectively resist the adversaries and enemies of freedom. We must contain totalitarianism.

The freedom scale that I imagine is a vertical scale with four quartiles. Although we do not have an objective scale with which to measure, we are free to subjectively categorize nations as allies, friends, adversaries or enemies to freedom, and to assess whether each nation is moving up the freedom scale toward greater liberty or moving down the freedom scale toward greater tyranny.

United States foreign policy must be guided by the principle that we will use our economic and military might to support those nations that are on the positive side of the freedom scale and are committed to greater freedom for their people, and to resist those nations that are on the negative side of the freedom scale and are moving in the wrong direction toward greater tyranny.

It is important to communicate to other nations that they are either with us, or against us. By pursuing a national strategy of seeking to engage in secure, strategic trade, we will use trade with other nations as a carrot to reward those nations that are with us and other freedom loving nations, and to restrict or deny trade status to those nations that are against us and going the wrong direction on the freedom scale. The degree to which we trade with other nations should directly correlate to where they are on the freedom scale.

Our military strength is obviously the big stick. By establishing American Enterprise Zones as force multipliers with nations that are of strategic interest to us economically and militarily, we will be able to expand our reach and capabilities while assisting nations in their economic development in a more stable and secure environment. We must communicate to all nations a willingness to work with them so long as they demonstrate a commitment to move in the right direction on the freedom scale.

PURSUE SECURE, STRATEGIC TRADE

International trade is, first and foremost, a national security issue. Every sovereign nation should recognize this truth, and pursue their own national interests when seeking to trade with other nations. Each nation should also be strategic in making decisions about trade with other nations.

Free-trade between nations is a myth. Even if free trade among nations were possible, just because the term has the word "free" in it, doesn't make the pursuit of free trade a good thing. Sovereign nations in the pursuit of their own interests will always tinker with any trade arrangements that exist with other sovereign nations. This behavior by sovereign nations should not only be expected, but should be encouraged, as every sovereign nation should be free to engage in activities that advance its own interests.

In order for free-trade to exist between nations, each nation must first permit the free market to operate within their borders without government restraint. No nation has a completely unbridled free market system in operation, nor is it an appropriate goal of any nation, as some level of useful regulation will always be necessary in order to accommodate growth without chaos. Government that is limited to that which is absolutely necessary to permit the free market to operate efficiently in a secure environment is the best model for free nations to pursue, but even if the ideal balance of the conservative principle of limited government were attained, the free market would not literally be absolutely free.

If two nations were to realize and maintain a degree of economic freedom that permitted the free market to operate at a level of freedom that is the maximum that any nation could achieve, then in order for those two nations to truly have free trade, both nations would have to have identical strategic and security interests that effectively made their borders of no practical effect. The situation becomes far more complex if the number of nations involved in a free trade arrangement increases. What is currently happening in the

European Union is an excellent example of how more than two dozen nations effectively erased national borders to allow the free flow of goods and people among the member nations. The EU seems to be on the verge of breaking up due to the compromise in the national security of the member nations that the arrangement resulted in.

Absolute free-trade requires not only the successful operation of the free market within the borders of each country; it essentially requires each nation to ignore their own national security and economic strategy, which will effectively erase the borders of each sovereign nation. The dangers of a sovereign nation giving up the security of its borders makes free-trade imprudent, and supports the notion that it is best for nations to abandon the concept of free trade in order to pursue secure, strategic trade.

Fair trade is a pipe dream. The pursuit of fair trade is a fool's errand and a waste of time, as it can only exist in an imaginary world. If free-trade or fair trade were to ever exist for a fleeting moment, it would take no time at all for circumstances to change and perspectives of those judging the circumstances to change so that the perception of free-trade or fair trade actually existing would evaporate.

What advocates for free-trade actually argue for, is trade that is simply *more free*. Advocates for fair trade are arguing for trade that is simply *more fair*. We should abandon both arguments and recognize that a nation's interests go beyond economic interests. We should focus instead on recognizing that it is incumbent upon sovereign nations to assure to themselves that the trading they do with other nations is secure, and in their strategic best interest. The United States must put America first.

Many Americans believe that the United States has suffered massive job losses because of unfair trading practices of our trading partners. In reality, the primary cause of lost jobs in the United States is the suicidal policies of the federal government that have severely restricted the operation of the free market in the United States. Instead of considering placing tariffs on foreign made goods, the federal government should pursue a policy of pursuing secure, strategic trade and implement the elements of this plan that would unleash the American economy by freeing all Americans to pursue their own individual economic self-interests.

As I mentioned earlier in this book, the cost of assuring that the importation of goods does not pose a threat to our national security should be borne by those doing the importing of the goods, which would be reflected in the final price of goods to the end-user. Furthermore, the United States is free to exercise its sovereignty in placing limits on the importation of products that, for strategic reasons, should be made in the United States.

If there is no national security issue or national strategic issue involved in generally reducing the trade imbalance with other nations, tariffs should not be used as a tool to bring about a change in that trade imbalance. Tariffs will simply put more funds in the national treasury while hurting the consumers of both nations. What will bring lasting change to a trade imbalance through the operation of the free market is if government removes impediments to the operation of the free market. Employment is suppressed and American companies have difficulty competing because of the countless ways that the federal and state governments tie the hands of American companies and American workers.

Our federal and state governments have hindered American citizens from engaging in free-trade within our nation. Through the implementation of this plan, or one of similar magnitude and direction, we will remove the restrictions that have been placed upon the American economy and permit We the People to innovate and work our way into again leading the world in productivity and in the export of goods and services. What we have to do is unleash the free market economy so that we have free-trade, or as close to free-trade as is possible, within our borders.

We should have no national minimum wage. Workers in rural America should be able to compete with workers in cities by working at whatever wage they find to be acceptable. Property rights should be restored to property owners so that property can be quickly put to use by entrepreneurs seeking to create enterprises. Unnecessary and hurtful regulations should be removed. Americans have been forced to compete in a global marketplace while having our hands tied behind our backs. It is time to free ourselves and unleash the New American economy.

AMERICAN ENTERPRISE ZONES

One way that we can promote liberty, economic prosperity and security to nations that are seeking to move up the freedom scale and develop closer ties to the United States is to enter into ninety-nine year leases for significant portions of land and resources within nations that are deemed to be compatible with the economic and national security interests of the United States.

Hong Kong is an excellent example of what can happen when an underdeveloped nation, such as China, entered into a ninety-nine year lease with Great Britain that led to the development of one of the most prosperous territories in the world that is also known for the economic liberty enjoyed by its citizens.

The United States can pursue American Enterprise Zones in much the same way, but with the caveat that the host nation must decide halfway through the ninety-nine year lease whether to reset the term to ninety-nine years. This would permit the United States citizens and companies that invest in the American Enterprise Zones to adjust their investment plans based upon an expectation of only having fifty years left on the lease, or based upon an extension of the lease to a full ninety-nine years remaining.

Hong Kong is of much smaller size than I would envision would be ideal for the United States to enter into American Enterprise Zones. What I envision is the scenario where the United

States and the host country are both motivated to bring the liberty and economic prosperity of the United States to a sizable portion of the host country. This scenario should not result in the exportation of American jobs to the host country if the United States has implemented this plan to unleash the new American economy within our borders, and the arrangements with the host country are properly structured to permit the free enterprise system to flourish in the American Enterprise Zone. Such a plan should allow the prosperity created in the American Enterprise Zone to spread to other parts of the host country, which will create a higher standard of living for the citizens of the host country.

The United States and the host country would first agree on an area that the United States would lease and be granted all authority to secure. United States citizens and business interests could then build infrastructure, develop resources and establish agriculture, manufacturing and distribution within the region. American expatriates and business interests and the local workers that they hire could then develop an economy that would also bring prosperity to the remaining portions of the host country.

The United States could maintain a small military presence that is augmented by private security forces that are loyal to the United States. The cost for supporting the small US military presence as well as any other investments by the United States in the venture could be paid for by the same flat income tax and sales tax that is proposed by this plan. A portion of excess tax revenue could be repatriated to the United States, and the balance reinvested into improving the local infrastructure of the host country.

These American Enterprise Zones would only be created if the United States and host country deemed it to be mutually desirable and advantageous. The host country would enjoy greater security and more rapid economic development. The United States would have greater influence and control over the peace and prosperity in the region of the host nation. The United States military would be more efficiently deployed and would be augmented by security forces that are loyal to the United States.

The United States would enjoy greater security if, in lieu of authorizing large sales of arms to nations that have the potential to later become adversaries, we entered into American Enterprise Zones with those nations. Such a plan would create exciting opportunities for American entrepreneurs and freedom loving patriots to be able to migrate to new lands in order to build a new life for themselves and their families while assisting other nations with their economic growth and security.

The movement of people and resources into American Enterprise Zones would be reminiscent of the mid-nineteenth century in the United States when young entrepreneurs in search of opportunity were encouraged to "go west, young man." If the citizens of the host country were happy with the first American Enterprise Zone established, and the host country and the United States were in agreement, a second American Enterprise Zone could then be established within the host country.

This concept of establishing American Enterprise Zones is not one of a new American colonialism, it is simply a great way to share the American dream with people anywhere in the world that yearn to have liberty, prosperity and security while also establishing an American military presence in allied countries at lower cost. This concept would not work with a nation that does not have a people and a government seeking to move up the freedom scale.

Before we can be in a position to advocate for exporting American freedom and prosperity, we must first take our country back and restore to ourselves the lost blessings of liberty that have been stripped from us by the entrenched establishment political class. If We the People succeed in implementing this plan or one of similar magnitude and direction, we will find many underdeveloped nations of the world eager to invite the United States to establish American Enterprise Zones within their nations.

By articulating and consistently following some very basic principles of foreign policy in our dealings with other nations over the long-term, the United States would have greater success with our friends and allies, as well as with our adversaries and enemies. The manner in which the United States walks softly and carries a big stick, and the manner in which we promote liberty and resist tyranny, can be tailored to each nation that we deal with, with adjustments over time based upon where they are on the freedom scale, and whether they are moving up or down the freedom scale.

PART V

FREE ENTERPRISE
UNSHACKLED

THIRTY-SEVEN

Dramatically Reduce Federal Spending

WE CAN CUT FEDERAL SPENDING IN HALF, AND THEN CUT IT IN HALF AGAIN

Congress has not unlimited powers to provide for the general welfare, but only those specifically enumerated.

– Thomas Jefferson

The powers not delegated to the United States by the Constitution, nor prohibited by it to the States, are reserved to the States respectively, or to the people.

– United States Constitution, Tenth Amendment

Most of the problems that our country faces will be resolved if We the People compel our elected officials to restore the balance of powers originally intended by the founders by respecting the 10th Amendment and simply limiting the federal government to the powers enumerated in the Constitution.

If we can get the federal government out of all activities that are not expressly authorized by the Constitution, we will not only unleash the New American economy, states will have freedom to differentiate themselves by exercising authority over larger areas of governance that will give citizens of the United States the opportunity to choose between conservative governance and socialist governance. We would see a dramatic reduction in federal employment, but for every federal job lost there will be at least five private sector jobs created.

221

ELIMINATE FEDERAL ENTITLEMENTS

The preamble to the Constitution establishes the function of the federal government to "promote the general Welfare," not the specific welfare of particular individuals or groups of individuals. The federal government has no constitutional authority to create or to administer entitlement programs.

The entrenched establishment political class has used wealth redistribution by means of entitlements to amass political power by creating a dependency upon the federal government by an ever-increasing percentage of the population. These unconstitutional programs are classified in the federal budget as "mandatory" or "nondiscretionary" outlays, whereas national defense is classified as "discretionary." The primary purpose of the federal government is to provide for the common defense, so the federal government has gotten the prioritization of expenditures backwards.

Entitlements represent a growing percentage of the federal budget. If the trend is allowed to continue, entitlement spending will not only result in a diminished capacity for our nation to defend itself, it will bankrupt our nation. The United States does not need entitlement reform; we simply need to get the federal government out of the entitlement business, which it had no business getting into in the first place. Each state would also do well to reduce or eliminate entitlement spending, as the growth in entitlements can quickly lead to insolvency.

DISMANTLE SOCIAL SECURITY

It has been said that Social Security is the "third rail" of American politics, meaning that anyone that touches it will find it fatal. On a subway line, the third rail carries the electricity that powers the subway trains, and anyone that touches it will most likely die by electrocution. The conventional wisdom in politics is that a political candidate or a political party that wants to substantially tinker with the Social Security system will be committing political suicide.

My view is that Social Security is the biggest Ponzi scheme ever foisted upon mankind, and that if allowed to continue, will lead our nation into bankruptcy. In other words, if we don't grab the third rail and rip it out, we will see it expand our national debt to a point where it will collapse our economy.

Some maintain that if we add the unfunded pension liabilities of the Social Security system, the true national debt is much higher than the approximately $20 trillion that is officially reported. The good news is that the Social Security unfunded pension liability is money that we owe ourselves, and we can do something to fix the problem. My plan to do so is really quite simple. First, we must admit that our nation is technically insolvent, and that we must fix the problem before it bankrupts our nation. If we recognize that Social Security was an ill-conceived concept to begin with, and that there is no merit in preserving the broken system, then we can implement a plan that will dismantle it in several decades.

The problem with kicking the can down the road, instead of dealing with the problem head-on, is that the problem gets bigger and more difficult to solve as time goes on. We the People have the liberty to get behind an equitable plan to dismantle Social Security and other entitlements, which will permanently fix the problem of entitlements, but will also permit the federal government to refocus on national security. We the People must work diligently to elect representatives that will have the courage to solve the problem of entitlements for us, and especially for our posterity.

Share the Cost

There is no way to equitably dismantle Social Security without requiring some sacrifice from every age bracket in our population. If one segment of the population is unwilling to share in the cost of dismantling the program, it will unfairly shift the burden to other segments of the population, so there must be a willingness of each segment of the population to share the pain.

Young people did not create the problem, but they will have to bear some of the cost of the solution now, so that it does not crush them in the future. Current retirees should not hold to the view that they have made it past the finish line and therefore should not be expected to share the cost of dismantling the program. Segmenting the population into several age brackets will allow us to spread the pain evenly among the population segments and rid ourselves of the ticking time-bomb that our government created.

Social Security Legacy Tax

In order to provide funding for the unwinding of the Social Security problem in a manner that includes all taxpayers in sharing the cost of dismantling Social Security, I propose what I call a "Social Security Legacy Tax" that will expire once the task is accomplished. The imposition of this temporary tax will be most palatable if it is introduced at the same time as the elimination of payroll taxes on all earned income, and at the same time as the implementation of the flat tax on all income.

My proposed Social Security Legacy Tax of 3% of all income would include taxpayers that are not presently part of the Social Security system. It is important to include all taxpayers in sharing the pain of dismantling Social Security, because there are many people that have exempted themselves from contributing to the Social Security system over the years, and it would be a shame to deprive them of the opportunity to be a part of the solution to the Social Security problem.

Congressmen and other government employees that are exempt from Social Security should pay the Social Security Legacy Tax on all income going forward. Those that have avoided earned income in order to effectively opt out of Social Security because they have had the opportunity to have most of their income classified as unearned income over the years should pay the Social Security Legacy Tax on all income going forward. This is one of the ways that the Social Security Legacy Tax can be used to make sure that every citizen makes a reasonable contribution to dismantling Social Security.

All American citizens will benefit from the dismantling of the Social Security system, and should therefore help bear the cost of dismantling the system. Those that are not part of the system will be limited to paying the Social Security Legacy Tax for as long as it takes to unwind the system. Paying this small tax in the context of a lower flat income tax in a reviving economy is a small price to pay compared to sharing in the collapse of our economy. The implementation of the Social Security Legacy Tax will also give us a tool for tweaking the share of pain absorbed by members of the several segments of the population that have been participating in the Social Security system.

Current Retirees

The obvious way that current retirees could share in the cost of dismantling the Social Security program would be to reduce the actuarial value of their expected benefits. There are a number of means by which we can reduce the expected benefits of current retirees, several of which have been proposed by elected officials, such as a reduction in cost-of-living adjustments, or indexing benefits based upon need. Current retirees, as well as new retirees entering the system, should be exempt from any Social Security Legacy Tax imposed on all sources of income.

As we experience success in implementing elements of this plan to save America, we will obviously be very sensitive to the impact that it has on retirees or those close to retirement, as they have fewer options for adjusting to the new paradigm as it unfolds. There are way too many moving parts to try to anticipate the impact on our seasoned citizens, so we should simply assure them that as We the People take our country back, we will also have their backs. We must take care of our seasoned citizens.

People Over Forty

In addition to a potential increase in the retirement age, this segment of the population would receive a reduced actuarial value of expected benefits while continuing to pay the current contribution rate. They could also be offered the opportunity to opt out of their Social Security benefits completely in exchange for the elimination of payroll tax deductions. Of those in that segment of the population that choose to opt out, those that paid into Social Security for at least eighty quarters would be exempt from any Social Security Legacy Tax, and those that paid into Social Security more than forty quarters, but fewer than eighty quarters, would only be assessed 50 % of any Social Security Legacy Tax going forward.

One additional caveat to this segment that I think is worthy of consideration is the notion that anyone that is between forty and fifty years old that has not already met the eligibility requirement of forty quarters of contributing Social Security taxes should be excluded from the Social Security program going forward. Anyone over fifty should be permitted to continue in the Social Security program even if they have not yet accumulated forty quarters of contributions.

People Under Forty

Everybody under the age of forty would be excluded from the Social Security program, and would no longer make payroll tax contributions. Those individuals under the age of forty that satisfied the requirement for forty quarters of contributions in order to be eligible for Social Security would only be assessed 50% of any Social Security Legacy Tax going forward. Since giving up what they paid into the system for more than forty quarters represents a significant portion of the sacrifice we are asking of them, a reduction in the Social Security Legacy Tax is warranted. People under forty would have many years to save and invest for their retirement using any investment options available to them.

Government Pension Programs

We need to take a hard look at the various pensions created by the establishment political class for themselves and their hirelings in the bureaucracy that they have created. We should not let them get away with the largess that they have voted for themselves at the expense of taxpayers.

Congress has granted to themselves lifelong pensions, even for those who serve only a single term in office. They have exempted themselves from the Social Security program, which we should take as recognition on their part that the Social Security program is an inadequate sham.

We need to examine what Congress has granted to themselves and their cronies and recover the purloined public funds and give all of them the same treatment that others receive from the Social Security system. Government pension programs at the federal, state and local level will present great moral and fiscal challenges as we grapple with the reality that our elected officials and their cronies have feathered their nests.

Thirty Years to Unwind

We can fix the problem of Social Security immediately by making the right decisions, but it will take thirty years or more to unwind. This plan that I propose is an example of how We the People could successfully dismantle the Social Security system without causing great harm to any one generation of Americans.

Shortfalls along the way would be made up by the general fund, but it is important that as surplus Social Security funds are collected, that the Social Security trust fund be protected from being raided again by spendthrift politicians. Within a thirty year timeframe, we could see sufficient funding in the Social Security trust fund to satisfy the actuarial value of all remaining liabilities. The Social Security Legacy Tax would be reduced over time and eventually eliminated once all of the remaining liabilities are funded.

By implementing a plan such as this one to dismantle Social Security, we will take a big step in getting the federal government out of the business of redistributing wealth through entitlements. People will enjoy the freedom to save, invest and plan for their future in their own way and on their own terms.

This plan to dismantle and unwind Social Security will not be necessary if we take the bold step of eliminating debt altogether by declaring a Year of Jubilee, which I will suggest that we do in the next chapter. If we truly cut the Gordian knot and eliminate all debt, and all mechanisms that permit price rigidity, then there will no longer be any pensions, or entitlements like Social Security.

If We the People make the bold move to initiate the reset of our financial system, instead of allowing globalists to do it on their terms, the free market will quickly establish a very clear path of new American prosperity that will easily permit us to replace the subsistence income for retirees that typical Social Security benefits provide. All segments of the population will benefit from the revived American economy, and those that are unable to participate due to health or disability will be cared for through the actions of individuals, charities, communities and states. There has never been, nor will there ever be, a need for the federal government to step in and provide any kind of specific welfare or entitlement program.

TRANSFER MEDICARE AND MEDICAID TO THE STATES

Medicaid and Medicare combined are about the same size as the Social Security program, but those costs are likely to spiral out of control. The entrenched establishment political class running the federal government has created a dangerous beast in Medicaid and Medicare, especially after the Obamacare expansion. We can end federal government involvement by simply moving Medicaid and Medicare from the federal government to the states, leaving it to the individual states to solve the problem in their states.

Proposals have been made to block grant Medicaid and Medicare funds to the states for administration of those programs. The easiest thing to do would be for the Medicaid and Medicare payroll deductions to go straight to the states and have the states figure out how to dismantle Medicaid and Medicare or to modify the programs in accordance with the will of the citizens of each state.

The federal government had no business creating Medicaid and Medicare, and we should remove those programs from the federal budget immediately. Again, the big losers are the establishment political class in both parties. By doing this, We the People can dramatically reduce the power of the federal government and the entrenched establishment political class.

If We the People are successful in realizing the magnitude and direction of the elements of this plan, and if we take the bold step that I propose in a later chapter of eliminating health insurance altogether, then we should also eliminate Medicare and Medicaid immediately in order to permit the free market to quickly adjust pricing in the healthcare market.

ELIMINATE FEDERAL UNEMPLOYMENT INSURANCE

The federal government has no constitutional authority to create or administer an entitlement program like unemployment compensation. Even if the concept had merit, which I don't believe it does, the federal government has no business being involved.

Since all powers not specifically granted by the Constitution to the federal government are reserved to the states or to the people, states have very broad authority, including the authority to establish unemployment programs. The citizens of each state will be wise to compel the legislature of their state to eliminate unemployment and other entitlement programs. States would also do well to refrain from imposing minimum wages to match the elimination of the federal minimum wage.

For those states that are not ready to eliminate entitlements like welfare and unemployment, there is a better way of dealing with the problem. Instead of paying people not to work, states could simply supplement employee wage rates that the state or local government consider to be too low.

Without the opportunity to draw unemployment, a recently laid off worker would go out and find the most appropriate job that he could find within a reasonable timeframe. Without the constraint of a minimum wage, the free market would create an abundance of job opportunities. The laid off worker could perhaps find two jobs, work a few more hours, and replace his lost wages. A state or local government that considered that worker's wages to be too low could then augment his average hourly rate at a much lower cost than the current cost of unemployment for that worker.

The benefits of this approach to eliminate unemployment compensation go way beyond the cost savings to the state or local government. The worker in this scenario would have the satisfaction of being gainfully employed instead of sitting around at home wishing he had a job. There is also the additional benefit that this approach actually contributes to real output, which translates into an increase in the average standard of living.

Eliminating the minimum wage and unemployment benefits in a free market environment where small businesses are liberated from the oppressive regulatory bureaucracy will permit anyone that wants a job to create his own job or to find two or three jobs to choose from. Such an unleashing of the American economic engine is not what environmentalists and globalists want for our country, but it is what American citizens need.

ELIMINATE FEDERAL WELFARE AND OTHER ENTITLEMENT PROGRAMS

All other forms of federal entitlement programs, such as food stamps, subsidized housing and student loans should be eliminated.

We the People need to eliminate all opportunities for the federal government to be involved in any kind of redistribution of wealth scheme that the entrenched establishment political class uses to accrue power. Americans need to be free to work and to improve their lot in life without hindrance. I believe that most people in need would rather receive a hand up instead of a handout. We must get government out of the entitlement business and out of the way of productive workers and businesses. We the People must block the federal government from pursuing any activity resulting in the redistribution of wealth.

Liberals, entrenched establishment politicians, environmentalists and globalists will rant and rave about how destructive it would be to get the federal government out of the entitlement business. The fear-mongers will try to frighten their constituent groups with the loss of the government largess that enslaves them. The naked truth is that eliminating federal entitlements will do nothing but strip establishment politicians of power and unleash the greatest economic engine the world has ever seen. We the People need to liberate ourselves and our posterity from the tyranny that robs us of the opportunity to live free, productive lives.

ELIMINATE DEPARTMENTS NOT CONSTITUTIONALLY AUTHORIZED

Many departments of the federal government were created for functions that, even if appropriate for government, should have been instituted by the states, not the federal government. Spending in these departments can be eliminated completely or reduced by as much as ninety percent.

Department of Health and Human Services

Most of the budget of the Department of Health and Human Services will transfer to the states with the transfer of Medicare and Medicaid. Continuing expenditures for appropriate federal programs like the FDA, Centers for Disease Control and the National Institutes of Health should be carefully reviewed for the elimination of unconstitutional or wasteful spending. Even in these areas of appropriate federal expenditure we could see as much as a 50% reduction in spending.

Eliminate the Department of Education

We can safely eliminate the Department of Education in its entirety. The federal government has no business being involved in education. Education is an important lifelong activity that can be more than adequately managed by parents empowered by free market educational opportunities.

Central authority and control of this very important aspect of life is, at best, a complete waste of time and resources, and at worst, undermines the foundation of a free society and works contrary to what is best for the general population. In a later chapter, I will present my plan for states to dismantle the public education system and replace it with a twenty-first century market-based lifelong learning approach that recognizes the responsibility and authority of parents to educate their children.

Eliminate the Department of Housing and Urban Development

The federal government has exceeded its constitutional authority in meddling with housing and urban development, creating serious problems in the housing market. We should trust the free market, not the government, to allocate resources for housing. For too long, liberal policies have favored the urbanization of America at the expense of small-town America. Federal government policies in housing and urban development are fatally flawed, and have led to the institutionalization of poverty. Democrats have effectively used this department to create modern-day plantations of exploited and dependent American citizens.

Department of Commerce

The Department of Commerce can be streamlined by eliminating functions that the federal government should not be involved in and consolidate the constitutionally appropriate functions of the Department of Energy, Department of Agriculture, Department of Labor, Small Business Administration and the Department of the Interior into the Department of Commerce.

Department of Energy

We should target the reduction of Department of Energy expenditures by ninety percent. If We the People are successful in compelling our government to unleash the free market to produce abundant, cheap domestic energy, a very limited Department of Energy budget will be needed to implement energy policy. This budget can be administered by the Department of Commerce, with perhaps a portion of the budget pertaining to nuclear energy being administered by the Department of Defense.

Eliminate the Department of Agriculture

All agricultural subsidies should be phased out over a short period of time. The free market can be trusted to establish agricultural commodity prices and to determine the appropriate allocation of resources in agriculture. All remaining legitimate activities related to agriculture that may be constitutionally appropriate for the federal government to continue to be engaged in can be consolidated into the Department of Commerce.

Eliminate the Department of the Interior

We should target a seventy-five percent to ninety percent reduction in Department of the Interior expenditures and consolidate all remaining constitutionally appropriate expenditures into the Department of Commerce. We should also eliminate the Bureau of Land Management and correct the unconstitutional practice of the federal government owning as much land as it does by transferring the vast Western lands and most national parks to the states.

Eliminate the Department of Labor

The federal government has no business being involved in labor issues, and the Department of Labor should be eliminated in its entirety, with any constitutionally appropriate functions, if any, transferred to the Department of Commerce. The NLRB should be disbanded, and any labor relations issues transferred to the states in which those issues arise. It is time for We the People to dismantle the unholy alliance between big government and big labor.

Eliminate the Environmental Protection Agency

We the People must compel Congress to eliminate the EPA and assign any necessary and constitutional functions that survive scrutiny to the Department of Commerce. We need a complete overhaul of the environmental laws and executive orders that have been causing so much destruction to our economy. We must repudiate the theology of radical environmentalism and embrace our God-given roles as stewards of our environment. We must not allow radical environmentalists that worship the creation instead of the Creator to continue to kill our economy and transfer jobs to countries that are very poor stewards of the environment.

Small Business Administration

As part of the Department of Commerce, the SBA budget should be reduced and reallocated to efforts that identify ways that the federal government can simply get out of the way of small business and allow the free market to operate without federal government interference. Providing a limited budget to a team of advocates seeking ways to unleash entrepreneurial activity through the operation of the free market is worthy of some consideration, as long as it only promotes the general welfare.

Abolish the IRS

Under the simple tax plan that I propose, the Treasury Department can oversee the collection of taxes without the Internal Revenue Service. The IRS is one of the most tyrannical arms of the federal government, where you are presumed guilty until proven innocent. We should simply abolish the IRS.

ZERO-BASED BUDGETING

Much wasteful federal government spending could be eliminated by requiring that all expenditures be reauthorized every year or two. Expenditures that are not reauthorized would simply be eliminated from the federal budget. No expenditure should be permitted to continue indefinitely without requiring the affirmative vote of Congress. By extracting the federal government from activities that are not constitutionally authorized, and by scrutinizing spending of all remaining departments, We the People should compel Congress to reduce federal government spending by 50%, and then work on reducing spending by another 50%.

With zero-based budgeting, portions of the federal budget would essentially reset to zero every fiscal year, and Congress would be required to rebuild the budget by reauthorizing spending line items in as much detail as is practicable. Congress would then have another shot at getting things done the right way, and the president should have the line item veto power to eliminate pork-barrel spending. Congress could still override a presidential veto for any programs that have the support for an override. Fat would be trimmed from the budget.

With an annual or bi-annual review, key questions could then be answered anew for each program in order to justify continued spending on the program. Is the program constitutional? Is the program necessary? Is the program effective? Can the program be more effectively administered, or the objectives more effectively realized by the states or perhaps by the private sector?

Instead of following the "use it or lose it" method of budgeting with the typical omnibus spending bills, continuing resolutions and threats of government shutdowns, Congress should do the job of authorizing all expenditures in the federal budget annually, or at a minimum, reauthorize half of the federal budget every two years.

This budgeting process also includes the authority that Congress has over the budget allocated to specific initiatives taken by the executive branch to administer or enforce the law. If Congress does not approve of the manner in which the executive branch chooses to spend money to enforce legislation, Congress should assert the power to eliminate line item funding from the executive branch with a simple majority vote. In essence, Congress needs to apply a "reverse veto" to any spending by the executive branch that Congress deems to not follow the law.

THIRTY-EIGHT

Solve the Debt Problem by Declaring a Year of Jubilee

WE THE PEOPLE CAN CUT THE CORDS THAT BIND US BY ERADICATING ALL DEBT

The modern theory of the perpetuation of debt has drenched the earth with blood, and crushed its inhabitants under burdens ever accumulating.

– Thomas Jefferson

When We the People successfully preempt the coming reset of the global financial system by abolishing the Federal Reserve and fractional banking, eliminating the minimum wage and taxes on all property, and dramatically reducing the federal budget by extracting the federal government from activities not delegated to it by the Constitution, we will see a collapse of asset prices.

The immediate collapse of asset prices and the natural deflationary forces that will kick in once prices have stabilized at a new equilibrium will result in a dramatic redistribution of wealth toward debtholders unless debt balances are indexed down or completely eliminated. Any mechanism by which debts are indexed down by some measure that equitably reflects the collapse in asset prices will lag behind the collapse in prices, creating uncertainty in the marketplace that may create an impediment to the full throttle operation of the economy.

Since worldwide debt escalated 40% from 2007 to 2014, and there seems to be no end to the debt binge that the United States has been on for decades, it seems that it is time that we face the fact that our nation is bankrupt. We should encourage other nations to join with us in dealing with the staggering problem of worldwide debt. The debt problem can be dealt with more completely and decisively if other industrialized nations will join with us in slaying that dragon.

We have at our disposal the option of employing a one-time solution of simultaneously declaring national bankruptcy, and declaring a Year of Jubilee, whereby all debts are canceled. In order to avoid future debt bubbles, we should also take the additional step of outlawing debt altogether, or establishing that every twenty-five years there will be another Year of Jubilee when all debts that have accrued by that time are canceled.

Since the escalation of debt has occurred without a substantial change in wealth worldwide, that escalation in debt has simply redistributed the claims to worldwide wealth, concentrating wealth more and more in the hands of fewer individuals and corporations. Declaring a Year of Jubilee whereby all debt is canceled will indeed redistribute wealth, as debtors will see their wealth increase at the expense of creditors. Part of that redistribution of wealth would reverse the redistribution of wealth that occurred with the escalation of debt, and part of the redistribution of wealth will create winners and losers that will see a net benefit or net loss from the escalation in asset values and debt followed by the collapse of asset values and the eradication of debt.

Since any reset of the global financial system will necessarily create winners and losers through massive redistribution of wealth and any massive redistribution of wealth will occur in an inequitable fashion, we should structure the eradication of debt in a manner that creates the greatest potential for economic revival while also achieving reasonable equity.

WORLDWIDE YEAR OF JUBILEE

If We the People prevail upon the leaders of our nation to take the bold steps in this plan, including the declaration of a Year of Jubilee by the United States, we could lead the nations of the world to join us in a worldwide declaration of a Year of Jubilee whereby the debts of all nations and all people are canceled. By allowing the escalation of debt to happen, most nations are nominally bankrupt. If all debt is simply wiped away and the borders of nations respected, all nations will be free to pursue their own national interests without being enslaved by debt.

If other nations of the world follow the lead of the United States and outlaw debt, then nations would not lend to nations. Nations could freely provide charitable support to nations in need. It makes no sense to run up the debt for some countries and later forgive portions of that debt. One day the roosters will come home to roost and all nations will be so burdened with debt that a New World Order with a new currency and global financial system will seem like deliverance, when in reality it will lead to the final and complete enslavement of the entire world.

We can choose to liberate ourselves from the globalist agenda, and encourage other nations to do likewise. It isn't difficult to see that there is an impending global financial collapse, and that global elites will then come forward with their plan to rescue the global economy. The merits of this plan to stop the globalist agenda may seem simple enough, but it will be difficult to get enough people to wake up and take the action necessary to get the job done.

YEAR OF JUBILEE IN THE UNITED STATES

If the United States declares a Year of Jubilee, the first order of business is to decide how to handle unsecured personal debts and real estate mortgages. Since the American worker and small business owners are the most important element of any plan to revive the American economy, the Year of Jubilee eradication of debt should bring the greatest economic liberty to the largest and most important segment of the United States economy. All credit card debt, student debt and other unsecured debt should be completely forgiven. All mortgages and liens against all single-family or duplex owner-occupied dwelling units should also be completely forgiven.

Mortgages on multifamily real estate units should be converted to an equitable sharing of equity based upon 50% of the loan-to-value ratio prior to implementation of the Year of Jubilee. A lender with an 80% loan-to-value would receive 40% of the equity. Landlords should be barred from evicting tenants for one year, with rent set at a maximum of a certain percentage of the total income of all occupants of the unit. At the end of the one-year transition period, landlords will then be permitted to charge market rents. This plan for handling rental housing units should be implemented simultaneously with the elimination of all federal entitlements, including housing subsidies.

We don't know how low housing prices will fall in order to reach a new equilibrium. We don't know how low wages will go in order to reach a new equilibrium. We don't know how low food and energy prices will go in order to reach a new equilibrium. What we do know is that an unfettered free market economy will quickly sort everything out. With the financial reset that will take place with the elimination of the Fed, fractional banking and debt, it is critical that people have the liberty to stay in their homes without fear of foreclosure or eviction. The elimination of debt and limiting rent to a percentage of income earned without the threat of eviction will permit us to immediately eliminate the minimum wage as well as all federal entitlements. It is imperative that we eliminate wage and price rigidity and all subsidies in order to permit the free market to establish new price equilibrium.

The next order of business is to see to it that the productive assets of business and industry continue to be employed in the production of energy, goods and services so that the burden of debt does not cause functional companies to become dysfunctional. By converting debtholders to equity holders based upon the collateral secured by loans, and by prohibiting the old debtholders from being able to seize control of the operation of the business or force liquidation of assets, we will minimize the disruption that the eradication of debt will cause upon economic output.

Corporations and creditors can be given a period of time to voluntarily rearrange their financial commitments to each other prior to the imposition of a sharing of equity so long as there is no disruption to operations caused solely by the negotiations. For each entity, debtholders in aggregate should receive equity in the entity that is equal to half of the percentage of aggregate debt in the capital structure of the entity prior to the eradication of debt. If debtholders represented 60% of the capital structure, debtholders would receive 30% of the equity. The declaration of the Year of Jubilee and the eradication of all debt would work like bankruptcy reorganization.

Parties in possession are the most trustworthy and competent to keep the wheels of the economy turning, which is why I propose that debtholders take a 50% haircut on the percentage of the capital structure that was represented by debt. This will assure that debtholders will have less than 50% of the control of each entity upon capital restructuring, as debtholders should not be permitted to operate the companies. I also believe that requiring a 50% haircut on the part of debtholders is equitable, because the issuers of debt bear a greater share of the responsibility in creating the debt problem, and most corporations understate the value of assets on their balance sheets. Whatever constraints are placed upon companies and creditors can be limited by time, which will allow for a period of transition for the free market to sort out the details.

OUTLAW DEBT

Libertarians may say that we must not outlaw debt, that we should permit parties to enter into transactions by mutual consent that do not hurt others. The argument that I would like to use to persuade my libertarian friends that We the People not only have the liberty to impose such a limitation on ourselves as we seek to pursue self-government in a manner that we deem fitting, but that eradicating debt is an important step in securing our liberty.

I trust that libertarians will agree that We the People should continue to prohibit slavery, even if one party is willing to sell himself in servitude to another party. Even though such a transaction may not hurt anyone else, Libertarians probably agree that it would violate the inalienable right of the party selling himself into slavery. The Bible teaches us that the borrower is servant to the lender, which means that the borrower is a slave to the lender. We have the liberty to outlaw debt, and we should consider doing so, for we do not have liberty so long as we have debt.

Instead of allowing those that created the crisis to "solve" the crisis, We the People should choose liberty instead and reject the New World Order that globalists wish to impose upon us. We should reject central banking and the centralized control of the global financial system by globalists, and make a bold move in restoring our political and economic freedoms. We the People have the option of choosing which chaotic path we take, one that brings a New World Order out of a global financial collapse, or one that intentionally collapses the global financial system in order to restore liberty. Each path has its own difficulties, but one leads to a new hope for a brighter day.

Role of Banks

The abandonment of the safeguards imposed by the Glass-Steagall act has permitted a very risky combination of commercial banks with brokerage houses and insurance companies. Those risks are eliminated if we eliminate the Fed and fractional banking, and declare a Year of Jubilee and outlaw debt. The role of banks would dramatically change. Banks would hold money of depositors and charge a service fee, or negative interest rate to safely hold the funds of depositors. Banks would be clearinghouses of transactions, earning a fee such as Visa or PayPal would. Banks would work as brokers in matching investors with investments such as brokerage houses do now, only with the added volume resulting from lifting the restrictions on individuals from making direct investments in small businesses. Banks would have to reinvent themselves in order to function successfully in an environment with no debt and no central bank.

Permit Direct Investment in Small Business

Small business is perhaps the most important element of the United States economy, and we should do all that we can to encourage and support small business. We the People must compel our leaders to find a way to permit the ordinary citizen to make direct investments in small businesses. This will be especially true if we choose to declare a Year of Jubilee and possibly even eradicate debt altogether by outlawing borrowing and lending.

Since most jobs in the United States are created by small business, it doesn't make sense that small businesses are denied access to equity markets. There is no need to require businesses to become public companies in order to raise equity from individual investors that are not qualified as sophisticated investors. There have been numerous cases of fraud at large, public companies. Even with the protection of SEC regulations, companies find ways to defraud investors of billions of dollars. It is time to permit small businesses to also raise equity capital from people other than limited sources such as venture capitalists, friends, family, or sophisticated investors as defined by the SEC.

In similar fashion to the way that modern technology using the internet permits crowdfunding sites to enable people to raise money for anything from health needs to taking a vacation, new technology platforms can be developed for small businesses to offer investment opportunities to individual investors to make equity investments in small business entities.

In the case of crowdfunding, people are making cash donations to proposals advertised by individuals for a variety of reasons that cannot possibly be monitored by any government agency for potential fraud. There are no underwriters or entities giving a seal of approval to requests for donations. Caveat emptor, let the buyer beware, is the guiding principle, as donors to crowdfunding projects are left to themselves to evaluate each project.

The Harvard Business School defines entrepreneurship as "the pursuit of opportunity beyond the resources presently controlled." What that means is that an entrepreneur is always looking to raise money in pursuit of some new business opportunity. If we value and want to encourage entrepreneurship, we should make it easy for entrepreneurs to get matched up with investors willing to back their idea, no matter how risky or outlandish it may seem.

THIRTY-NINE

Judicial Reform

COURTS SHOULD ESTABLISH JUSTICE BY SEEKING TRUTH AND RIGHTEOUSNESS

And I charged your judges at that time, saying, Hear the causes between your brethren, and judge righteously between every man and his brother, and the stranger that is with him.

– Deuteronomy 1:16

Although it causes much consternation for liberals, the laws of Western civilization are deeply rooted in the laws of God set forth in the Bible. The Ten Commandments and other biblical laws and principles form the basis of most laws in the United States. Moses commanded the judges that he established to judge righteously, for it is the duty of government to punish evildoers, to commend the righteous and to protect the poor and weak.

The judicial system in the United States is terribly broken as a result of attorneys and judges colluding to pervert righteous judgment. The truth does not matter, for the convoluted process that has been invented that they call Rules of Civil Procedure subvert and suppress the truth. Judges no longer hear the causes that are under dispute, for those causes are overshadowed by the legal maneuverings of conniving lawyers. Judges no longer seek the truth in matters before them, for they become preoccupied with ascertaining whether attorneys are presenting laws and legal precedents that merit the consideration of the court. The American justice system bears no resemblance to the procedures that God prescribed for establishing justice, for it is no longer a straightforward matter of searching out the truth and arriving at righteous judgment.

The legal system is very unfriendly to a pro se litigant that chooses to defend himself against a lawsuit or to initiate a lawsuit to recover damages asserted in his claim, for simply choosing to pursue a matter without legal representation will almost always result in prejudice against the party that chooses to take a low-cost, simple approach to the matter being litigated. This is especially true in the case of a pro se litigant that actually works hard to follow the Rules of Civil Procedure. Most judges are former lawyers that have a vested interest in supporting trial lawyers in maintaining barriers to the valiant few that would dare take on the legal system without hiring one of their brethren to represent them.

TORT REFORM: DRAMATICALLY REDUCE CIVIL LITIGATION

One of the biggest reasons for our broken judicial system is that wrongdoers are not sufficiently motivated to do the right thing. This is particularly true for large corporations that calculate, based upon a probability distribution of potential outcomes, they are better off financially to do the wrong thing rather than do the right thing. Instead of doing the right thing, some companies that have deep pockets will blatantly violate a contract with an attitude that communicates "so sue me."

By making some simple changes to the way that our system of justice penalizes wrongdoers, we would see a dramatic reduction in the number of cases litigated and the length of time that it takes to litigate those cases.

Another huge problem with the judicial system is that attorneys in most cases have an incentive for the case to litigate for as long as possible. The terrible truth about lawyers is that they always work for themselves. Attorneys are never truly working for their clients, regardless of what they may say. Although attorneys may inform their clients that they are welcome to seek alternative counsel, they know that in most cases, clients effectively grant the attorneys they hire a monopoly on each case. Not only do attorneys generally work for themselves and milk every case for as much money as they can, they can be the most abusive bullies, many treating their clients in a manner that no typical business could get away with in the way they treat their customers.

Loser Pays Court Costs and Attorney Fees

The way the system works right now, litigants are generally responsible for their own attorney fees. Litigants will look at a case dramatically differently if they know that they will have to pay the legal fees of the prevailing party should they lose the case. Since the party has no direct knowledge or control of precisely what the other party's legal bills are, they will have to consider an ever-growing potential liability that they will incur if they lose the case.

Most people involved in litigation have no desire to spend their time and energy in that process, and are eager to resolve the case at the earliest possible time, unless they are pursuing a strategy to use the realities of the current broken judicial system as a club to beat up the other side. Under the current system, litigants frequently use mounting legal costs as a lever to accomplish their objectives. By changing to a system that requires the loser in a lawsuit to pay the attorney fees of the winner, wrongdoers will have much greater motivation to avoid litigation, and to settle quickly whenever their misdeeds result in litigation.

Loser Pays Double Damages

In addition to the current system not penalizing wrongdoers for running up legal bills for the prevailing party, the current system generally limits the liability of wrongdoers to actual damages that are determined by a judge or jury. Habitual wrongdoers know that they can work the system to their financial advantage because the worst case for them in a probability distribution of potential outcomes is usually limited to making the other party whole for actual damages. They know that they can most often succeed in reducing the estimates of actual damages, and that there are other far more attractive potential outcomes that make the expected value of litigation very attractive to them.

The motivation for wrongdoers to defraud others and work the system in order to optimize the outcome for themselves will completely evaporate if the loser must provide restitution that is twice the actual damages proven. If we simply go to the Bible for guidance in this matter, we find that wrongdoers routinely had to pay twice the amount of the actual loss to the prevailing party:

For all manner of trespass, whether it be for ox, for ass, for sheep, for raiment, or for any manner of lost thing which another challengeth to be his, the cause of both parties shall come before the judges; and whom the judges shall condemn, he shall pay double unto his neighbor.
–Exodus 22:9

To put it simply, wrongdoers should have to pay a penalty for their wrongdoing. Making the loser pay double the actual damages will dramatically reduce the frequency of wrongdoers working the system to their advantage and will provide additional incentive for litigants that genuinely believe that they are right and just in their cause to more quickly come to terms on an amicable resolution to the dispute. Litigation resolves quickly if all parties are properly motivated to settle.

Loser Pays Consequential Damages

The current system generally does not allow for consequential damages, even though many cases could demonstrate that the wrongdoing of the losing party in the litigation led to additional consequential damages to the prevailing party. Introducing this element to the judicial system would be another way to apply additional pressure to wrongdoers, especially those that know they are in the wrong. Properly motivated by a system better designed to penalize wrongdoing, those that might be inclined to do wrong based upon the strategy for financial gain will be disinclined by a different set of potential outcomes. There would be far fewer breach of contract claims, and a much higher percentage of cases that are settled very early in the process.

Require Early Mediation

Combined with all of the above changes, requiring litigants to participate in mediation efforts prior to discovery would result in the quick resolution of many cases that otherwise clog up the courts. Litigants could state their positions to experienced mediators and benefit by the assessment of the mediator as to the merits and likelihood of success of each party. With the other changes imposed upon the parties, there should be ample motivation for finding common ground to settle most cases.

Another important change to our judicial system that would speed things along and result in a higher level of judicial integrity is if judges became more proactive in their management of each case. Instead of permitting lawyers to drive the process, justice would be served if judges became active in making early inquiries into the case and ordering specific discovery from the litigants in order to limit opportunities for obfuscation.

Permit pro se Representation by Corporations

Individuals that are involved in litigation may represent themselves pro se, but the current system requires corporations to hire attorneys to represent them in litigation. Habitual wrongdoers and their attorneys use this reality to apply great leverage in matters that might be fairly easy for corporations to handle at low-cost if they could do so on a pro se basis. We should level the playing field by allowing corporate officers to represent corporations with or without assistance from attorneys.

Trial lawyers, habitual wrongdoers, large corporations and the insurance industry may thrive in the current judicial system, but most litigants that are not professional litigators simply want to have their day in court and move on with their lives. Anything that will minimize, expedite and simplify the litigation process will be helpful to the economy by liberating the producers in our economy from being bogged down in senseless litigation.

Prohibit Class-Action Lawsuits

Attorneys are almost always the only winners in class action lawsuits, so they would be the only losers in most instances if class-action lawsuits were prohibited by law. Trial lawyers love class-action lawsuits and make millions gathering thousands of clients that stand little chance of receiving significant sums of money in a process that most frequently only pays off for the attorneys pursuing the litigation.

Trial Lawyers to Weep and Wail

By making a few simple changes to the system, both parties to litigation would have strong motivation to be very careful that they are not in the wrong. Making the penalties much greater for the wrongdoer will dramatically increase the motivation for parties to settle cases instead of litigating. Trial lawyers will be big losers if these changes are implemented, so expect them to fight tooth and nail and raise every conceivable argument against such changes.

TRANSFORM OUR COURTS

Judges should have broad latitude in conducting hearings, trials and proceedings in pursuit of the truth of a matter before them. Rules of Civil Procedure should not take a higher priority than the truth and in seeking righteous judgment. If judges have the instruction to seek the truth and to do right by the litigants, and if the loser pays double, there will be far less litigation and perversion of justice.

Judicial precedent should be abandoned in favor of judging the merits of each case without perverting justice by the citing of erroneous rulings by other judges in other venues. Congress has the authority to define the jurisdictions of courts and to make wholesale changes to our judicial system. Daniel Horowitz has suggested that Congress should strip courts of jurisdiction over immigration, election law, marriage and other matters that should not come under the purview of the court system.

Our judicial system has become so irredeemably broken that it is perhaps time for us to completely replace our judicial system with one that is geared toward the discernment of truth and establishing righteous judgment. Part and parcel to overhauling the system will be to retrain lawyers to seek the truth, and to speak the truth, for attorneys are the most notorious liars, and live in a gray world that they have created for themselves.

Just days before his death on February 13, 2016, Supreme Court Justice Antonin Scalia led the Supreme Court in a decision to put a lower court action on hold pending the conclusion of appellate action and review by the Supreme Court. The Clean Power Plan, implemented in August 2015 by the Obama administration under the Clean Air Act would have had disastrous consequences for our economy if it had been permitted to stand, pending appeal. Even if the plan was overturned it would have caused great damage, as is often the case when bad laws or executive actions cause great damage until they are set right.

This unprecedented decision by the Supreme Court was the first time that the court had stepped in and intervened in a lower court decision before the matter was brought to the Supreme Court. We need to see more such action by the Supreme Court in order to rein in the judicial tyranny that we have been suffering through. Although it is not the subject of this book, I believe that there are many questions surrounding the suspicious and untimely death of Justice Scalia that we should demand answers to.

Another glaring example of judicial tyranny that makes it imperative that We the People compel Congress to strip the federal courts of jurisdiction is the way that rogue federal judges shut down perfectly lawful and constitutional executive orders by President Trump to limit immigration from countries that he deemed to be potential threats to our national security. Federal statute gives the president broad authority to limit immigration:

> *Whenever the President finds that the entry of any aliens or of any class of aliens into the United States would be detrimental to the interests of the United States, he may by proclamation, and for such period as he shall deem necessary, suspend the entry of all aliens or any class of aliens as immigrants or non-immigrants, or impose on the entry of aliens any restrictions he may deem to be appropriate.*

–8 US Code Section 1182 (f)

The fact that rogue federal judges with the support of the rogue Ninth Circuit Court of Appeals and the Fourth Circuit Court of Appeals could interfere even momentarily with such a critical duty of the President to protect our nation from potentially dangerous immigrants should be of grave concern to every freedom loving American. Add to this egregious action of the federal courts the manner in which the federal judiciary has overstepped its bounds in matters of election law and marriage, and we have great cause to call for the solution to the problem that Daniel Horowitz prescribes in his book *Stolen Sovereignty*.

FORTY

Free-Market Energy

PERMIT THE FREE-MARKET TO PRODUCE CHEAP, ABUNDANT, DOMESTIC ENERGY

Conservation may be a sign of personal virtue, but it is not a sufficient basis for a sound, comprehensive energy policy.

– Dick Cheney

For decades, United States energy policy has been dictated by radical environmentalists and crony capitalists. The Washington cartel has given lip service to the idea of the United States achieving energy independence while pursuing policies that make energy independence impossible. We the People must demand the changes necessary to unleash the domestic production of abundant, cheap energy that will permit our economy to come roaring back.

ALL OF THE ABOVE ENERGY POLICY

Energy is the lifeblood of economic activity, so the United States cannot afford to jeopardize national security and economic liberty by continuing our dependence upon foreign sources of oil or by experimenting with expensive emerging technologies for generating energy that are not yet economically viable or scalable. We must insist that our nation pursue all viable energy options without picking winners and losers by subsidizing new technologies and penalizing energy sources that we used to build our nation.

Fossil Fuels

The United States has been blessed with vast amounts of coal, oil and natural gas. Instead of relying so much on oil from Middle

253

Eastern nations that hate Western civilization, we should completely liberate our coal, oil and natural gas industries so that we may not
only be energy independent, but so that the United States could
become a major exporter of energy to our allies.

Our economy is dependent upon energy, and we must recognize that, until the free market is able to produce solar power cost-
effectively, we must continue to rely on fossil fuels to get the job
done. We have been relying on fossil fuels anyway by tying the
hands of our own people and importing fossil fuels at great cost to
our economy and our security. We the People must put an end to
this foolishness immediately by compelling our leaders to remove
all restrictions on the development of fossil fuels and eliminating
the heavy penalties imposed upon our fossil fuel industries, especially on coal.

It makes no sense to penalize United States fossil fuel production when we have been tying our hands and letting our international competitors, particularly China, pummel us to death with
imported goods that are made with the same fossil fuels that we
have regulated into disuse. It's time for the gloves to come off, to
tell environmentalist liberals to go take a hike and get back to the
business of making our economy second to none.

Hydroelectric Power

Nothing better illustrates the hypocrisy and stupidity of the
United States energy policy for the last few decades than what has
happened, or should I say not happened, with respect to the development of hydroelectric power in the United States. Hydroelectric
power is one of the safest, cleanest and most environmentally
sound methods of producing electricity available, yet our nation has
woefully neglected the development of new hydroelectric capacity.

One of the advantages of hydroelectric power is that power
from hydroelectric plants with reservoirs is "dispatchable," meaning
that when demand is low on the power grid, power from hydroelec-

tric plants flowing into the power grid can be quickly shut down by using the electricity generated to store energy in the reservoir by pumping water back into the reservoir. The power grid has to be balanced, with power coming from non-dispatchable generation sources like nuclear power plants balanced by dispatchable generation sources like hydroelectric and natural gas power plants.

China has embraced hydroelectric power in a big way in its quest for cleaner energy and greater energy independence. In recent years, China has added hydroelectric capacity at a greater pace than the United States, Brazil and Canada combined.

Environmentalists effectively shut down the development of hydroelectric power back in the 1970s, which is where the hypocrisy comes in. Environmentalists successfully fought against new hydroelectric projects because of the vast expanses of land that would become submerged. Environmentalists have a zeal for protecting flora and fauna, and seem to hold the position that somehow deems the current state of any environment to be superior to any altered state that can be imagined. Radical environmentalists simply want to eliminate the impact of human activity from the earth.

Because of environmentalist activism, we have missed out on pursuing the most environmentally sound method for increasing the generation of power, and we have also missed out on the great benefits of creating massive reservoirs of water. Environmentalists seem to want to protect every drop of rain water from the time it falls to earth until the time it reenters one of the oceans. The truth is that, as good stewards and prudent planners, we should pursue the addition of hydroelectric capacity and the corresponding development of vast reservoirs of water with all of the determination that we can muster.

Environmentalists that are so concerned about the threat of rising sea levels should vigorously support the idea of storing vast quantities of water inland so that in some small way it may mitigate the impact of rising sea levels. I don't buy the argument that our world is threatened by man-made climate change, but you would think that environmentalists that do would want to do everything possible to save the planet, including killing two birds with one stone by generating clean power and storing water.

We should embark on a new era of hydroelectric power development with a special emphasis on the storage of water, especially in parts of the country that are more arid. Instead of letting all the water from the eastern United States continue to flow into the Atlantic and the Gulf of Mexico, we should use our ingenuity to transfer water west of the Rocky Mountains, creating an abundance of water so that the Western states don't have to fight over it. We can enter into agreements with Canada to transfer water from Western Canada into the Western United States.

The vast reservoirs of water that we should create to store water for power generation, drinking and irrigation will result in the loss of the use of some land by humans and animals, but the lakes created will provide not just power and water, but vast areas for humans and wildlife to enjoy the altered environment. If human activity is leading to an increase in sea level on the magnitude of inches or a few feet, this kind of approach, especially if pursued worldwide, would reduce carbon emissions and offset the rise in sea level. If the greatest fear of environmentalists was realized, and both polar ice caps melted, sea levels would rise by more than 200 feet, which we could never stop, even if we stopped using fossil fuels altogether.

If this approach were used worldwide, an abundance of clean energy and water could be available to every place on earth until the great drought of the coming Great Tribulation, when all bets are off, as the earth will be plagued by drought, famine, pestilence and war on a scale never seen before. Although imminent, we don't know when that day will come, but until then we can use our God-given intellect and the sweat of our brow to solve any problems that we face.

Wind and Solar Power

Since almost all energy comes from the sun, it seems that the immediate generation of power from sunlight would be the most sensible way to harness the power of the sun. Through the use of fossil fuels, we are harnessing power that originated from the sun long ago. Through the use of hydroelectric power, we are harnessing energy that originated from the sun when water evaporated and was carried by winds caused by the effect of the sun on our atmosphere, resulting in the collection of rainwater at a higher elevation with stored energy that can be harnessed by a hydroelectric dam. When we burn ethanol, palm oil or wood, we are harnessing power that originated from the sun.

We should permit the free market to pursue solar power options, and not try to force our economy to adopt technology that is not quite developed to the point of large-scale usage. It makes no sense to develop large-scale projects in the desert that function like power plants do, when the obvious solution is to use solar panels on a small scale for homes and businesses to generate power in a decentralized fashion. This is how satellites and remote cell phone towers are powered. We should simply have more patience in allowing the development of technology to catch up with our dreams of a solar powered world.

Generating power by huge windmills that are very expensive, unsightly and rarely seem to be turning makes no sense. Environmentalists seem to be a little mixed up on maintaining consistency in their objections to the environmental impact of oil drilling as compared to windmill farms. They just will not suffer the coastline of the Carolinas, Florida or Virginia to be blighted by an occasional oil rig, but they will embrace rows of windmills on the tops of mountains and on coastlines because they think it is more environmentally sound. All subsidies on solar power and wind power should be eliminated so that the free market may determine the pace at which those technologies advance.

Nuclear Power

When considering cost, efficiency, safety and environmental impact, nuclear power may very well be the best option for the large-scale generation of electricity until solar power becomes more cost-effective and efficient. Nuclear power has no carbon footprint, and has a good safety record compared to other options. When it comes to the storage of spent nuclear fuel, the federal government should get Yucca Mountain back on track and allow nuclear power to once again flourish.

ELIMINATE ALL SUBSIDIES AND PENALTIES

It makes no sense for the government to meddle with the free market and artificially stimulate developing technology while burdening existing technology. Federal and state governments should refrain from penalizing legacy methods of power generation such as coal-fired power plants.

The free market is more than capable of replacing old technologies of power generation with new technologies at a pace that makes sense. Government subsidy of new technologies will result in an overinvestment in technologies that have not yet become right for widespread use. Solar energy makes great sense once the technology is developed for the cost-effective production of power coupled with battery technology that will permit homeowners and small businesses to safely store power.

The pursuit of renewable energy through subsidies for ethanol in the United States and palm oil in Third World nations like Indonesia create very undesirable unintended consequences. In the United States, vast quantities of land has been reallocated to the production of ethanol instead of being used to grow food for livestock and human consumption, resulting in escalating food prices. Indonesia has seen innumerable peat bog fires that have been set intentionally in order to clear land of peat bogs so that palm trees can be planted for palm oil production. It is ironic that the pursuit of renewable energy from palm oil in order to reduce carbon emissions from fossil fuels has resulted in massive carbon emissions from peat bog fires, but government tinkering with markets often produces such unintended consequences.

We the People should press the federal government to eliminate subsidies on biofuels and to eliminate the federal mandate that requires a certain percentage of ethanol be used in gasoline and permit the free market to determine appropriate levels of biofuels used in our vehicles.

ENCOURAGE MICRO-POWER GENERATION

There should be no federal subsidies of any energy source or method of power generation, but there should also be no impediments to permitting individual homeowners, businesses or municipalities from generating power at the local level. States would also do well to stay out of the business of picking winners and losers by subsidizing specific methods or technologies used in the generation of power. Government policy should encourage all safe means of generating power by all parties connected to the power grid.

Since homeowners and businesses have no choice but to buy electricity from a single source for each point of delivery, federal law could assure that excess power generated by a homeowner or business must be purchased by the supplier of electricity that is granted the local monopoly to supply power to the home or business that generates excess power. At present, some suppliers of electricity offer net metering that effectively repurchases excess power generated by the user at the same price charged per kilowatt hour to the end user.

As the capacity to generate power at the customer level increases, it will be necessary and equitable for excess power to be repurchased by the utility at a discount off the price charged the home or business, but utilities should also be required by law to repurchase electricity generated by homes and businesses.

Encouraging more decentralized production of electricity at the local level by municipalities, businesses and homes will permit us to reduce the vulnerability of the power grid in the United States. We must strengthen the grid and reduce our vulnerability by modifying our current structure of having three power grids to one of having hundreds of smaller power grids that can be isolated when there is a problem so that any threat can be contained.

END COUNTERPRODUCTIVE POLICIES

In their quest to pursue their liberal agenda, environmentalists and globalists have implemented numerous policies that have an implicit bias toward validating the myth that humans are destroying the planet, and their goal of establishing a New World Order dominated by global elites of the entrenched establishment political class. Many policies implemented by the federal government not only have the opposite result of the one intended by the policy, but the unintended consequences of the policy result in undermining our ability to develop and use energy efficiently, and in many cases result in much wasted energy.

The free market system is more reliable then government at any level in achieving more with less, and allocating resources in a sensible fashion. Virtually everything the government does results in suppressing liberty and real output while causing damage to our economy and environment. We will not belabor the point, but I would like to consider some examples of how government policy itself contributes to the very energy and environmental problems they seek to mitigate.

Stop Defining CO_2 as a Pollutant

The decision to include CO_2 as a pollutant under the Clean Air Act has been so destructive to our economy. Environmentalists started the "green" movement to presumably advocate for making our world more green, as in more verdant and lush. Vegetation thrives on CO_2, so it would seem logical that environmentalists would welcome more carbon dioxide emissions so that we would have more plant life, which by the way would throw off more oxygen for human consumption. Some have argued that the ideal level of CO_2 in the atmosphere for optimum conditions for plant life is five times the current level of CO_2 in the atmosphere today. We don't have to curtail human activity in order to save the planet.

End Public Education

There are many reasons to bring an end to public education. One reason that environmentalists should support the end of public education is that there would no longer be a need for kids to be driven or bused to school and back, which would dramatically reduce traffic and pollution. Since most environmentalists are liberals, they would be conflicted with the prospect of shutting down their preferred method of indoctrinating our kids in order to help protect the environment.

Massive amounts of wasted energy and the resulting emissions is but one of the many unintended consequences and other pitfalls of public education. Typical zoning laws result in most kids going to schools that require transportation to get there, and parents usually work at locations that are at some distance from home. In addition to kids being bused or driven to school, many parents endure long commute times to their places of employment in order to enroll their children in what they consider to be superior schools. One of the benefits of my plan to get the government out of education will be a dramatic reduction in the energy consumption required to deliver the inferior product that the public education system presently delivers.

Vehicle Emission Standards

The federal government fixation on vehicle fuel efficiency standards makes absolutely no sense. The policy of requiring auto and truck manufacturers to meet increasingly unrealistic fuel efficiency standards as a proxy for measuring the emissions performance of the vehicles produced is entirely flawed. President Barack Obama might have felt like he was doing the right thing when he mandated that auto and truck manufacturers increase efficiency, but that action only exacerbates the problem that fuel efficiency standards create for our economy.

Vehicle fuel efficiency measured in miles per gallon has no value in the evaluation of the performance of specific vehicles, as it does not take into account the many variables that should be considered when evaluating vehicle performance. An environmentalist that thinks driving a smart car at 40 miles per gallon is a superior moral choice to someone with a family of six that drives a suburban at 20 miles per gallon ignores variables like comfort, safety and payload capacity, not to mention the annual miles driven for each vehicle. These variables are simply not captured by simply looking at a measure of miles per gallon fuel efficiency.

It seems that environmentalists would not be satisfied if auto and truck manufacturers could produce cars and trucks that only emitted CO_2. Since CO_2 is not a harmful emission, the only thing that should matter when evaluating the performance of engines is the amount of harmful emissions per gallon of fuel consumed, as compared to other engines of similar horsepower. For this reason, miles per gallon fuel efficiency standards should be abandoned.

FORTY-ONE

Free-Market Healthcare

REPEAL OBAMACARE, OUTLAW HEALTH INSURANCE AND GET GOVERNMENT OUT OF HEALTHCARE

A time to break down, and a time to build up.

– Ecclesiastes 3:3

The notion that health insurance coverage equates to adequate healthcare is a fallacy that liberals used to foist Obamacare upon us. Assuring that all Americans have health insurance coverage may sound like a noble cause, and naming the legislation the Affordable Care Act may have been intended to lead us to believe that the real objective of Obamacare was to assure that Americans have access to affordable healthcare, but the real intent of Obamacare was to cause irreparable harm to the health insurance industry and to so transform the healthcare market that there would be no choice but to adopt a single-payer healthcare system.

We should not discount the possibility that there was evil intent behind the passage of Obamacare. A decision was made to implement Obamacare with full knowledge that it was not going to work, perhaps in order to pursue the Cloward and Piven strategy to overwhelm the entitlement laden federal budget. Obamacare has worked as it was designed and intended to work.

REPEAL OBAMACARE

Obamacare has destroyed the health insurance market, and if we do not repeal it immediately, we will have a broken healthcare system that will lead to a lower standard of healthcare at higher cost. We the People must compel Congress and President Trump to resist the temptation to try to fix the health insurance market. Obamacare has effectively destroyed the private health insurance market in this country, so We the People must take this opportunity to compel Congress to make it illegal for insurance companies to issue health insurance contracts altogether.

Obamacare is the biggest job killer ever foisted upon the American people. It must be repealed without a federal government designed replacement, as any replacement will be just as bad as Obamacare. It was through the operation of the free market that the United States created the greatest healthcare system in the world, not the actions of the federal government. The longer that we wait to repeal Obamacare, the longer it will take the American healthcare system to recover.

Barack Obama and his Democrat co-conspirators in Congress are so confident that they have succeeded in the permanent takeover by the federal government of the American healthcare system that they are taunting President Donald Trump and the Republican House and Senate with the challenge to replace Obamacare as part of any effort to repeal Obamacare. They know that if Congress buys into their false narrative that the only way to repeal Obamacare is to immediately replace Obamacare, they will succeed in their objective of preserving their intentional takeover of one sixth of the American economy.

We the People are serious about the mandate that we gave President Trump and the Republican Congress to completely repeal Obamacare, and to "drain the swamp" as Donald Trump puts it. We the People are tired of the spineless Republican members of the entrenched establishment political class cowering in fear over the childish threats of the liberal left. Liberals know that they have Congress between a rock and a hard place if Congress accepts the premise that they have to replace Obamacare in order to repeal it. Congress faces the wrath of We the People if they do not repeal

Obamacare, yet Democrats know that Congress fears repealing Obamacare without a replacement because doing so will be very disruptive in the short run.

Replacing Obamacare is a losing proposition, especially if it means the delay of the repeal of Obamacare. Congress is faced with a complex equation with numerous known and unknown variables for which there is no solution.

OUTLAW HEALTH INSURANCE

A little bit of useful regulation is all the free market needs to fix the problems created by Obamacare. Useful regulation will also fix the numerous problems in our healthcare system that preexisted Obamacare, many of which were created by the meddling in our healthcare system by the federal government.

Barack Obama threatening to shut down the government, or taunting President Trump and Congress with the notion that they cannot simply repeal Obamacare without replacing it, is like one brother licking the last few cookies left on a plate so that his older brother will not want to eat any of the cookies, leaving all of the cookies for him to eat. The threat is neutralized when big brother simply smiles at his little brother while taking a bite out of one of the cookies.

By creating the current crisis in the health insurance market and sabotaging all reasonable means by which we can salvage the health insurance market while dismantling the deleterious effects of Obamacare, liberals may have given us the perfect opportunity to fix all of the problems they have created in the health insurance and healthcare markets with one slice at the Gordian knot. Of all of the problems created by liberalism in the last fifty years, there is no problem so large and impactful that provides greater opportunity for such a simple and straightforward solution as the problems created by the passage of the Affordable Care Act and the opportunity that We the People now have to fix it.

Insurance companies and the health insurance policies that they sell do nothing to improve healthcare or add value to the healthcare system. The basic function of health insurance is to spread the risk of the financial burden of unanticipated healthcare events, which is something that we can collectively do without any involvement of insurance companies. We the People now have the opportunity to insist that our government permit us to spread the risk of catastrophic healthcare events in a much more cost-effective and equitable manner.

A Single-Payer System

Government involvement in the healthcare system leads to higher costs. Instead of increasing government involvement to eventually move to a single-payer system leading to lower quality healthcare at higher cost, if we get the government out of the equation and eliminate health insurance as an option, we will then have a single-payer system where the single-payer is the patient in each healthcare transaction.

When the patient pays for healthcare in a free market driven, competitive environment such as we have seen with elective surgeries such as plastic surgery and Lasik eye surgery, costs are driven down dramatically. Why should We the People continue to pay for ever-increasing health insurance premiums, deductibles and co-pays in the current structure, when we can change the structure so that prices will collapse to about what the co-pay or deductible would be under the current structure?

Life Without Health Insurance

One of the benefits of eradicating health insurance altogether is that whenever we hear that someone we know has a significant healthcare cost arise, we will know without question that they alone must bear that cost unless assistance is volunteered by others. We will have no question that there is a need, and that if we volunteer assistance to meet that need it will not simply displace insurance money or government assistance.

Since it is more blessed to give than to receive, we will receive great blessing by the opportunities presented to us to give to others that have healthcare needs in a free market healthcare environment without insurance company or government involvement.

Without the involvement of third-party payers like insurance companies and the government, we should expect the average cost of medical procedures currently covered by insurance or government programs to drop at least 70%. Full implementation of most of the elements of this plan that will permit the free market to establish prices will lead to a deflationary trend in healthcare costs, as it would with other segments of the economy.

In addition to lower prices, mutual assistance and crowdfunding that will make healthcare costs less burdensome, Healthcare providers will likely compete for patients facing catastrophic events such as cancer. Just as defense attorneys compete to represent the notorious criminal charged with a heinous crime at no cost to the criminal, cancer centers will most likely compete for patients and perhaps charge nothing, possibly even offering to provide housing for family members like Ronald McDonald House does.

Free Market Alternatives to Health Insurance

In a scenario where the government is not involved in the healthcare market and insurance companies are not permitted to sell health insurance policies, the vast majority of Americans would be better off financially. Since there would be no monthly expense for health insurance premiums, routine healthcare costs would be easily managed, and people would have several options to handle high cost or catastrophic healthcare needs.

For decades there have been affinity group mechanisms for sharing healthcare needs. In such plans, members share monthly in the payment of certain healthcare costs of other members submitted to the administrator of the plan. Since members in such plans pay directly for healthcare costs, much greater scrutiny is given to healthcare costs. Prices are still artificially high presently due to government involvement in paying for healthcare costs, but if health insurance is outlawed, and government gets out of making healthcare payments, healthcare prices will collapse and the healthcare community will have to get used to being accountable for costs to the patient.

Crowdfunding through sites like GoFundMe are a more recent manifestation of innovative ways to spread risk and share costs by millions of Americans willing to participate in helping perfect strangers with healthcare needs that seem to be insurmountable to them. Such platforms are incredibly efficient, as there is little cost of administering sites that bring people with needs together with people that are inclined to give toward such needs. The percentage that a site retains for providing the service is primarily a redistribution of wealth from the donor to the site, with very little true cost. Free-market healthcare will drive those transaction costs even lower as new providers enter the crowdfunding market.

Crowdfunding is an option that shows great promise for We the People to self-insure ourselves against catastrophic healthcare costs while also encouraging a resurgence of the charity that brings out the best in people instead of a reliance upon the government to take care of someone that is in need.

GETTING GOVERNMENT OUT OF HEALTHCARE

The days are numbered for the insurance industry to provide health insurance plans, for either health insurance goes away because we see the full implementation of a single payer system of healthcare, or We the People compel Congress to make health insurance plans illegal. The only chance of implementing free-market healthcare is if we can get government out of healthcare.

Eliminate Medicaid and Medicare

The most direct path to getting the federal government out of the healthcare market is to transfer Medicaid and Medicare to the states, repeal Obamacare, and outlaw health insurance. States that pursue the full implementation of this plan will then eliminate Medicaid and Medicare and any other involvement in the healthcare market in their state in order to permit the free market to complete the transformation of the healthcare market. States that do not embrace the magnitude and direction of this plan will have much difficulty controlling healthcare costs.

We can let liberal states flounder in their effort to provide socialized medicine to their citizens while conservative states pursue free-market healthcare, but it would be better to implement a solution that will eliminate all third party payments for healthcare. In addition to compelling Congress to repeal Obamacare and outlaw health insurance, We the People should also compel Congress to eliminate Medicare and Medicaid altogether by including those programs in legislation that outlaws insurance. The federal government created a mess of these programs, and states would benefit if the federal government fixed the problem that they created.

Eliminate VA Hospitals and Clinics

When considering the steps we must take to get government out of healthcare, we must not neglect to include the solution to the problem with the VA hospital system. We have failed our veterans by relegating them to a substandard healthcare system. We must correct this national sin by simply eliminating all VA hospitals and clinics, and permitting our veterans to fully participate in the world's best healthcare system.

When healthcare prices collapse to what the free-market healthcare system will establish as the new price equilibrium without third-party payments by insurance companies and government, our veterans that are generally healthy will be able to afford healthcare.

We can trust our veterans with an honor system that permits any veteran that asserts that his healthcare needs are related to service in the military to look to the federal government for reimbursement of those healthcare costs.

Most veterans that I know are patriots that signed a blank check to the government for an amount up to and including their life, and could have accomplished any objective with few resources, yet ask so little from our government in return. Trusting them with an honor system to cover service related healthcare is the least we can do for them. How can we not help a veteran with healthcare, food, clothing or housing if they tell us that their need arises from their service to our country? How can we not trust them?

Veterans that cannot honestly make the assertion that their healthcare needs are related to their military service will join with the rest of us in participating in free-market healthcare. We the People will all be in the same boat when it comes to paying for healthcare, and we will be far better off trusting in the free market instead of the government to meet our healthcare needs.

Free-Market Healthcare

Free-market healthcare will permit our healthcare system to thrive and innovate, meeting the needs of patients and providing all those employed in the healthcare system with the satisfaction of helping others, while making a reasonable living without the burden of interference by government and insurance companies making their jobs more difficult and less fulfilling.

If there was a way to salvage Obamacare, it would then be necessary to outlaw employer provided health insurance plans in order to permit the portability of plans and to correct the damage done to small business in this country. Giving big business an unfair advantage in procuring lower cost large group health insurance plans makes it more difficult for small businesses to attract quality employees in order to compete with big business. Small business is where most jobs are created, and if we continue to allow insurance companies to sell health insurance policies, we would need to fix this problem. The problem goes away if we repeal Obamacare and outlaw health insurance policies.

The involvement of insurance companies and the government in making third-party payments for prescription drugs, particularly under Obamacare, leads to artificially high drug prices. Drug companies are able to engage in price gouging, because under the current broken system, doctors are afraid to not prescribe medication, and insurance companies are virtually required to provide the medication, no matter what the cost is. One thing is certain, if We the People implement free-market healthcare by eliminating health insurance and government payments, the free market will permit nowhere near the pricing that drug companies are currently able to extract from third-party payers. Big Pharma will lose their opportunity to price gouge.

FREEDOM CELL ACTION

In seeking to use a backdoor option to create a single-payer healthcare system in our country by foisting Obamacare upon us, Barack Obama and his big government, liberal Democrat cohorts gave us an incredible opportunity to take what they have intended for evil, and to turn it into good. By destroying the health insurance market and threatening the healthcare market, Democrats have made the choice easy for us.

The entrenched establishment political class is good about talking the talk about the need for entitlement reform, but never having the courage to do anything about it. Many RINO Republicans made campaign promises to repeal Obamacare if given the opportunity, and indeed even voted for Obamacare repeal when they knew that it would be vetoed by Obama. Barack Obama and the Democrats have given us a compelling reason to get our government completely out of healthcare by repealing Obamacare and eliminating all socialized medicine programs like Medicaid and Medicare in one slice of the Gordian knot.

There is no doubt that our congressmen and senators will fail to see the opportunity to restore free-market healthcare, or that they would have the courage to do so if they saw the opportunity. That is why We the People must rally behind this plan or one of similar magnitude and direction. We must clamor for commonsense changes that will extract our federal and state governments from activities that they should not be engaged in. We the People must clamor for President Trump to advocate for bold, transformational changes, and we must replace Democrats and RINO Republicans in the House and Senate with transformational conservatives that will get the job done.

FORTY-TWO

Free-Market Education

GOVERNMENT MUST PERMIT PARENTS TO FULFILL THEIR GOD-GIVEN RESPONSIBILITY TO EDUCATE THEIR OWN CHILDREN

Ever learning, and never able to come to the knowledge of the truth.
– 2 Timothy 3:7

When you step back and look at the public education system in America, you can't help but wonder where the education of students is in the hierarchy of priorities of those running the system. Regardless of what they claim to be doing, the result is the dumbing down of American students. While the quality of education slips and other problems abound, the education elite and the entrenched establishment political class say that the solution is to throw more money at the problem.

What is really happening in our public schools is the systematic indoctrination of our children in accordance with liberal theology of big government. There is a battle going on for the hearts and minds of our children, and We the People are losing. If we are to stem the tide, we must dismantle the nineteenth century model of education that was hijacked and allow 21st century free-market opportunities for truly educating our children to prevail.

THE EDUCATION FUNCTION OF OUR PUBLIC SCHOOL SYSTEM

Ostensibly, the true function of the public education system is to educate our children so that they can live productive lives. As is often the case, government bureaucrats think that government does all things well, and is therefore better qualified to educate young people than parents are. Federal, state and local governments have teamed up to spend incredible sums of money to realize inferior outcomes to what parents aided by the private sector can accomplish at a fraction of the cost.

The Bible teaches us that in the end times, knowledge will increase. Through advances in science and technology in recent decades, we have seen an unprecedented explosion in knowledge. For millennia, knowledge increased in a fairly linear fashion, but in the last fifty years we have seen knowledge grow exponentially. Although the body of knowledge that the average person or the best and brightest among us is able to master has increased dramatically in recent decades, our knowledge as a percentage of all knowledge has been decreasing. As we become more knowledgeable individually, our ignorance, as measured by what we do not know, grows!

A Renaissance man in the eighteenth or nineteenth centuries was capable of knowing a much higher percentage of the body of knowledge that existed at that time than a Renaissance man could know today. Despite the opportunity that the average person has today to become informed about a vast array of knowledge from various fields, the most committed student focused on acquiring knowledge will lose ground every single day.

Given the exponentially increasing body of knowledge, and the limited capacity that any one person has to master even a small percentage of that knowledge, who has the legitimate right, authority or competence to say what is necessary or appropriate for children to learn from birth to eighteen years of age?

Leave it to government to, in a world of ever-increasing knowledge, appropriate to itself the power and authority to develop curriculum that is then prescribed to all students and entitled "common core." Only parents have the right and the responsibility to determine what is best for their own children. Parents have the God-given right and responsibility to train up their children in the way they should go. It is time for We the People to take control of educating our children.

THE INDOCTRINATION FUNCTION OF OUR PUBLIC SCHOOL SYSTEM

The primary function of our public education system has become that of indoctrination. Notwithstanding any claims by the political class or the education elite that they have the idealistic purpose of educating children, experience has shown that their real agenda is to indoctrinate our children in the doctrines of liberal theology: anti-God secular humanism, evolution, political correctness, multiculturalism, revisionist history, anti-Americanism and a whole host of other destructive doctrines.

Parents have the right, authority and privilege of indoctrinating their own children as to values, religious instruction, and political persuasion. Government has abused their access to children that was acquired under the false pretense of education and has engaged in violating parental rights by indoctrinating children in the ways of big government.

THE DAYCARE FUNCTION OF OUR PUBLIC SCHOOL SYSTEM

Public education serves the ancillary function of day care for children for many Americans. Households that require both parents to work, single-parent households and parents that abdicate their responsibility for nurturing their children result in heavy dependence upon the daycare function of public education. Government uses this dependency, as with all dependencies that liberalism seeks to create, to make it very difficult to change the status quo.

We must not permit the dependency on the daycare function of public education to dissuade us from finding a way of bringing an end to the status quo public education system and permit parents, with the help of the free market system, to pursue education for their children, to arrange for the appropriate supervision of their children and most importantly, to indoctrinate their children with the faith and values that they espouse.

THE ILLS OF PUBLIC SCHOOLS

Set aside, for the moment, the dismal failure of our public schools to properly educate our children. There are a host of other serious problems that have cropped up in our schools.

Our schools, since they are gun free zones, have become very visible and obvious targets for mass shootings and terrorist attacks. There is some evidence that the San Bernardino terrorist couple was considering an additional terrorist attack against a school in San Bernardino. This would have added a mass shooting by terrorists to the carnage inflicted on Columbine and Sandy Hook. Sadly, it seems inevitable that we will someday see terrorist attacks on our vulnerable public and private schools.

Decades ago, serious problems in public schools consisted of kids putting chewing gum underneath their desks, talking in class, being late for class and such innocuous problems. In contrast, gang violence, drugs, bullying, and sexual assaults on our children by fellow students, teachers, coaches and administrators are all very real problems in our public schools today.

The problems with public schools, and therefore an additional motivating factor for parents to choose to opt out of public education, grew worse in 2016 with the outlandish Obama mandate that public schools permit the use of bathrooms, locker rooms and such by transgender students.

All things considered, it is well past the time when We the People should force the federal government to completely withdraw from any influence or control over the education of our children. We the People in every state of the union should force our states, counties, cities and towns to reject the public education model and permit the free market to do more with less.

21ST CENTURY EDUCATION

We must dismantle the failed, archaic nineteenth century model of public education and replace it with a 21st century model that restores the responsibility for educating children to the parents of those children. We the People must diligently pursue free-market education that delivers far superior results at dramatically lower cost. We must reclaim the lost precious liberty to educate and train up our children in the way they should go.

We must recognize that all education is self-education. Even in a classroom with a teacher at the front, education does not happen unless the student willingly participates. The words of the teacher at the front of the class are of no effect if the student does not pay attention, listen, think and reason, consciously using his God-given intellect to acquire knowledge.

So much discussion has been expended on the appropriate teacher to student ratios at various age levels of students. By limiting our thinking to a model with a teacher at the front of the classroom and discussing how many students should be in a classroom, we isolate ourselves from the reality that learning does not happen in a ratio of one teacher to X number of students. Learning actually happens in a ratio of X teachers to one student. From a very young age, we all learn from the input of many teachers that are constantly teaching us.

Children are born with such a desire to learn and grow and experience life that they need no motivation to learn. Children are like little sponges learning constantly. After children learn so much, so fast from birth to age five, we then stifle their education by putting them into classrooms with other children the same age for many hours in a day, primarily learning from just one person. No wonder kids are bored out of their minds in school! A 21st century model of education should unleash the learning potential of each student instead of restricting and throttling back on the natural God-given appetite for learning that children have.

The best model for education is that of a one room school-house, where each person is in their little bubble, their schoolhouse, and they are in charge of the pace at which they learn. Thankfully, no two people are exactly alike. People have different God-given abilities, interests and preferences. For any subject, people will learn at different paces. Why put fifteen or twenty people of the same age into a classroom and expect to not have incredible inefficiency in matching education to the individual?

The reason why I use person instead of child in my one room schoolhouse description of education, is because education is not limited to children. The 21st century model of self-education will recognize the value of continuous lifelong education and encourage people of all ages to productively learn in their one room school-house. Children that, for one reason or another, did not advance very far academically will be able to quickly make up lost ground. Adults that want to learn new things or refresh their knowledge of certain subjects would have easy access to the academic modules that they would like to master.

The exponential increase in knowledge comes with a remarka-ble vehicle for delivery of education, that of the internet and the advent of distance-learning. Anyone can learn anything, anywhere, anytime, and can have an unlimited number of teachers impacting their life at all times. There are risks that such access to information brings, but what a wonderful world of opportunity we all have to learn new things!

Academics

The 21st century model of education will permit students to pursue a more robust and diverse palette of studies than the current archaic nineteenth century model of education could ever hope to deliver. The free market can quickly develop thousands of educa-tion modules that students could use to customize their own educa-tion to match their skills and interests. The means of delivery of educational modules and the proctoring of quizzes and tests to establish proficiency in the subject matter at low cost is already well-established, and will only get better.

As we were going through school, many of us were told more than once that something, usually misbehavior, was going to go on to our "permanent record." I doubt that there is much, if anything, that I could find from my "permanent record" from elementary school or junior high school. So much for a permanent record for those of us over thirty! Technology today permits the accumulation and retention of vast amounts of data on each of us. It is scary to think about what information is collected about each of us, and the ways such information could be used for malevolent purposes, but it would be clearly a simple matter for a permanent academic record to be compiled for every student going forward.

As each student chomps away ferociously at all of the modules available to them to learn, they would be building a transcript of all of their academic performance for those modules that earn academic credit. With numerous distance-learning platforms in current operation, it is simply a matter of dramatically expanding the course offerings so that the breadth and depth of academic opportunities become available to children as well as adults.

If a standard course load is six courses per semester, gifted students could sail through two or three times the material typically required for an academic year, and students that are challenged could put as much time as they needed into each module to master the material, pass the tests and then move on. In this model, no child would truly be left behind.

Daycare

One of the beauties of the self-paced, individualized approach to the 21st Century model of education that I envision is that the academic modules, testing and proctoring would all be cloud-based. All that any student would need would be internet access from a smart terminal with a camera for proctoring purposes. Parents would have the liberty to schedule and coordinate the opportunities for their child to have internet access with the daycare options that they have available to them. Daycare options include anywhere a child might be throughout the day. What this might look like for each child is as individualized as each child.

Parents should have the liberty to determine how to supervise their children and their education. Some parents may choose to have each child under close supervision until the late teenage years, while other parents may choose to trust their children with greater degrees of freedom to live life day-to-day. If given the opportunity, children are remarkably capable human beings, and certainly have the capacity for much greater independence and autonomy than most people would give them credit for.

If the option of providing daycare at public school is eliminated because we eliminate public schools altogether, parents will have the responsibility for arranging appropriate supervision as well as opportunities for their children to pursue distance-learning. There is no limit to the ways that resourceful parents may accomplish their God-given responsibility to care for and educate their children.

Indoctrination

The authority and responsibility to indoctrinate children must be restored to parents, and governments at all levels must refrain from interfering with that indoctrination. Parents have the right to customize the education of their children to conform to the faith that they adhere to without interference by government, which has succeeded in removing God from public education.

Parents have many options for guiding the education of their children in the 21st century model of education that I propose. Most people will avail themselves of the technology for cloud-based distance-learning, but some, such as the Amish, will choose to educate their children without the benefits and risks of technology. These alternative approaches should not be denied to parents because the state decides that it knows best.

People of like faith should have the liberty to use their house of worship, or any other facility that they choose to use, to establish learning centers that will provide cubicles for students to pursue their studies in an environment that also functions as the daycare solution for the children. This could take the form of a one room schoolhouse at a church, or at a location set up by a homeschooling group, or in a neighborhood. Parents should be the final authority on what is best for the education and daycare of their children. No government authority should be able to conclude that a space is too small to use, a distance is too far to walk or that a child is incapable of the independence granted to the child by the parent so long as there is no obvious danger. Unnecessary interference by the nanny state should not be tolerated.

Severing the Nine-Month Tether

One of the negatives of the archaic public education system is the nine-month tether that keeps a family tied down to a location for the nine-month school year. In the past, people did not notice this nine-month tether because they were generally tied down by a fifty week tether because of the manner in which most people were employed with two weeks of vacation annually.

In the 21st century, we are seeing a growing percentage of people that are no longer tied to a work location by a fifty week tether. Many people now have the liberty to perform their work from wherever they are. For many of us, this is a wonderfully liberating thing that allows us to contemplate living and working in different locations for significant periods of time. For some, that liberty is limited by the nine-month tether of the school year for their children. Eliminating public education and embracing the 21st century model of education will free families from the nine-month tether, allowing them to contemplate an unlimited number of scenarios for combining living, working and playing while providing their children unprecedented opportunities for learning.

Severing the nine-month tether and pursuing my 21st century model of education affords families great opportunities for travel, which will enhance the lives and education of all members of the family. Families could purposefully choose to live life differently by mapping out a short-term or long-term plan for living life, working, ministering or playing in different parts of the United States or the world. Such opportunities to enhance our lives are only limited by our imagination.

Socialization

For years I have heard the arguments of many that one of the drawbacks of homeschooling is that children do not learn how to relate to other people, that somehow their social growth is stunted by what many assume to be the isolation of homeschool kids from others that denies to them opportunities for socialization. I think that this thinking is utter foolishness because I believe that the complete opposite is true. In my experience, I have observed that homeschool children tend to be more socialized than the average child attending traditional schools.

Parents that homeschool their children, or "unschool" their children, or pursue any other variation of the 21st century model of education that I propose, have the liberty to give their children far greater opportunities for socialization than traditional education would ever hope to provide.

In my 21st century model of education, children will have opportunity to engage and interact with people of all ages as they live out their lives while pursuing their education, which should include learning how to work. Children that live daily life surrounded by people of all ages that they can learn from will fare much better than children stifled by being sequestered with large numbers of children that are close in age.

Sports

Some will say that my 21st century model of education will deprive children of organized team sports, and the opportunities that some will have to become highly paid professional athletes. My response to that concern is that it would be a good thing if the 21st century model of education results in deemphasizing organized team sports. It would also be a good thing if professional teams would have to organize their farm leagues a little bit differently.

I am sure that many parents that have the flexibility to work anywhere they want to would avail themselves of the opportunity to travel with their star athlete children, whether it be soccer, baseball, hockey or some other sport. Club sports would flourish in the 21st century model of education that I envision, but I am hopeful that with the deemphasizing of organized sports with the loss of the public school option, kids would learn once again to play pickup soccer, baseball, football and basketball in the communities where they spend their time.

Vocational Training

One of the great opportunities of the 21st century model of education that I envision is for children to learn to work at a young age. There are many jobs that children under the age of sixteen are capable of performing, and it is a shame to deprive children of the opportunity to work. One of the great blessings of family owned businesses is the opportunity to employ your children in the business at a young age. We the People should not only resist any effort by government to take that opportunity away from family owned businesses, we should also advocate for children to be granted the liberty to work, so long as they work in a safe environment.

A child that receives some vocational training in addition to the pursuit of his individualized academic education will be so far ahead of the typical child educated by the current public school system. A child that learns to work with mom or dad or other family member, or local business that they can walk to from home will learn skills that will be just as useful as academic training. Some employers may provide opportunities for children of employees to participate in a work-study program that gives the child a few hours of paid work along with access to a smart terminal in a cubicle in a company learning lab that they can use to work on their academic modules. We are only limited by our imagination as to how we reorganize the way that we live, work and educate our children.

Adult Education

The cloud-based 21st century model of education that will flourish if we shut down the public education system will provide an unprecedented opportunity for adult education. Any adult at any education level can create a profile on any of the platforms that will develop and quickly start devouring education modules to advance their education. As the free market develops platforms and education modules with the tutoring, testing and proctoring features that will be necessary for implementation, adults will have unlimited academic and practical living modules that would soon be available to anyone, anywhere at any time.

No matter how stunted the education happens to be for any specific individual, that person will have the liberty to pursue self-education at his own pace. This is why we need not worry about trusting parents with the education of their own children. Even if a parent really messes up, their children will eventually be able to catch up and surpass where they imagined that they could be in terms of their accumulated skills and knowledge.

Permanent Academic Record

When we finally put an end to our disgraceful public education system, the free market will quickly produce all of the elements needed for the cloud-based 21st century model of education. That permanent record that we heard of growing up will finally exist, but hopefully just the academic record! The capacity for our children to learn, excel and develop skills will be unleashed, and children will grow up with a record of their academic achievements that they can take pride in, and that will open new doors of opportunity for learning to them.

TRANSFORM HIGHER EDUCATION

Once a child has mastered the modules required for admission to college, there will be no reason to hold that child back because of age, for they will be free to continue their self-education with cloud-based institutions of higher learning that are focused on education, and not indoctrination. We the People have a great opportunity to take back the education of our children all the way through college without giving them over to anti-God, anti-American liberals to indoctrinate.

The 21st century model of self-education through cloud-based distance-learning permits every student to acquire an academic education while learning skills in working along the way. It will be most advantageous to most kids to continue to acquire their post-secondary education this way while working and earning a living. Students should also be able to pursue college degrees without incurring any debt. The free market should drive the net cost of all education down to near zero.

Free-market education at the college level should lead to a consolidation of bricks and mortar educational institutions and to the dramatic growth of cloud-based distance-learning higher education models that will serve the needs of increased demand from all age groups of the population. It's basically about putting the cookies on the lower shelf so the kids can reach the cookies. If education is either free or inexpensive, and can be accessed by anyone at any time, then there should be a huge increase in demand for education by people that would not otherwise attend traditional bricks and mortar universities.

High cost bricks and mortar colleges and universities will be necessary for some parts of some fields of study. If student loans are not an option because We the People have outlawed debt, and colleges and universities want the best and brightest students to attend, then the free market will find a way for providing the subsidies necessary to attract the best and brightest students without the need for government subsidies. Bricks and mortar universities would compete for the best students, and students would compete for slots available at those bricks and mortar universities.

There will be a consolidation in the numbers of bricks and mortar universities, but there will also be a huge opportunity for the best colleges and universities to combine cloud-based distance-learning with segments of attendance at the bricks and mortar facilities to create value added hybrid educational opportunities that should be in great demand by companies and students.

If We the People are successful in transforming the archaic nineteenth century educational system that now indoctrinates our children into this self-directed, cloud-based 21st century model of education, and we eliminate student loans and government subsidies as options, then we will unleash free-market education that will produce better educational outcomes at lower cost to the benefit of all American citizens.

FORTY-THREE

Restore Property Rights

WE MUST REVERSE THE DEGRADATION OF THE RIGHT OF OUR CITIZENS TO ACQUIRE, ENJOY AND DISPOSE OF PROPERTY.

All men are created equally free and independent, and have certain inherent rights, of which they cannot, by any compact, deprive or divest their posterity; among which are the enjoyment of life and liberty, with the means of acquiring and possessing property, and pursuing the obtaining of happiness and safety.

– George Mason

Property rights are essential for free people to exercise their God-given rights, and for the proper functioning of the free enterprise system. In order to unleash the potential of the United States economy to productively employ the more than 100 million underemployed Americans, We the People must clamor for our government to release the stranglehold it has on the free use of land and other real property.

ELIMINATE PROPERTY TAXES

As I mentioned in my chapter proposing a constitutional amendment to eliminate taxes on all forms of property, the assessment and collection of real estate taxes by government renders property owners as tenants, and not true property owners. The first step in restoring our right to own real property is to eliminate the authority of any government entity to tax real estate.

The obvious question that arises if we eliminate property taxes is where cities and towns will generate the revenue to continue to function. Most tax bills that I have seen reflect that approximately 50% of the property tax revenue goes toward public education. Cities and towns that choose to implement my twenty-first century plan for free-market education would no longer have that cost to bear. Further reductions in the budgets of cities and towns will be realized by using a zero-based budgeting process that will bring all expenditures under scrutiny on a regular basis.

Just as We the People should clamor for the federal and state governments to get their fiscal houses in order, We the People should also compel our towns, cities and counties to get their fiscal houses in order. It is well established that smaller towns and cities manage to provide public services at a lower cost per capita than larger cities. Many small towns utilize volunteer fire departments, so law enforcement could be provided in similar fashion by deputizing responsible citizens to assist a smaller police force in enforcing the law. User fees for services like trash collection could be assessed, and the services privatized.

After the town, city or county that presently assesses property taxes gets their fiscal house in order, the dramatically reduced need for funding will be easily provided by using several funding mechanisms available, such as sales tax, gas tax, income tax or a surcharge on the usage of water or electricity as a proxy for the level of burden placed upon local services by the occupants of properties.

Since all cities, towns and counties nationwide would share the same need to figure out how to fund operations without property tax assessments if the amendment I propose to eliminate property taxes is ratified, they will all have the same tools in their toolbox to work with, giving everyone a level playing field.

The only risk of a taxing authority seeing an exodus of citizens would be in cases where fiscally irresponsible decisions are made by tax and spend entrenched establishment political class types. If we are successful in getting the federal government out of all activities that properly belong to the states, there will be appropriate pressure on states, and the towns, cities and counties within each state, to get their fiscal houses in order. That will be a very good thing, as sharp differences in fiscal performance will contrast the policies of liberal and conservative state and local governments.

LIMIT ZONING LAWS

One of the greatest impediments to economic growth is the aggressive implementation of restrictive zoning laws by local governments that severely limit real estate development. I'm still trying to decide if it would be an overreach by the federal government to limit the opportunities for states and local governments to impose property use restrictions, or if it would be an appropriate step to protect one of our God-given natural rights. It would be nice to take care of the problem by constitutional amendment or federal law, but at this time, let's assume that it is a power reserved to states, and it is up to We the People of each state to compel our states to limit property use restrictions such as zoning laws. Any state that eliminated property taxes and limited the use of zoning restrictions would have a tremendous competitive advantage over other states.

Someone could compile a book of anecdotal evidence from law-abiding, hard-working, entrepreneurial Americans that have been stymied in their efforts to live productive lives by the insane restrictions that have been imposed upon land use and real estate development. Such a book would be interesting, but nothing would expose the insanity better than if one or several states took the bold action of simultaneously eliminating property taxes and limiting property use restrictions, as well as limiting the use of building codes to life safety issues only.

These and other actions proposed in this plan would free the economy of any state from the tyranny of the environmentalists, globalists and nanny state central planners that think they can do a better job planning and managing economic growth than the free market will do with limited government involvement. If property owners had greater freedom to do what they want to do with their property, business development would happen at a very rapid rate, and we would see a boom in innovative housing that would make housing affordable again. We would see explosive growth in small business because entrepreneurs and innovators could once again thrive and drive economic growth.

LIMIT EXTORTION OF PROPERTY DEVELOPMENT

One of the well-known phrases from the movie, *Field of Dreams*, is "if we build it, they will come." This phrase articulates an inspirational concept that motivates entrepreneurs to marshal the resources to build something that doesn't presently exist. One need not develop or build pathways for people to use to get to what you have built, for if it is worthwhile, people will beat a path to your door, and you will not have to advertise what you have built, for the word will spread like wildfire.

This is why it is wrong for nanny state central planners in cities and towns to extort anything from property developers in exchange for permission to go forward with a proposed project. If planners believe that a project creates a need for road widening or a new traffic light, it should not be the responsibility of the developer of the project to pay for those improvements. The developers of a project may find it in their best interest to provide funding for such improvements, but it should be voluntary, and not a requirement to gain approval for the project.

REIN IN THE TYRANNY OF HOMEOWNER ASSOCIATIONS

Millions of Americans are being duped into giving up property rights in return for what is presented as benign membership in homeowner associations. This insidious trend for homeowners to voluntarily submit themselves to what amounts to another layer of tyrannical government is conditioning Americans to become passive and compliant in accepting encroachments on their constitutional rights. Property owners are being conditioned to expect to ask permission from their HOA board to make very simple changes or additions to their property, such as planting a tree or painting their front door.

Neighbors become adversaries when tyrannical board members seeking a little bit of power abuse that power by reigning over the members of the Association. Homeowners are deprived of the right to enjoy their property and are subjected to all manners of abuse that go unchecked by state law and judicial systems that favor the realtors, property management companies, developers and attorneys that profit from establishing and maintaining the associations.

There is no way to get away from homeowner associations in communities of condominiums and townhouses, but the percentage of new construction of single-family homes that are governed by homeowner associations has reached an alarming level in some states. The construction of shared amenities in communities leads to the formation of homeowner associations, but even communities without shared amenities are being forced to form associations to maintain retention ponds that local authorities require to manage storm water issues related to development.

EMINENT DOMAIN

Government use of eminent domain to acquire private property from citizens should be limited to public projects like roads, bridges and a border wall with Mexico. State and local governments should be barred from taking property by eminent domain for private or public projects such as housing or sports arenas. To be equitable, and to put the burden of proof on the state or local government in order to protect private ownership of property, compensation for property taken by eminent domain should be twice the market value of the property taken. On the flipside, property owners should be barred from seeking injunctive relief from legitimate and lawful eminent domain takings.

TYRANNICAL ENVIRONMENTAL LAWS

We should all be advocates for prudent environmental stewardship, but We the People should also clamor for federal, state and local governments to bring an abrupt end to the radical environmentalist actions that have been foisted upon property owners throughout the country. I would love to see volume one of a compilation of anecdotal evidence of the abuses that property owners have endured at the hands of the federal government.

We have heard horror stories of how the federal government has used regulations promulgated under the Waters of the United States (WOTUS), otherwise known as the Clean Water Rule. As if environmental regulation in this country was not onerous enough, the Obama administration EPA redefined waters of the United States subject to the Clean Water Act of 1972. This action was so onerous that it rendered farmers violators of federal law for simply plowing their own land, resulting in outlandish fines being levied against farmers that were found in violation of the more stringent definition.

What was originally intended to cover navigable waters in the United States has been so abused as to include virtually all land where any amount of water is standing for any period of time. The EPA should be completely abolished and a more sensible policy of environmental stewardship pursued. Until such time as the EPA is stripped of its abusive authority, We the People must clamor for states and the federal government to get their boots off the necks of property owners.

RIGHT TO GROW FOOD AND RAISE LIVESTOCK

It seems logical that when we consider our natural rights that have been enumerated by our founders, we would conclude that our right to grow food and raise livestock on property that we own or rent is also a natural, God-given right. How can we enjoy our other God-given rights if we can't feed ourselves?

Government bureaucrats think they have the right to dictate when and where we have the liberty to grow food and raise livestock. One of the vulnerabilities that our nation faces is the fact that the vast majority of our population is not even remotely connected to agriculture. During the Great Depression, the population of the United States was approximately 130 million, and the vast majority of the population was engaged in agriculture or only one step removed from somebody that was. In the United States today, we have more than 300 million people in this country, with very few engaged in, or even two or three steps removed from someone that is engaged in agriculture.

Growing food and raising livestock locally is a lost art in America today. It is understandable that specialization and mechanization has led to large farms that have relatively few employees, given the acreage involved, that produce vast quantities of food for all of the rest of us to enjoy. What makes no sense, however, is depriving Americans of the freedom to grow food and raise livestock when it is such an important life skill that also provides sustenance.

During World War II, Americans were encouraged to plant victory gardens in order to augment the capacity of our nation to produce food. Americans made the sacrifices necessary to scale back domestic consumption in order to rapidly build our capacity as a nation to wage war. Our nation has lost the resiliency that it once had. We also seem to lack the national character that we had at the time of World War II, which makes it doubtful that we can survive another national crisis of the magnitude of World War II.

We the People should not only refrain from hindering those among us that would be inclined to grow food or raise livestock, we should encourage it. We should encourage independence and resiliency on the part of all of our people, and permitting Americans to exercise their God-given right to grow food and raise livestock on property that they own will be one small step toward reestablishing that independence and resiliency. Taking small steps like this will also help restore our national character.

REMOVE FEDERAL GOVERNMENT IMPEDIMENTS TO THE USE OF PROPERTY

The Constitution only grants the federal government the authority to own property that is needed to build forts, magazines, arsenals, dockyards and other buildings that are needed for the operation of the federal government. This is one area where the federal government has dramatically overstepped boundaries set by the Constitution, as the federal government has amassed vast quantities of land that is not essential to the operation of the federal government.

The federal government owns approximately 20% of land in the United States, including more than half of the land in some Western states. We the People should compel the federal government to eliminate the Bureau of Land Management and transfer all unnecessary federal lands to the states. Additionally, we must call for an end to the abuse of the Antiquities Act, whereby vast quantities of land have been designated monuments by Barack Obama and prior presidents. All of these efforts have deprived Americans of land with which to live productive lives.

If We the People are successful in removing all of the federal and state imposed impediments and restrictions upon property, and we are successful in implementing much of this plan, we will see unprecedented economic growth and prosperity. As we battle the entrenched establishment political class and their globalist puppet masters for our economic liberty, We the People must be equally diligent in guarding against the federal government trying to limit our right to own and use money of any type, or to enter into barter transactions.

FORTY-FOUR

Next Steps

PROMOTE THIS PLAN AND ORGANIZE FREEDOM CELLS

Where there is no vision, the people perish.

— Proverbs 29:18

When I speak of promoting this plan, please bear in mind that I am always speaking of implementing this plan, *or one of similar magnitude and direction.* I don't have all of the answers, but I am confident that the full implementation of this plan would solve most of the problems that we face. When you have to jump across a twenty foot chasm, a twelve foot leap will not work. Articulating this bold, comprehensive and transformational plan to turn our country around is easy compared to the Herculean task of getting enough patriots on the same page, and getting We the People to clamor with one voice for transformational change. That is the hard part, which is why we must not only promote this plan, but also do some community organizing so that We the People may speak as one and act as one.

Publishing this plan to save America is just the first step in my personal plan of action for doing what I can do to articulate a bold, comprehensive and transformational plan that I believe is necessary to save our nation from distress, as well as to organize patriots all over this great nation to get behind this plan or one of similar magnitude and direction. Although far from perfect, this book will have to be good enough to get the conversation going, which will lead to improvements in the plan along the way. There are many improvements that I would like to make to this book, but what is urgently needed right now is to organize patriots to rally behind this plan or one of similar magnitude and direction to take our country back, and to become actively engaged in promoting specific action steps that will turn our country around.

Fellow patriot, if you are in agreement with most of the elements of this plan, then mention this plan to other patriots when you are discussing the problems that our nation faces and the bold ideas for solving those problems. Use social media to promote this plan and to encourage others to join Freedom Cells. Call your local conservative talk radio host and promote the plan generally, as well as specific elements of the plan. Contact the offices of your congressman and Senator, and ask that they consider the merits of the bold ideas articulated in this plan.

Join or form Freedom Cells, starting with your local precinct, and recruit other patriots in your precinct to join you in dominating your local precinct with the transformational principles and actions set forth in this plan. Operate your precinct Freedom Cell like the Freedom Caucus of the Republican Party in your precinct. If you are a member of the Republican Party and are registered in your precinct, you don't have to have permission of precinct leadership to meet with fellow patriots that join with you to form your precinct Freedom Cell.

After you get your precinct Freedom Cell organized, find out who the elected leaders of the precinct are and request regular meetings of the precinct. Hold precinct Freedom Cell meetings a few days prior to your Republican precinct meetings so that members of the Freedom Cell can get on the same page. Use wisdom in dealing with the existing precinct leadership, as most of them will either embrace what we are doing, or will eventually come around in due time. Learn the rules of your local Republican Party organization and follow those rules judiciously in taking over leadership of the party from the precinct level all the way up to the state party organization.

Continue to be involved in any Tea Party or any other group promoting freedom and conservative activism, for Freedom Cells are intended to augment the organization of patriots, not displace existing groups that are like-minded. Any like-minded groups that substantially embrace the specific actions articulated in this plan are already Freedom Cells. Beware of any group that is co-opted by the entrenched establishment political class, and work diligently to keep your Freedom Cells completely independent and autonomous.

Work with other Freedom Cells to articulate an action plan to eliminate corruption and take on the entrenched establishment political class at the state and local level. If candidates for office do not substantially support the specific action items in this plan or a plan for your state or local government that We the People put together, reject them and find a like-minded candidate to run for each office. Consider running for office yourself.

Freedom Cells within the Republican Party should function in the same way that the House Freedom Caucus does. Freedom Caucus members in the House, and Senators Mike Lee, Ted Cruz and Rand Paul are examples of the kind of candidates we should back to run against RINO Republicans in every single Republican primary. Work to compel your state Republican Party to select Republican general election candidates by closed caucus or closed convention. Recruit patriotic, freedom loving Democrats that are fed up with the illiberal left to assist us in replacing Democrats in office with candidates that support this plan.

As long as the entrenched establishment political class is in power, We the People cannot trust our government to correct the problems that our country faces. As President Ronald Reagan said, government is not the solution to the problem, government is the problem. It is up to We the People to transform our country, but we cannot do so if we do not organize into groups like Freedom Cells with tens of millions of patriots doing their part to get behind a plan that will get the job done.

I have identified a bold, comprehensive, transformational plan that will turn our country around if We the People are successful in getting on the same page and getting organized. I am calling for patriots to get behind this plan and to form Freedom Cells in order to organize our efforts and permit us to speak with one voice as we clamor for transformative change. As the Lord tarries and I live in health, I will continue to improve upon this plan with input from other patriots, and to promote this plan and assist patriots in organizing Freedom Cells.

I have shared with you my vision for taking our country back, and my vision for organizing patriots to rally around the cause. I ask you, dear patriot, to contribute some of your time, talent and treasure to the effort to save our country. Will you answer the call? Is there not a cause?

Made in the USA
Columbia, SC
07 September 2017